To John Ward, Solicitor of Donegal Town
A great tactician of litigation and a generous mentor

and

In memory of Gerard Barry of RTÉ
A journalist whose standards never dipped

FOREWORD

This book is in many senses a unique work, aimed at both journalists and lawyers, but of equal appeal to those with a passing interest in public affairs and the increasingly complex field of defamation and libel.

It provides a basic grounding in terms and definitions, and a map of the various jurisdictions in which actions have been brought and defended. It also charts some of the more recent hazards which have emerged for the working journalist.

More significantly, it deals with the fundamental changes brought about by the Defamation Act 2009 which provided the legal basis for a Press Council and simplified the law for both plaintiff and defendant.

Defending defamation actions presents the Irish media with a multi-million bill annually. Unlike other areas of litigation, the outcome is difficult to predict, as the *Kinsella* case amply demonstrated, and the defendant is consequently more likely to settle. The 2009 Act improves matters, but defamation remains a significant preoccupation for broadcasters and the print media.

On the other side of the argument, the proliferation of media in recent times, and what many regard as the coarsening of the public debate, mean that the ordinary person must feel that the scales are weighed against them, and to that extent the Act maintains a balance, even if some feel the protection it affords to public figures remains on the generous side.

This book will be a valuable guide for the ordinary citizen, and for working journalists, who frequently feel excluded once the process of defending an action is initiated by their employers.

Yvonne Murphy has drawn from her own experience as a journalist, which is when I had the pleasure of working alongside her. Those who know her will not be surprised that she had the energy and found the time to complete this updated edition while chairing a high profile Commission and carrying out her other judicial duties.

Her co-author Donal McGuinness is a well-known junior counsel who worked for many years as a solicitor before joining the Bar.

David Davin-Power

PREFACE TO THIRD EDITION

It is always gratifying to authors of books of this kind when a further edition is called for. The imperative for the second edition was the delivery of various judgments of the Superior Courts including *de Rossa v Independent Newspapers*, *Irish Times Ltd v Murphy* and *O'Brien v Mirror Group Newspapers Ltd*. The imperative for this third edition is the belated arrival of the long-awaited statutory reform in the area of defamation in the form of the Defamation Act 2009, and other initiatives such as the establishment of the Press Council and the Press Ombudsman. In this regard, it must be acknowledged that the late Mr Brian Lenihan as Minister for Justice, and Mr Michael McDowell as Attorney General and later as Minister for Justice, were significant reformers of the law. But it must also be chronicled that, during this period of law reform, the promised Privacy Act was abandoned or "parked", as Mr Lenihan said. There was, of course, considerable media opposition to this measure but it would be unfair to attribute its abandonment solely to this factor. Only time will tell whether the combination of the 2009 Act, the Press Ombudsman and the Press Council will prove the cynics wrong and demonstrate that there is no need for a privacy law.

The Defamation Act 2009 brings about a complex situation. It came into force on January 1, 2010, and it applies to defamations published after that date. Accordingly, for the foreseeable future, journalists and lawyers will have to bear in mind both the old and the new law. It is more than likely, given the slow progress of cases through our courts, that the old law will continue to be relevant for several years.

This book takes the approach of dealing with the old law and the new law on particular topics and addressing them individually. Any reader of this work will come to appreciate that it would be pointless to try to deal with the new law though it were entirely separate and distinct from its predecessor. The Oireachtas has ordained a long period of overlap and the structure of the book recognises this. In some areas, the old law has been re-enacted.

As with the previous editions, this book is written primarily for working journalists and for students of journalism and cognate subjects. Its "mission statement" is to help to allow journalists to participate in media and media/legal decision-making as equal parties.

It aspires to inform such decisions as to whether a particular article or statement can be published, whether an apology should be offered, and the myriad of tactical and legal decisions which have to be taken on both sides in the course of litigation. It is not a work for academics or for practitioners, who are already served by *Gatley* and *Duncan and Neill*, or, in Ireland by *MacDonald* and *Cox* and *Media Law in Ireland* by Eoin Carolan and Ailbhe O'Neill. But neither is it one of those very brief guides which are too often the only alternative to these tomes. The former give too much insight and information to be really useful to or readily absorbed by a focused, working journalist. The latter provides snippets of information but insufficient depth and context to give any real understanding of the law of defamation. We hope that this book fills the considerable gap between them.

The first two editions of this book were solely by the first author, Yvonne Murphy, who worked for several years as a journalist, first in RTÉ and later in the print media, before practising at the Bar and later becoming a Judge. All these experiences are reflected in her book. She has been joined for this edition by the second author, Donal McGuinness, whose experience as a barrister, and formerly as a solicitor, enables him to bring to the book the very necessary insights provided by a busy practice in this time of very rapid development of the law.

The authors wish to express their gratitude to Paul O'Higgins SC, Chairman of the Bar Council, and to Hugh Mohan SC and Ita Mangan BL, who read the text at various stages and offered very useful suggestions. We have also benefited from reading a paper on the new legislation written by Eoin McCullagh SC. However, none of the foregoing persons are responsible for any errors or infelicities in the text, which is wholly the responsibility of the authors.

We would also like to thank the team at Thomson Reuters, Catherine Dolan, Frieda Donohue and Nicola Barrett, for their support in the publication of this book.

Yvonne Murphy & Donal McGuinness
June 2011

PREFACE TO SECOND EDITION

This is the second edition of this book. In the intervening years there have been a number of significant judgments in this area of the law. Among those discussed are: *De Rossa v. Independent Newspapers Ltd*; and, more recently, *O'Brien v. Mirror Group Newspaper Ltd.*

The role of the courts and that of the media was explored in considerable detail in the Supreme Court judgment in *The Irish Times Ltd. v. Murphy.*

Finally, I would like to acknowledge the great assistance I received from Adrian Hardiman and Elizabeth Senior in the compilation of this edition.

Yvonne Murphy
The Circuit Court
December 2000

PREFACE TO FIRST EDITION

This book is designed principally for students of journalism, media studies and related areas. It is hoped that working journalists will also find it useful.

The book seeks to redress two main needs. The first is to give readers a sound general overview of the legal system, specifically the courts and the reporting thereof and the legal profession. There is an increasing public interest in the working of the courts and legal affairs in general. For most people, journalists are the principal source of information on these topics.

Secondly, the book addresses the areas of the law which are of most interest to journalists in their day to day work. The areas of libel, contempt and relations with sources are of significant interest to working journalists. I have tried to steer a middle course between the complexities of the technical works on the subject and the very brief handbooks which are often the only alternative. The treatment of the technical areas is perhaps fuller than usually found in books for a non-legal audience. It may in the end prove more digestible.

Particularly in relation to libel, an effort is made to go beyond the details of the law into their pratical application in actual cases. There is a considerable emphasis on tactical as well as technical aspects. It is hoped that the chapter on pleadings and other procedural steps will enable practising journalists to feel less excluded from the process of preparation for trials than is often the case at the moment.

Yvonne Murphy

Dublin,
December 1996

CONTENTS

CHAPTER ONE

THE COURTS AND OTHER QUASI-JUDICIAL BODIES

The Constitution provides for the administration of justice in public, in courts established by law, by judges appointed in the manner provided by the Constitution. The important pieces of legislation giving effect to this are:

1. The Courts (Establishment and Constitution) Act 1961.
2. The Courts (Supplemental Provisions) Act 1961.
3. The Courts and Court Officers Act 1995 and the amendments to these Acts.

THE JURISDICTION OF THE COURTS

The jurisdiction of a court means the power of a court to hear and decide a case. The work of the court is divided between its criminal and its civil jurisdiction.

Criminal Jurisdiction

Article 38 of the Constitution provides that no person shall be tried on any criminal charge save in due course of law and that, with three exceptions, no person shall be tried on a criminal charge without a jury. The exceptions are:

1. Minor offences which may be tried by courts of summary jurisdiction, i.e. the District Court;
2. Special courts, like the Special Criminal Court, may be established to try cases where it has been decided that the ordinary courts are inadequate to secure the administration of justice and the preservation of public peace and order; and
3. Military Tribunals may be established for the trials of offences against military law and also to deal with a state of war or armed rebellion.

The District Court

The District Court sits at 118 provisional venues throughout the country and 11 venues in Dublin. Sittings usually occur at least once a month, but are more frequent in populous areas. In Dublin, a number of District Courts operate at the same time. Sittings to deal with juvenile business are held separately from other sittings of the court. Generally, the venue at which a case is heard depends:

i. In criminal proceedings, on where the offence was committed or where the defendant resides or carries on business or was arrested.
ii. In civil cases, on where the contract was made.
iii. In licensing cases, on where the licensed premises are situated.

In the District Court a judge sits alone without a jury.

The criminal jurisdiction of the District Court falls under the following headings:

i. Minor offences triable in a summary way before the District Court. This makes up the great bulk of the work of the District Court, and these offences are mainly statutory in origin.
ii. Indictable offences specified in the appropriate legislation which are triable summarily on the basis that in the view of the judge, the facts alleged constitute a minor offence; that the accused, on being informed of his/her right to be tried by a jury, does not object to being tried summarily; and that, in the case of certain offences, the Director of Public Prosecutions has consented to a summary trial.
iii. Indictable offences (other than certain offences including rape, aggravated sexual assault, murder, treason and piracy) where the accused, when before the District Court, pleads guilty and the judge is satisfied that he/she understands the charge. With the consent of the Director of Public Prosecutions the judge may deal with the cases summarily, otherwise, the accused is sent forward to the Circuit Court for sentence. When before the Circuit Court he/she may withdraw his/her plea and alter it to "not guilty" in which case trial takes place.
iv. Indictable offences not triable summarily. In this case a Book of Evidence is served on the accused. The judge considers the material before him/her to make sure the documents are in order. He/she sends the accused forward to the Circuit Court or Central Criminal Court for trial.

Book of Evidence

When a person is charged with a serious crime which, for one reason or another, cannot be disposed of in the District Court, and will have to be tried by a higher court, the judge can remand the accused while the State's case is being prepared. This preparation takes the form of assembling what is known as a Book of Evidence which is served on the accused.

There are time limits within which the book should be served but they are more readily observed in the breach than in the observance. If a District Court judge feels the remand period is being abused he/she can strike out the charges.

The Book of Evidence consists of a statement of the charges, the list of witnesses whom it is proposed to call, statements of their evidence and a list of the exhibits it is proposed to use at the trial.

Procedure in Summary Matters

The usual procedure adopted by the District Court in summary matters is that, following an application, a summons is served on the accused indicating the nature of the offence and its time and place of commission and requiring the attendance in court of the accused to answer the charges. The accused can seek the statements of witnesses prior to the trial of the case.[1] If the defendant has been arrested and brought to court the procedure is by charge sheet.

The Circuit Court

The country is divided into eight circuits for the purposes of the Circuit Court.

Indictable Offences

The Circuit Court has original jurisdiction in relation to indictable offences except for treason, murder, attempted or conspiracy to murder, piracy, certain serious offences under the Treason Act 1939 and the Offences against the State Act 1939. Criminal trials under the Competition Act 2002 are dealt with in the Central Criminal Court. The trial will normally take place in front of a judge sitting with a jury on the circuit on which the offence has been committed or where the accused person has been arrested or resides. Under the Court and Court Officers Act 1995, where an accused person has been sent

---

[1] *Cowzer v Kirby*, unreported, High Court, Barr J., February 2, 1991.

forward for trial to a Circuit Court sitting other than in the Dublin Circuit Court, the judge of the Circuit Court before whom the accused is triable, may on the application of the prosecutor or the accused, if satisfied that it would be manifestly unjust not to do so, transfer the trial to the Circuit Court sitting within the Dublin Circuit. The Circuit Court judge's decision in this instance to grant or refuse the application is final and unappealable.

The Indictment
When an accused person is sent forward for trial the prosecution must prepare an indictment. This document sets out the formal charge which the Director of Public Prosecutions or in certain instances the Attorney General prefers against the accused.

The Arraignment
The next stage in the process is the arraignment. By this is meant the accused is brought before the Circuit Court and the charges against him/her as set out in the indictment are read out and he/she is asked whether he/she wishes to plead guilty or not guilty. The accused and his/her lawyers will already know what the State's case is from the Book of Evidence. If the State decides that it is not proceeding with the trial it will normally enter a nolle prosequi[2] at this stage.

Plea Bargaining
Plea bargaining is no longer a feature of the Irish criminal justice system. If the accused pleads not guilty to the charges, then a jury has to be empanelled.

Selection of a Jury
Suitability for jury service is now decided by the Juries Act 1976, as amended by the Civil Law (Miscellaneous Provisions) Act 2008. Subject to that legislation, every citizen aged 18 years and upwards who is entered in the Dáil Register of Electors in a particular jury district is qualified. A person is liable to serve if called upon, unless at the time they are called they are ineligible or disqualified. Persons who are deemed ineligible include the President of Ireland, people concerned with the administration of justice, for example, a practising barrister or a solicitor, members of An Garda Síochána and prison and welfare officers, members of the defence forces and persons who are illiterate.

---

[2] Refer to p.272 of the glossary for an explanation of this term.

In addition, people can be disqualified for jury service; if, for example, they have been convicted of a criminal offence attracting a certain type of prison sentence. There is also a process whereby people may be excused from jury service. Those excused by right include those who served on a jury within the past three years or others who may be excused at the discretion of the County Registrar of the court, and among that group would be people like medical practitioners who cannot be spared from certain jobs. A person over the age of 65 may apply to be excused on that ground. Others who are excused include those who were excused by a judge in a previous case. If a person gets ill, they can apply to be excused from jury service, but if summoned to attend a person must attend unless excused, disqualified or ineligible. Deaf people can now serve on juries following a recent High Court decision. It will be up to the trial judge to rule on the matter in any particular trial.

The Ballot
Usually the 12 people selected to serve on any particular jury are selected by ballot in open court. Literally, the County Registrar puts all the numbers of those called for jury service on a particular day into a bag and picks them out at random. Both the prosecution and the defence have a right to object to a particular jury member. Two forms of objection can be taken, one is peremptory, which means that no cause has to be shown as to why either side do not want that particular juror serving on the jury. Both the prosecution and the defence have seven challenges of this sort and once their respective challenges have been exhausted they can then challenge further members of the jury provided they can show cause. In practice this is rarely done, although both the prosecution and the defence usually use up their peremptory challenges.

The Verdict
Once the jury is sworn in, the trial proceeds and results in an acquittal, a conviction or disagreement. There can also be a direction. If, at the end of the prosecution's case, an application is made to the judge that based on the evidence given, there is no case to answer then the judge may direct the jury as a matter of law to find the accused not guilty or he/she may refuse to grant such a direction.

Appellate Jurisdiction of the Circuit Court
The other main area of work with which the Circuit Court deals is appeals from the District Court. Such appeals take the form of a

complete rehearing and it is open to the accused to call new evidence if he/she wishes. The Circuit Court can vary any sentence imposed in the District Court and it also has the power to increase the penalty imposed. Its decision on appeal is final.

The Central Criminal Court

The High Court exercising its criminal jurisdiction is known as the Central Criminal Court and it sits in many venues throughout the country. It formerly sat exclusively in Dublin. It has exclusive jurisdiction in relation to such areas as murder, attempted murder, rape, and for criminal trials under the Competition Act 2002. It normally tries these cases in a similar manner to the procedure in the Circuit Court.

The Court of Criminal Appeal

The Court of Criminal Appeal comprises three judges, one of whom must be the Chief Justice or an ordinary judge of the Supreme Court nominated and the other two judges must be from the High Court. The Court of Criminal Appeal's jurisdiction is to hear appeals from the Central Criminal Court, the Circuit Court and the Special Criminal Court and Military Courts.

The Special Criminal Court

The Offences Against the State Act 1939 provides for the establishment of the Special Criminal Court, which may be brought into force whenever the Government is satisfied that the ordinary courts are inadequate to secure the effective administration of justice and the preservation of public peace and order. Its most recent period of establishment has been since 1972.

Various challenges were made to the constitutionality of the court and the powers of the DPP but the Supreme Court has upheld its validity and the powers of the DPP.[3] Three members comprise the court but no person can be appointed unless he/she is a judge of the High Court, the Circuit Court or the District Court, a barrister or a solicitor of not less than seven years' standing or an officer of the defence forces not below the rank of commandant. In practice, since

---

[3]   *Re MacCurtain* [1941] 1 I.R. 83; *State (Bollard) v The Special Criminal Court*, unreported, High Court, Kenny J., September 20, 1972; *Eccles v Ireland* [1985] I.R. 545 (Supreme Court).

the mid 1980s, the court usually comprises a combination of those holding judicial office. The court sits without a jury.

The Government may, by order, declare particular offences to be "scheduled offences" under the Offences Against the State Act 1939. Once scheduled, if the offence is indictable, the District Court judge must send the case to the Special Criminal Court unless the DPP directs otherwise. If a person is charged with a scheduled offence, which is to be tried summarily, that case must also be sent to the Special Criminal Court if the DPP makes a specific request to that effect. A person appearing before the court on a non-scheduled offence may also be tried in the Special Criminal Court if the DPP certifies in writing that the ordinary courts are inadequate to secure the effective administration of justice and the preservation of peace and order. Provision was made in s.8 of the Criminal Justice (Amendment) Act 2009 to designate certain "gangland" type offences as offences which the ordinary courts should no longer deal with and are now dealt with in the Special Criminal Court.

Military Courts

The system also provides for the establishment of Military Courts, called courts martial. The jurisdiction is to try people for an offence against military law committed by such a person whilst subject to military law as an officer or man. Membership of the court is confined to officers of the defence forces, not less than five in the case of a general court martial and three in the case of a limited court martial.

The Supreme Court

An appeal from the Court of Criminal Appeal may lie to the Supreme Court if the Attorney General or the Court of Criminal Appeal certifies that the decision involves a point of law of exceptional public importance, and that it is desirable in the public interest that the opinion of the Supreme Court be taken. There are other appeals to the Supreme Court, the most interesting being an appeal to the Supreme Court from the High Court on a case stated from the District Court once leave to appeal has been obtained from the High Court.

Civil Jurisdiction

While undoubtedly the criminal courts provide constant copy for journalists of all sorts, cases within the civil area are also now covered quite intensively, particularly by the print media. Procedure plays an important role in the running of the civil cases before the Irish courts. There are complex sets of rules and regulations which govern civil proceedings. The Rules of the Superior Courts are constantly under revision. These govern the procedure in the High Court and the Supreme Court. Similarly, there are rules for the District Court and rules for the Circuit Court. In all cases the rules are subject to ongoing scrutiny and revision and are supplemented by what are known as practice directives. These are directives which judges issue to attempt to make the system run more efficiently.

In considering the civil jurisdiction of the courts, it is important to bear in mind that the vast majority of cases settle without going into court at all. Some cases settle once an initiating letter has been written by a solicitor to the other side whereas others take some time longer to settle.

Small Claims Court

A new initiative which has been started in recent years is the introduction of Small Claims Courts. The small claims procedure is operated by the District Court. They deal with claims of up to €2,000. In order to avail of the service both sides must be agreeable in advance to be bound by the findings of the court. From January 2010 the Small Claims Courts can also deal with certain types of cross border claims. The small claims procedure has been amended by Statutory Instrument No. 519 of 2009. The Courts website *www.courts.ie* provides full details of how to make and defend claims.

The District Court

The main areas of civil jurisdiction for the District Court are:

General   The civil jurisdiction of the District Court in contract and most other matters is where the claim or award does not exceed €6,348.69. Excluded from those areas are defamation, false imprisonment and malicious prosecution, which must be taken in a higher court.

Family Law   Under the huge volume of family law legislation passed in the last 20 years, the District Court plays a major role in areas dealing in the main with maintenance, custody and barring orders. Again, it is precluded from granting a decree of judicial separation or decree of divorce. It also deals with applications by the Health Service Executive under the Child Care Act 1991.

Licensing Another major area covered by the District Court relates to licensing matters. The court deals with objections to the renewal of a licence, transfers, exemption applications, etc.

Miscellaneous District Court judges also preside over the Children's Court.

Finally, it should be noted that the District Court is presided over by a judge sitting alone and anyone dissatisfied with the decision of the District Court can appeal to the Circuit Court.

The Circuit Court

The Circuit Civil Court, like the District Court, is presided over by a judge alone and is a court of record. Like the District Court it is an extremely busy court when exercising its civil jurisdiction.

General It deals with a wide range of cases in the tort and contract areas. For example, actions for defamation, false imprisonment and malicious prosecution can be taken in the Circuit Court. The main restriction on the court is that in general it cannot award more than €38,092.14 in damages. The principal exception is defamation cases where it can now award up to €50,000. If both parties to the action consent, then it can have unlimited jurisdiction but this rarely happens.

Land It can resolve any matter relating to land where the rateable valuation is under €252.

Landlord and Tenant Another major area dealt with by the Circuit Court is cases relating to the granting of new leases and those covered by the Landlord and Tenant (Amendment) Act 1980.

Equity Suits Here again the court has the ability to deal with a wide range of equity matters, e.g. injunctions with a special proviso that the rateable valuation of the land does not exceed €252.

Family Law Under the Judicial Separation and Family Law Reform Act 1989, the Family Law Act 1995 and the Family Law (Divorce) Act 1996, the Circuit Court is the main court dealing with all family law matters. When exercising its jurisdiction it is known as the family court and it can deal with judicial separation and divorce and all the consequential orders that arise from a judicial separation or divorce. It can also deal with nullity cases.

Licensing Matters   The court can grant new licences or declaratory orders that premises are suitable to be licensed. It also deals with the granting of new restaurant licences.

Appellate Jurisdiction of the Circuit Court   The Circuit Court also deals with civil appeals from the District Court, which is by way of a full rehearing. The Circuit Court deals with appeals from the Employment Appeals Tribunal, the Appeals Commissioners and Mental Health Tribunals.

The High Court

Under our Constitution the High Court has original jurisdiction to determine all matters and questions whether of law or fact, civil and criminal. Since the Courts Act 1988, juries sit in the High Court only to determine actions for defamation, false imprisonment and malicious prosecution on the civil side. Before that they heard all personal injuries cases. In practice, the work of the High Court is divided into a number of areas:

Personal Injuries Litigation   There is no limit on the amount of damages which the High Court can award in a personal injuries case. A great deal of the work of the High Court is taken up with the hearing of such cases. The court also deals with any contract case that is worth more than €38,092.14. Following the introduction of the Personal Injuries Assessment Board (*www.injuriesboard.ie*), a great deal of work that was formerly done by the Circuit Court and High Court in this area is now being dealt with by the Board.

Chancery   Another major wing of the High Court deals with chancery matters.

Companies and Bankruptcy   Under the Companies Act 1963 and the Bankruptcy Act 1988 the High Court has exclusive jurisdiction in both of these areas.

Constitutional Areas   Another area of exclusivity to the High Court is the determination of the constitutional validity of legislation.

Judicial Review Proceedings A major growth area for the High Court is judicial review proceedings. Individuals or bodies seek orders of certiorari, habeas corpus, and mandamus against decision-makers of all kinds.

Family Law The High Court has concurrent jurisdiction with the Circuit Court in relation to divorce and legal separations. Generally speaking it would tend to deal with what are termed "ample resources" cases. It also deals with applications under the Hague Convention relating to the care and custody of children who are removed from one jurisdiction to another.

The Supreme Court

Matters decided in the High Court can be appealed to the Supreme Court but the appeal does not take the form of a full rehearing of the case. Most appeals are limited to points of law. In addition, the Supreme Court, under Art.26 of the Constitution, can decide on the constitutionality of any proposed new legislation. These matters are referred to it by the President after consultation with the Council of State.

The European Court of Justice

The European Court of Justice is part of the European Union. It adjudicates upon the law in the EU and its rulings are binding on the Irish courts.

The European Court of Human Rights

The European Court of Human Rights is part of the Council of Europe and not of the EU. It investigates breaches of the European Convention on Human Rights. It is located in Strasbourg. The Convention was incorporated into Irish law by the European Convention on Human Rights Act 2003. The significance of this court will be dealt with from a journalistic perspective later.

Judicial and Quasi-Judicial Bodies

There are a range of tribunals and other judicial and quasi-judicial bodies that deal with specialist legal problems. This chapter deals with only a number of them because the list is quite exhaustive and what have been selected here are the more common ones which the media are likely to cover in the course of a day's work. While these bodies are not courts within the meaning of Art.34 of the Constitution, they nevertheless have to act judicially and must hear all sides of a case and are subject to judicial review in the High Court if they fail to act correctly.

Employment Appeals Tribunal   The Employment Appeals Tribunal (EAT) was set up under s.18 of the Unfair Dismissals Act 1977. In the main it deals with unfair dismissal cases. It can also, amongst other matters, deal with disputes relating to minimum notice, maternity protection and redundancy. A typical tribunal will comprise the Chairperson who is a lawyer—either a solicitor or barrister—and a representative nominated by the Irish Congress of Trade Unions and one person nominated by the employers' organisation IBEC.

A person dismissed from his/her job can refer the issue of the dismissal to a Rights Commissioner who will deal with the matter in an informal way, but it is more usual for the matter to be referred directly to the EAT. While the headquarters of the tribunal is situated in Dublin, divisions of the tribunal travel throughout the country to hear cases at different venues. Section 66 of the Unfair Dismissals Act 1977 places the burden of proving the fairness of a dismissal on an employer. If there is a dispute about the fact of dismissal, then the employee has the burden of proof. The hearings of the EAT are generally in public. The tribunal usually reserves its decision and the reasons and conclusions are provided to the press in written form if there is a request to do so. Each side bears its own costs for the tribunal but the finding of a tribunal can be appealed to the Circuit Court which can award costs to one side or the other. This decision in turn can be appealed on a point of law to the High Court.

Coroner's Court   The Coroners Act 1962 prescribes the procedure under which an inquest must be held and in which a coroner's jury must be summoned to issue a verdict on the death of a person. It is severely limited by the Act to what it may or may not decide. No decision can be given which would in any way implicate the person in a criminal law sense, nor can the court decide to make a finding of unlawful killing. A controversial area which it cannot deal with is the question of bringing in a verdict of suicide. A coroner is usually either a lawyer or a person with a medical qualification and will often possess both qualifications.

Criminal Injuries Compensation Tribunal This tribunal was established by a scheme which was introduced by the Government in 1974 but it has been amended many times since. Once again the tribunal comprises three persons, either barristers or solicitors. Prior to 1986 a person who was injured as a result of a criminal act could apply to the tribunal for compensation. Since that date the tribunal only has the power to award special damages as a result of a criminal act. There is provision for compensation to be paid where the injuries result from a riot or from the activities of an illegal organisation.

Mental Health Tribunals Since November 1, 2006 the Mental Health Tribunals Division of the Mental Health Commission is responsible for establishing mental health tribunals for patients admitted to psychiatric hospitals on an involuntary basis. Patients involuntarily admitted have the right to attend their mental health tribunal if they so wish.

Patients have the right to be represented at the mental health tribunal by a legal representative who is appointed by the Mental Health Commission.[4] The Mental Health Commission also arrange for an independent medical examination of the patient to be carried out by a consultant psychiatrist. The function of the mental health tribunal is to revoke or affirm the admission or renewal order.

The mental health tribunal must consist of the following members:

- A legal member (a barrister or solicitor who will act as chairman)
- A lay person
- A consultant psychiatrist

A tribunal clerk may be in attendance at mental health tribunal hearings and witnesses may be required to attend. Mental health tribunals also consider proposed transfers to the Central Mental Hospital and proposals related to psycho-surgery.

An appeal lies to the Circuit Court from a decision of a mental health tribunal only on the issue as to whether the patient is suffering from a mental disorder as defined by the Mental Health Act 2001. If the Circuit Court overturns the decision of the tribunal, the order admitting the patient to the hospital is discharged and the patient is released from hospital. The patient is entitled to legal representation at the appeal.

---

4 Section 17 of the Mental Health Act 2001.

Tribunals of Inquiry

A tribunal is basically an extraordinary enquiry into some dramatic public event or events. In this general sense they have been around a long time: they were well known to the Romans and the Greeks. As long ago as the fifth century BC, the Athenians had what amounted to a tribunal of inquiry into the disastrous conduct of their military incursion into Sicily. In the late 1600s, the diarist Samuel Pepys, who also held the high civil service appointment of Secretary to the Naval Commissioners, records vomiting in an anteroom to the House of Commons so anxious was he at being called as a witness at an inquiry into naval provisioning. Extraordinary investigations, such as those of US special prosecutors enquiring into the affairs of President Clinton and the very innovative South African Truth and Reconciliation Commission, have attracted world-wide attention.

It is important to realise that one can have an enquiry in any legal form. Examples of such enquiries include the first Dublin Monaghan bombings of 1974 and the Ferns inquiry. Both were non-statutory without any special legal form at all. But the classic tribunal of inquiry is an inquiry established under the terms of the Tribunals of Inquiry Act 1921, one of the last statutes of the United Parliament of Great Britain and Ireland passed before Irish Independence. This Act was amended by the Tribunals of Inquiry (Evidence) (Amendment) Act 1979. This was the statutory basis of such tribunals as the Stardust Tribunal of the 1970s, the Kerry Babies Enquiry of the 1980s and the Whiddy Island Shipping Disaster Tribunal of the same era, the Beef Tribunal, the Hepatitis C Tribunal, the McCracken Tribunal into Dunne's Stores Payments, the Moriarty Tribunal, the Flood Tribunal (now known as the Mahon Tribunal) and the Smithwick Tribunal, all of which have been convened under the same statutory authority. These Acts permit the passage of a resolution by the Dáil to the effect that it is expedient that a tribunal of inquiry be established into "definite matters of urgent public importance". The motion must also be passed in the Seanad. When this has occurred, the Executive may establish a tribunal to enquire into such matters.

Fundamentally, the distinction between a tribunal so established and any other form of special enquiry is that a tribunal to which the Acts relate has special powers in relation to compelling the attendance of witnesses and the disclosure of documents and other ancillary matters. Such powers are also provided to other bodies, e.g. Companies Acts Inspectors under different statutes and the Director of Corporate Enforcement.

The general circumstances in which tribunals are established have been well described by the Salmon Report on Tribunals of Inquiry in the UK as follows:

> "It is essential that on the very rare occasions when crises of public confidence occur, the evil, if it exists, shall be exposed so that it may be rooted out, or if it does not exist, the public shall be satisfied that in reality there is no substance in the prevalent rumour and suspicions by which they have been disturbed."

As the list of recent tribunals given above indicates, tribunals have been established into major disasters (Stardust and Whiddy), very peculiar circumstances of public interest occurring on a one-off basis (the Kerry Babies Enquiry), and allegations of commercial or political, or mixed commercial/political malpractice like the current Mahon and recent Moriarty tribunals.

It is very obvious that tribunals may easily traverse some of the territory more often dealt with either in the courts or in the Oireachtas. But they are in no sense a substitute for these more normal ways of doing business and are, properly speaking, regarded as extraordinary measures. The late Chief Justice Hamilton remarked that the Beef Tribunal which he chaired would have been unnecessary had proper questions been asked and answered in Dáil Éireann. Sometimes a tribunal actually enquires into the activities of bodies which should, perhaps, have addressed the matters before the tribunal at an earlier stage, such as the Revenue Commissioners.

It is also clear that tribunals of inquiry, by reason of their powers, may encroach upon and to some extent set aside what would otherwise be inviolable rights of citizens such as the right to silence, the right to privacy and the right to confidentiality of documents and records. For these reasons a somewhat complex set of provisions are made in the statutes and these have been further expounded in decided cases taken by persons aggrieved by tribunals' powers. In particular, in *Goodman International and Laurence Goodman v The Honourable Mr Justice Liam Hamilton, Ireland and the Attorney General*,[5] it was held that the proceedings of a tribunal of inquiry were not an administration of justice and their powers and duties were not judicial functions. On the contrary, a function is limited to conducting an inquisitorial enquiry and making a report of its findings to the Oireachtas. It follows from

---

[5] [1992] I.R. 542.

this that findings of fact made by a tribunal are not conclusive or binding on any other court or body.

This aspect has caused certain difficulties in public understanding. For example, after the McCracken Tribunal into Dunne's Stores payments, many people expressed bewilderment as to why charges or civil proceedings were not immediately brought, based on the findings. But this could not have occurred because the findings of a tribunal of enquiry are not binding or conclusive. The reasons for this relate to the extraordinary powers given to tribunals. In particular, the fact that a person may be compelled to attend and answer questions, produce documents and even incriminate him/her(self), means that his/her ordinary constitutional rights are set aside to that extent. Constitutional justice requires that certain provision be made to counterbalance this fact: accordingly, what a person says in a statement to the tribunal is not admissible against him in any criminal charge, save that of lying under oath to the tribunal itself. Thus, in the case of *DPP v Susan O'Keeffe*[6]—a case taken against a journalist after the Beef Tribunal— Ms O'Keeffe was charged with obstructing the tribunal by refusing to answer certain questions. But the case against her collapsed when it proved impossible to prove in evidence at her criminal trial the record of what she said to the tribunal, because of the statutory privilege conferred in the relevant section of the 1979 Act. A similar result would no doubt follow in any other case where a person was charged on the basis of what he had said to the tribunal. In *Lawlor v Judge Flood*,[7] it was held that the Flood Tribunal could not compel a person to attend for questioning before counsel to the tribunal in advance of a public sitting, for various reasons including that it was not obvious that such privilege attached to disclosures in that context.

A tribunal of inquiry under the 1921 and 1979 Acts is, accordingly, simply a body given special powers for the purpose of allowing it to report to the Oireachtas. It is not a court, either ordinary or special, its findings do not bind any person and it cannot of itself inflict any censure or penalty. That at least is the position in law: quite clearly in practice a person's reputation can be severely affected by what goes on at a tribunal.

---

[6] Unreported, Circuit Court, 1994.
[7] [1999] 3 I.R. 107.

Reporting a Tribunal

Since the passing of the Defamation Act 2009, there is a statutory privilege attached to reporting on a tribunal. Before that, it was in any event beyond doubt that such reports attracted a common law privilege by reason of the unique public interest. To avail of this privilege, however, a report must be fair and accurate, though it need not be contemporaneous. Prudence therefore suggests that such a report should be balanced, should not emphasise one person's account at the expense of another, and should in general presentation, including headlines, be fair. Particular difficulties may arise for journalists because of the very long duration of some tribunals: it can be difficult to recall accurately contradictory evidence which may have been given months or even years earlier. Moreover, some evidence which tends to defame an individual may be given months or years before the person in question gets an opportunity to reply: in such circumstances it is well to point out that the relevant person has yet to be heard. In general, the practices advised in relation to court reporting are applicable to the reporting of tribunals as well.

Commissions of Investigation Act 2004

This Act allows for the establishment of commissions from time to time to investigate and report on matters considered to be of significant public concern. More recently, this vehicle was used to investigate such cases as clerical child sex abuse in the Dublin Archdiocese, the Leas Cross Commission of Investigation and the banking collapse in Ireland.

As most of the proceedings of such commissions are held in private, journalists only tend to become involved when commission reports are published. The commissions themselves do not publish their own reports. The Minister who commissions the report has responsibility for its publication. Like tribunals, commissions have also been given statutory powers of compellability in relation to witnesses and the production of documents.

CHAPTER TWO

THE LEGAL PROFESSION

In Ireland the legal profession is divided into two main branches: solicitors and barristers.

SOLICITORS

Solicitors deal directly with clients and handle all sorts of legal business. The profession is governed by the Law Society of Ireland. Until recently, a law degree guaranteed admission to the profession but that was changed by a High Court decision.[1]

Qualifying as a Solicitor

To qualify as a solicitor in Ireland, you must:

- Pass the preliminary examination or receive an exemption from it.
- Pass the final examination-first part (FE–1).
- Secure a training contract.
- Attend the Professional Practice Course 1 and pass the course examination.
- Spend a period of 11 months as a trainee solicitor in a training solicitor's office.
- Attend the Professional Practice Course 2 and pass the course examinations.
- Serve the remainder of the two year term of apprenticeship following completion of the Professional Practice Course 2 course.

The Law Society have published a very useful booklet giving full details of what is involved in qualifying as a solicitor and it can be downloaded from their website *www.lawsociety.ie*.

---

[1] *Bloomer v Incorporated Law Society*, Irish Times Law Reports, November 6, 1995.

During training the student is paid a nominal amount and works in the office where they are training or in some other office which has the approval of their trainer.

The solicitor was always seen as the person who prepared the case for the barrister to advocate in court and who traditionally spent a good deal of time in the office working on conveyancing, wills, probate and preparing cases for litigation. Today, with the rise in new types of law, for example, family law and employment law, solicitors are as entitled as barristers to litigate these matters and in some cases have taken on that responsibility. Until recently, solicitors have tended not to exercise the right of audience in the courts. Now, especially in country areas, it is notable that solicitors are handling cases in the Circuit Court. While it may well happen in the future, we do not, as yet, have solicitor advocates as in Northern Ireland. Apart from a handful of solicitors, advocacy in the higher courts tends to be the preserve of the Bar. Qualified solicitors are commissioners for oaths and can become notaries public.

The Law Society investigates any allegation of misconduct by a solicitor and can impose various penalties on the solicitor, up to and including, applying to the President of the High Court to have the solicitor struck off the rolls. This means that the solicitor can no longer practise as a solicitor.

All solicitors must carry compulsory professional indemnity insurance. This means that if a solicitor acts negligently his clients can take comfort in the fact that proper compensation will be paid.

The Law Society has stringent controls for ensuring that solicitors do not in any way mishandle their clients' money. The Law Society operates a compensation fund into which each solicitor pays to ensure that if a solicitor does defraud a client, the client will be refunded their money.

The introduction of lay persons on various committees dealing with solicitors' misconduct has ensured that all client complaints are now thoroughly investigated by the Law Society.

The rules governing the conduct of solicitors are principally contained in the Solicitors Acts 1954, 1960 and 1994.

BARRISTERS

Barristers are known collectively as the "Bar" and also as "Counsel". The term derives from an old practice where barristers practised at the "bar" of the court. Originally the bar was a partition separating the judges from the ordinary person attending court but all that distinction is now gone and only the term barrister has survived. A barrister generally gets his work from a solicitor. In recent times there is limited direct access from other professions such as accountants and surveyors. When a barrister is given work by a solicitor it is termed "briefing" a barrister. Traditionally, barristers wore wigs and gowns when they were conducting a case in court but since the introduction of the Court and Court Officers Act 1995 the wearing of the wig is optional. In courts dealing with family law and Children Court matters, the wearing of the wig and gown is prohibited. When a barrister is practising at the Bar for 10 years or more he/she can apply to the Government to become a senior counsel or "Silk", which entitles the barrister to use the words Senior Counsel (SC) after his name as opposed to junior counsel who use the letters BL. A senior counsel will wear a gown of silk rather than cotton in his practice. It is also the practice for clients with relatively serious cases to employ the services of a senior counsel, in addition to a junior counsel.

Qualifying as a Barrister

The Honourable Society of the Kings Inns is the body which governs entry to the profession of barrister-at-law. The society provides courses of education and training for students, conducts examinations, and confers the diploma in legal studies and degree of barrister-at-law. The diploma in legal studies takes two years to complete and the degree course takes one year to complete. In addition to the one year full time degree course offered by the Kings Inns there is also an option of completing a two year modular degree course subject to certain conditions. Only holders of the degree may be called to the Bar of Ireland by the Chief Justice and admitted to practice in the courts of Ireland as members of the Bar of Ireland.

There is an annual entrance exam for admission to the barrister-at-law degree course which comprises the following subjects: law of contract, criminal law, Irish constitutional law, law of evidence and law of torts. In order to be eligible to sit the entrance exam a candidate is required to hold either an approved degree or an approved postgraduate diploma. Details of how to qualify as a barrister are on the Kings Inns website *www.kingsinns.ie*.

Discipline within the Bar

Complaints of misconduct against barristers are investigated and adjudicated upon by the Barristers Professional Conduct Tribunal. The Tribunal consists of seven members, five of whom are practising barristers appointed by the Bar Council and two lay people, one nominated by IBEC and the other by the ICTU.

Other Training

Other training in the legal area is provided by the universities and by private colleges. There are also opportunities to study law by night. Many Institutes of Technology offer opportunities to study for not only a basic law qualification, but also in some cases, a postgraduate qualification in law.

THE JUDICIARY

1996 saw one of the great expansions of the judiciary in Ireland. The Court and Court Officers Act 1995 (the "1995 Act") provided for a substantial increase in the number of judges involved in the administration of justice and also brought about minor changes in the method of appointment and provided for the training of judges. Currently there is legislation for 147 judges in total, of whom, at the time of writing, 76.03 per cent are male and 23.97 per cent are female.

The Supreme Court

The Supreme Court comprises the Chief Justice and seven ordinary judges who are known as judges of the Supreme Court. The Supreme Court may sit in two or more divisions. In addition, they may all sit at the same time, particularly on cases of major public significance.

The High Court, Circuit and District Courts

There is legislation providing for 37 High Court judges (one of whom is the President of the High Court), 38 Circuit Court judges (one of whom is the President of the Circuit Court), and 64 District Court judges (one of whom is the President of the District Court).

Judicial Appointments

The main change introduced by the 1995 Act was the establishment of what is known as the Judicial Appointments Advisory Board. The Board consists of:

   i. The Chief Justice.
   ii. The President of the High Court.
   iii. The President of the Circuit Court.
   iv. The President of the District Court.
   v. The Attorney General.
   vi. A practising barrister nominated by the Chairman of the Bar Council.
   vii. A practising solicitor nominated by the President of the Law Society.
   viii. Not more than three ordinary lay people appointed by the Minister for Justice and Law Reform.

Establishment of the Board has led to advertisements being placed for judicial appointments and applicants interested in the post are required to complete an application form. The Board considers applications and sends forward the names of suitable persons to the Minister for Justice and Law Reform. The Government then nominates suitable persons to the President who actually appoints judges. The Board publishes an annual report detailing the number of applications it receives for each vacancy. This information can be accessed on the web at *www.courts.ie*.

Qualification of Judges

Two major changes were introduced by the 1995 Act in relation to the appointment of judges. One was the ability to take into account service in the European Court of Justice (the "EU Court") either as a judge of the Court of Justice, a judge of the Court of First Instance or as an Advocate General. Taking the totality of such service or amalgamating such service with practice at the Bar, the person seeking the appointment must be able to show at least 12 years' standing for an appointment to the Supreme or High Court. Another change saw the introduction of practising solicitors of not less than 10 years' standing, being eligible on the same basis as practising barristers of similar standing, for appointment to the Circuit and District Courts. In a further legislative development, solicitors are now eligible for appointment to the High and Supreme Court benches on the same basis as barristers. High Court and Circuit Court judges who are appointed after the enactment of the Court and Court Officers Act 1995 may serve until the age of 70. Judges appointed prior to the 1995 Act may serve until the age of 72.

District Court judges hold office until they reach their sixty-fifth year. On attaining the age of 65 they may retire if they so wish, or they may apply each year to extend the retiring age up to 70 years. This is done by writing to the Supreme Court Office, Four Courts, Dublin 7, who will contact the Office of the Chief Justice. A meeting is then held to consider the application for an extension and the judge will be notified of the decision thereafter. The committee who makes the decision on the application comprises the Chief Justice, the President of the High Court, and the Attorney General.

Judges can only be removed for stated misbehaviour or incapacity and then only on a resolution passed by both Houses of the Oireachtas.

Further details of changes made in the 2000s for judicial qualification can be found in the 2009 report from the Judicial Studies Advisory Board at *www.courts.ie*.

Judicial Salaries

Judicial salaries are set in accordance with civil service guidelines and sanctioned by the Department of Finance. As of September 2008, the rates for an ordinary judge of the different courts are:

Supreme Court judge:	€257,872
High Court judge:	€243,080
Circuit Court judge:	€177,554
District Court judge:	€147,961

The Presidents of each court are paid a higher salary than an ordinary judge of the court. At the time of writing the Minister for Finance stated that starting salaries for new judges would be less than those currently operable.

Court Sittings

The sittings of the courts are determined by statute but basically the legal year is divided into four terms for the Supreme, High and Circuit Courts. The Hilary terms starts in January and usually runs through to

March. The Easter term follows that, starting after Easter week until just before Whit Sunday. Trinity term starts some time after Whitsun until July 31, and the Michaelmas term starts on the first Monday of October until December 21. No formal change has been made in these terms but because the business of the courts has increased substantially over the past decade, judges are available throughout the vacation periods to hear applications. Some judges who are in the course of hearing a lengthy case will require everybody in attendance during the vacation periods so that the conduct of the case can be expedited.

The vacations for the District Court are, the entire month of August, nine consecutive days commencing December 23, and six consecutive days commencing on the Thursday before Easter. The District Court does not sit on Good Friday.

Director of Public Prosecutions

The Director of Public Prosecutions is appointed by the Government to advise on matters of criminal law. He heads up the State prosecution service and is completely independent in his functions.

Attorney General

The Attorney General is the legal adviser to the Government. He or she is appointed to the Government and will sit at the Cabinet table. He or she may or may not be a TD. The policy in recent years has been to appoint a senior barrister although it is possible now for a solicitor to be appointed to the office of Attorney General. The Attorney General has the option of representing the Government on serious legal cases involving the Government.

Other Court Officers

A number of other court officers need to be mentioned.

The Master of the High Court

The Master of the High Court is authorised by law to exercise limited functions and powers of a judicial nature within the scope of Art.37 of the Constitution. He sits in the Four Courts and deals with a wide range of motions that assist in the orderly conduct of a case. He cannot rule on any dispute of fact and must send such a matter forward to the

High Court. His orders can be appealed to the High Court. The Master's considerable workload deals typically with matters such as discovery, procedural motions, summons and special summons.

The Taxing Master

The Taxing Master of the High Court deals effectively with any dispute relating to the costs of a particular action. He too sits in the Four Courts and his decisions may be appealed to the High Court.

County Registrar

These positions are advertised and appointed directly by the Government. Each county has a County Registrar who is responsible for the administration of the Circuit Court and who, under recent legislation, have been given wide-ranging powers.

County Registrars perform a number of quasi-judicial functions conferred on them by statute, for example, holding motion hearings, case progression hearings and taxation of costs. An appeal against their decisions is to the Circuit Court. Their powers are not too dissimilar to the Master of the High Court except that he or she can, with the consent of all parties, assess damages and try any issue of fact.

In practical terms the County Registrar is a person with whom journalists, particularly local reporters, have contact and it is not uncommon to see a reporter sharing the same bench as the County Registrar at the Circuit Court level.

Court Registrars

Another important element in the administration of the courts is the role played by the High Court Registrars. Each High Court judge will have a Court Registrar sitting with them. Again from a journalist's point of view the court registrar can be of invaluable assistance, particularly if the case is of a technical nature.

In the District Court the judge is assisted by a District Court clerk who can provide great practical assistance to journalists covering those courts.

Finding out what goes on in the Courts

Each day a list is published indicating cases listed for that particular day and also giving advance warning of cases that are likely to be heard in the future. This is called *The Legal Diary* which is now available on the Courts Service website. It is also posted up in the Round Hall of the Four Courts. This list indicates in what courts the matters are going to be heard and what judge is likely to hear the case. It also provides information on motions that are before the courts, appeals, and in Dublin, covers not only the High Court but also the Circuit Court, both criminal and civil. Outside Dublin, journalists have to rely on the various Circuit and District Court offices or the court registrars to let them know what cases are proceeding and when they are likely to proceed.

Details of what is going on in the courts can also be accessed through the Courts Service website *www.courts.ie*

This site also carries full details of all judgments given in recent years.

The site is maintained by the information office of the Courts Service which also keeps useful statistics in relation to court activities.

The office can be contacted at: (01) 888 6495

Media Relations Service

Mr Gerry Curran is the current Media Relations Advisor to the Courts Service. He acts in an advisory role in relation to media matters. In relation to the judiciary, he can arrange corrections, alterations, press statements or issue notices to the media on a judge's behalf.

Tel: (01) 888 6469, (01) 245 8304
Email: gerrycurran@courts.ie

CHAPTER THREE

PRESS AND BROADCASTING SUPERVISION

Initially a voluntary body, the Press Council of Ireland, was established in June 2007. The Press Council subsequently received statutory recognition in April 2010 following a ministerial order made pursuant to the Defamation Act 2009. This Act laid down the minimum requirements for the recognition of the Press Council by the Minister.[1] The Press Council has 13 directors, seven "public interest" directors, five owners and publishers and one journalist. The Press Council is funded by members' subscriptions. As a recognised body under the 2009 Act, qualified privilege will attach to reports and decisions of the Press Council as well as those of the Press Ombudsman. In addition, subscription to the Press Council and adherence to the Code of Practice for Newspapers and Periodicals will strengthen the entitlement of those organisations to avail of the new defence of "reasonable publication" as contained in the Defamation Act 2009. Non-members of the Press Council will be required to have in place an equivalent fairness regime or to operate an equivalent and publicised code of standards to avail of that defence.

According to Professor Tom Mitchell, the first chair of the Press Council:

> "The Press Council has a twin mission: to promote and protect press freedom, but also to provide a check on press behaviour by giving those who feel wronged by the actions of the press a simple, comprehensive mode of redress. It is a clear, unequivocal mission, designed to serve the public interest, and it should, and I believe it does, command the general support of the public, and of government, and of the media itself."[2]

Code of Practice

The Code of Practice adopted by the Press Council sets standards for the press in reporting news and information. The code which is contained in Appendix 3(a) binds all press organisations and journalists to a set of core principles.

The principles embodies in the code may be summarised as follows:

Truth and Accuracy
There is an obligation on the journalist to strive for truth and accuracy, and if there has been a "significant" inaccuracy, then there is a corresponding obligation to publish an apology promptly and with due prominence.

---

[1]   Section 44 and Sch.2 to the Defamation Act 2009.
[2]   *http://www.presscouncil.ie.*

Distinguishing Fact and Comment
While able to strongly advocate views, the reporting of any comment, conjecture or rumour or unconfirmed reports must not be reported as if it were fact. Conflicts of interest are to be disclosed and the publication must not be influenced by undisclosed interests.

Fairness and Honesty
In relation to the procuring and publishing of the information, material must not be obtained through misrepresentations or subterfuge unless such methods are justified in the public interest.

Respect for Rights
The Code recognises the constitutional protection to one's good name and so no press organisation may publish matter based on malicious misrepresentation or unfounded accusations. There is an obligation to check facts before publication.

Privacy
Recognition is given to the protection of privacy, as protected by the European Convention on Human Rights and by the Constitution. The Code however does not prevent the publication of "matters of public record or in the public interest". The Code expects sympathy and discretion in circumstances of personal grief or shock. The treatment of stories about "public persons" is specifically dealt with. Public persons include those who hold public office, deal in public affairs or follow a public career, or who have sought publicity for their activities. The publication of details of the private lives of public persons may be justifiable under the Code if the publication relates to the validity of the person's conduct, the credibility of his public statements, the values of his publicly expressed views or "otherwise in the public interest" (see Chapter 11 on privacy law).

Protection of Sources
Journalists are permitted to protect their sources. But it must be remembered that the code does not take precedence over the law (see Chapter 10 on contempt for a discussion on the law and protection of sources).

Court Reporting
The newspaper and periodical are obliged to respect the presumption of innocence for those persons who are charged with offences but whose cases have not yet been heard. No reporting should take place of any matter in such a manner that would prejudice a fair trial (see Chapter 4 on the law on court reporting).

Prejudice

Newspaper and periodicals are not permitted to publish material that is likely to cause "grave" offence or incite hatred against groups or individuals on the basis of their race, religion, nationality, colour, ethnic origin, gender, sexual orientation, marital status, disability, illness or age or membership of the travelling community.

Children

Special care is required when seeking or presenting information about children under 16. Journalists and editors must have sufficient regard for the vulnerability of children. Matters such as parents' consent, sensitivity of the information and whether there is a public interest to be served must be considered. Just because a child's parent is in the public eye cannot be used as the sole justification for publishing details of a child's private life.

Publication by the Press Ombudsman or Council

Newspapers will, if requested by the Press Ombudsman or the Press Council, print a copy of a decision in relation to a complaint by either the Ombudsman or Press Council with due prominence.

The Press Ombudsman

The Press Council also established an Office of the Press Ombudsman. The role of the Ombudsman is to receive complaints from the public, consider their validity, and attempt to resolve them by conciliation. Significant or complex cases may be sent by the Ombudsman to the Press Council for decision. Appeals from the Ombudsman's decisions are also decided by the Press Council.

The Office will accept complaints about any article in a newspaper or periodical published in Ireland. It will also accept complaints about individual journalists with respect to any breach of the Code. In order to be considered by the Ombudsman, the complaint must be delivered in writing, whether electronically or otherwise, by a person directly affected within three months of the publication or the behaviour complained of. Resolution of the complaint is attempted by a process of conciliation and if that does not resolve the matter, then a determination is made by the Ombudsman or the Press Council if referred to it by the Ombudsman.

The decision of the Ombudsman may be appealed to the Press Council. If a complaint has been upheld, the publication in question will be required to print with due prominence the Ombudsman's decision, which as previously stated is one of the principles of the Code in any event.

Complaints Received

More than 200 of the 351 complaints received by the Office of the Press Ombudsman in 2009 presented prima facie evidence of a possible breach of the Code of Practice, according to the Report of the Press Ombudsman, Professor John Horgan. Of these complaints, 53 were either successfully conciliated or decided upon by the Press Ombudsman or Press Council.

Most of the remaining complaints that presented prima facie evidence of a breach of the Code were not pursued beyond a preliminary enquiry by the complainant, or were informally resolved between the complainant and the publication prior to the Press Ombudsman's Office getting formally involved.

As was the case in 2008, the majority of complaints in 2009 were made under Principle 1 of the Code of Practice, relating to Truth and Accuracy.

Readers should also note that the National Union of Journalists also operates a voluntary code of practice which is reproduced in Appendix 3(b).

The Broadcasting Authority of Ireland

Until relatively recently, the Broadcasting Commission of Ireland and the Broadcasting Complaints Commission exercised control over the broadcasting industry in Ireland. The Broadcasting Act 2009 established the Broadcasting Authority of Ireland (the "BAI") to regulate the industry. This body was established pursuant to that Act on October 1, 2009. Within the umbrella of the BAI are two Committees, the Contract Awards Committee which licenses independent broadcasters, and the Compliance Committee which requires broadcasters to comply with broadcasting codes and rules.

Complaints

The Broadcasting Act 2009 requires every broadcaster to give due and adequate consideration to a complaint, provided the complaint is made in good faith and is not of a frivolous or vexatious nature. Broadcasters are required to publish a code of practice for the handling of complaints that maps out the relevant procedures for following a complaint within that organisation. A member of the public must first attempt to address that complaint with the broadcaster and have a right of complaint to the BAI should the complaint to the broadcaster prove unsatisfactory. The 2009 Act provides for the correction of incorrect facts or information which has been broadcast about a person, if the information has impugned that person's honour or reputation. The BAI has established a right of reply scheme that maps the process for addressing such an issue. This scheme along with many other helpful publications may be viewed on the BAI website at *www.bai.ie*.

CHAPTER FOUR

REPORTING ON WHAT IS SAID IN THE COURTS AND SIMILAR BODIES

COURT REPORTING UNDER THE CONSTITUTION AND STATUTE

Article 34.1 of the Constitution provides that:

> Justice shall be administered in courts established by law … and, save in such special and limited cases as may be prescribed by law, shall be administered in public.

The effect of this provision is that the open administration of justice is to be the norm; exceptions must be prescribed by law (as opposed, for instance, to the discretion of the judge), and what transpires in public may of course be reported to the public. This puts beyond doubt the existence of the common law qualified privilege in relation to such matters.

From a media point of view two questions arise in relation to any particular kind of hearing or proceeding:

1. Can the matter be reported?
2. If so, is the report privileged?

Can the Matter be Reported?

Hearings Otherwise than in Public

There is a variety of unconnected statutory provisions providing for hearings "in camera", "otherwise than in public" or "in chambers". There are other provisions affecting the type of material that can be published, e.g. prohibiting material identifying certain persons.

Restricting the Press

The Supreme Court considered this area in *The Irish Times Ltd v Murphy*.[1] In this case four non-nationals were charged with importing

---

[1] [1998] 2 I.L.R.M 161.

and possessing cocaine with intent to supply. The trial judge imposed an order prohibiting the media from reporting the evidence that would be given in the course of the trial until its conclusion. He ordered that they were to report merely the fact that the trial was proceeding and its venue, the names and addresses of the accused, the nature of the crimes alleged, and the fact that a fifth accused had pleaded guilty to the charge of possession with intent to supply. The basis for this decision was the risk that the trial would be prejudiced by contemporaneous reporting of it in the media resulting in a necessity to discharge the jury. In reaching this conclusion the trial judge appeared to take into account the misreporting of a previous and unrelated trial and some inaccurate reporting in the newspaper two days previously. *The Irish Times Ltd, Independent Newspapers (Ireland) Ltd, Newsgroup Newspapers Ltd, Examiner Publications (Cork) Ltd* and *RTÉ* sought an order of certiorari quashing the judge's decision. They were refused the order in the High Court and appealed to the Supreme Court.

The Supreme Court allowed the appeal and in the course of his judgment, Hamilton J. said that they could give:

> "… some guidance for the future which may be of help to trial judges and journalists as well as the public in general because the issues raised are of outstanding constitutional importance, *viz,* the right of accused persons to fair trial and the freedom of the press to report court proceedings, allied to which is the public's right to know what goes on in the court of law as well as the rights of the parties on occasions certainly to require that proceedings in which they are involved be eligible for publication."[2]

The Supreme Court also held[3]:

> "(1) In a democratic society, justice must not only be done but be seen to be done. By administering justice in public, respect for the rule of law and public confidence in the due administration of justice is maintained and safeguarded.
>
> (2) Justice is administered in public on behalf of all the inhabitants of the State, who have a right and a responsibility to be kept informed of what happens in courts of law. It follows that all such inhabitants are entitled to a fair and accurate report of proceedings in the courts, and that the media are entitled to give such an account to the wider public.

---

[2] [1998] I.L.R.M. 161 at 176–177.
[3] [1998] I.L.R.M. 161 at 162.

(3) The effect of the impugned order, which prohibited the media from contemporaneous reporting of these proceedings, was to deprive the wider public of knowledge of these proceedings. Accordingly, the trial was not held 'in public' within the meaning of Article 34.1 of the Constitution, despite the entitlement of the public, including the media, to attend in court.

(4) Article 40.6.1° (i) of the Constitution, which guarantees freedom of expression, is not confined to mere expressions of convictions and opinions, but includes the right to impart facts and information. The freedom of the press guaranteed by this provision includes the right to report and comment on proceedings in courts of law.

(5) However, the right of an accused to a fair trial is one of the most fundamental constitutional rights afforded to persons and, on a hierarchy of constitutional rights, is a superior right.

(6) A court may therefore interfere with the rights of the media to publish contemporaneous reports of proceedings before it where that is necessary in order to protect the right of an accused person to a fair trial. However, in order to exercise this jurisdiction, the trial judge must be satisfied:

(a) that there is a real risk of an unfair trial if contemporaneous reporting is permitted; and

(b) the damage which any improper reporting would cause could not be remedied by the trial judge either by giving appropriate directions to the jury or otherwise.

(7) In the instant case, the trial judge was not entitled to assume that the reporting of proceedings would be anything other than fair or accurate. Furthermore, he was not entitled to assume that any inaccuracy or unfairness as might arise could not be remedied by appropriate rulings and directions to the jury.

(8) There was no evidence before the court which would justify the conclusion that there was a real risk of an unfair trial if contemporaneous reporting of the trial was permitted. In the circumstances, the learned trial judge erred in law in making the impugned order."

The Chief Justice also referred to two previous cases, *D v Director of Public Prosecutions*[4] and *Z v Director of Public Prosecutions*.[5] Both of

---

[4] [1994] 2 I.R. 654.

[5] [1994] 2 I.R. 476.

those cases were again relevant from a journalist's point of view because they dealt with applications to prohibit the holding of trials due to alleged prejudice arising from pretrial publicity and Chief Justice Hamilton again reiterated the principle he had enunciated previously:

> "Having regard to the fundamental role of juries in our criminal justice system, it is fundamental that for an accused to have a trial, not only that the trial should be conducted in accordance with fair procedures but the jury should reach its verdict in a criminal case by reference only to the evidence lawfully admitted at the trial and not by reference to facts alleged or otherwise contained in statements or opinions gathered from the media or some other outside sources because fair procedures incorporate the requirement of trial by a jury unprejudiced by pre-trial publicity and capable of concluding a fair determination of facts on the evidence as presented at the trial."

It should be noted that in neither the *D* or the *Z* cases were the applicants successful in stopping their trials because of pretrial publicity.

Provisions for Hearing Otherwise than in Public

Section 45(1) of the Courts (Supplemental Provisions) Act 1961 provides:

> Justice may be administered otherwise than in public in any of the following cases:
> (a) applications of an urgent nature for relief by way of habeas corpus, bail, prohibition or injunctions;
> (b) matrimonial causes and matters;
> (c) lunacy and minor matters;
> (d) proceedings involving the disclosure of a secret manufacturing process.

These, of course, are in addition to other cases prescribed by law. In relation to "applications of an urgent nature" for reliefs of the kind mentioned in s.45, the rationale for this exception to the constitutional requirement of open justice is purely a practical one. A person seeking very urgent relief such as habeas corpus (an order to vindicate his right to liberty) or certain kinds of injunction may not be able to wait for a scheduled sitting of the court. He may have to apply late at night or over a weekend wherever a judge can be found. For example, a person may seek habeas corpus because he is threatened with deportation within the next few hours, or may seek an injunction against a newspaper about something which is due to be published in the following day's edition. Applications of this kind are often heard in a judge's home or other convenient place. It may be impractical in certain circumstances to hear them publicly.

Moreover, applications of this kind rarely determine the entire issue between the parties. In the case of habeas corpus the most that can be obtained is a "conditional order" and in the case of an injunction, an interim order. In each case, there will be a full hearing shortly afterwards with the other side on notice and before a court sitting in the ordinary way.

It is now established that the rationale behind this exception is the urgency and not the nature of the relief itself. In the well-known case of *Agricultural Credit Corporation v Irish Business*,[6] application for an interim injunction was made at a judge's home on the basis, amongst other things, that the article in question relied on leaked documents in relation to which the plaintiff was entitled to confidentiality and the protection of its copyright. The High Court granted an interim order. The plaintiff then gave notice of the order to a variety of media interests stating that the hearing by order of the judge had been held in camera and that the fact that the order had been made could not be published. It is not clear how much support this contention had in the order itself. However, when the case came up for interlocutory hearing an application to hear the case in camera was refused on the basis that the hearing was, unlike the interim hearing, not an urgent one and accordingly s.45(1)(a) could not apply.

It follows from this that the mere fact that the application is for an injunction does not in itself justify a hearing otherwise than in public. Moreover, the reference to urgency must be interpreted as an indication of a degree of urgency so great that a normal sitting of the court cannot be awaited and not merely to the fact that there is a degree of urgency attaching to the application.

---

[6] *Irish Times*, August 9, 1985; September 10, 1985.

Matrimonial Matters

By virtue of a variety of statutes, this general reference in s.45 has been applied to virtually every kind of family proceedings. With varying forms of words, it applies to separations, divorces, maintenance applications, Family Home Protection Act applications, applications for protection and barring orders, the Adoption Acts and, where a party requested, at least two applications for declarations of paternity.

The rationale for this restriction is so that family matters can be determined in what the former Chief Justice O'Higgins described, in the context of a guardianship case, as "a decent privacy". This is absolutely essential because countless persons would be deterred from instituting or defending proceedings of a very intimate nature if they were liable to be reported. In *Re Kennedy & McCann*,[7] it was stated in the strongest terms that any publication which interferes with this privacy will be regarded as a serious contempt of court even where (as in that case) one of the parties had positively sought such publicity.

However, if matrimonial proceedings are associated with other proceedings (an application for a non-matrimonial injunction; an attack on the Constitutionality of a statute) the protection will be strictly limited to the part of the proceedings which can be described as a matrimonial cause or matter. In such circumstances, however, the judge may request that the identities of parties or other details would not be revealed.

Matters Concerning Children

As far as minors are concerned, there is a considerable degree of overlap with the matrimonial jurisdiction. The prohibition here applies to applications for the maintenance of children, matrimonial or otherwise, guardianship matters, applications under the Child Care Acts and certain proceedings under the Succession Act. Where a child is a defendant in a criminal proceeding the media are entitled to be present but the anonymity of the minor must be preserved by not naming him or publishing other identifying material.

Proceedings Involving the Disclosure of a Secret Manufacturing Process

This might relate to certain applications involving the use of patented processes and similar matters. Again, the rationale is the fear that persons would be put off reporting to the courts at all if a secret process

---

[7] [1976] I.R. 382.

in which, perhaps, they had invested a great deal of time or large amounts of money, had to be publicly revealed.

Criminal Cases

A very wide range of provisions apply to different sorts of criminal proceedings. In particular, the fact that criminal cases are of a sexual nature should be a warning to a journalist to investigate his or her right to report.

Sexual Offences

The usual rule in relation to sexual offences now is that the public are excluded from the hearing. Bona fide representatives of the press are, however, permitted to remain. Any known material likely to lead members of the public to identify the victim cannot be published. After conviction, it may still be impossible to identify the defendant if to do so would tend to lead to the identification of the victim.

Miscellaneous Provisions for Hearing Otherwise than in Public

Income Tax Appeals

Appeals to the Circuit Court from the Income Tax Appeal Commissioners are held in camera but cases stated to the High Court (that is, requests for guidance by the Commissioners or a Circuit Court judge raising specified points of law) are heard in public.

Confidential Information

Applications under s.205 of the Companies Act 1963 (oppression of minorities) may be heard in camera:

> If, in the opinion of the court, the hearing of proceedings under this section would involve the disclosure of information the publication of which would be seriously prejudicial to the legitimate interests of the company … .

Examinership

The Companies (Amendment) Act 1990 which, inter alia, provides for the appointment of an examiner to a company and that an application for such an appointment may be made "otherwise than in public" if the court considers that the interests of the company or of the creditors as a whole so require.

Mental Health
The Mental Health Act 2001 expressly[8] prohibits the publication or broadcast of any matter likely to lead to identification of a patient in an appeal to the Circuit Court against an admission order involuntarily detaining the patient in a psychiatric institution under that Act. Breach of this provision is a criminal offence under the Act.

Affairs of Banks
The Credit Institutions (Stabilisation) Act 2010 came into force on December 21, 2010. This Act was brought in to make provision for the financial crisis in Ireland and to allow for the stabilisation of certain banks in the wake of the International Monetary Fund Programme of Financial support for Ireland. The Act gives new powers to the Minister for Finance to make new types of order that relate to a banking institution such as a "direction order",[9] a "subordinated liabilities order",[10] or a "transfer order"[11] of the assets or liabilities of the institution. These are all powers given to the Minister subject to the supervision of the High Court, to intervene in the affairs of financial institutions for the purposes of stabilising those institutions.

Section 59 of the Act makes it a criminal offence to publish the fact that the Minister proposes to make or has made any of those orders.

In any case, where an application is made under the Act to the High Court, the court may make an order that any application or part of it may be heard in private. The court may also impose restrictions on publication of any material that might be commercially sensitive arising on any such application under the Act.

Is the Report Privileged?

The Defamation Act 2009 deals in a fairly comprehensive way with the circumstances that give rise to a defence to a defamation action on the grounds of absolute privilege. A journalist must know when he or she has the protection of that privilege before reporting on what other people have said.

---

[8] Section 19(9) of the Mental Health Act 2001.
[9] Refer to p.266 of the glossary for an explanation of this term.
[10] Refer to p.275 of the glossary for an explanation of this term.
[11] Refer to p.276 of the glossary for an explanation of this term.

Common Law and Privilege

The law has always recognised that the public has an interest in receiving fair and accurate reports in certain proceedings, such as proceedings in courts and parliament, and various other proceedings such as tribunals, notwithstanding that the proceedings may contain statements defamatory of individuals.

To qualify for common law privilege, the report of such proceedings must be fair and accurate, though not necessarily verbatim. A summary is perfectly acceptable so long as it is a fair summary. If proceedings last over a number of days the media is entitled to report them as they occur. However, it is not acceptable to carry an accurate report of the plaintiff's or prosecution's case and to fail to reflect the defendant's attack on it either by cross-examination or otherwise at all. Some years ago the media in reporting a criminal case gave considerable prominence to prosecuting counsel's opening speech and then failed to report the evidence for either side or the fact that two days later the defendant was acquitted. Such a report is not of course "fair and accurate".

However, if a report is generally fair and accurate a slight inaccuracy will not deprive it of privilege although a significant inaccuracy will have that effect.

The report must be confined to what transpired in court including documents read or exhibited therein. If there is an issue as to the admissibility of certain evidence or documents, it is unwise to report their contents until this issue has been determined.

Common law privilege does not extend to reporting a matter which is blasphemous, indecent or seditious, or (of course) contrary to statute. It should be noted that s.14 of the Censorship of Publications Act 1929 provides:

> (1) It shall not be lawful to print or publish or cause or procure to be printed or published in relation to any judicial proceedings—
> (a) any indecent matter the publication of which would be calculated to injure public morals, or
> (b) any indecent medical, surgical or physiological details the publication of which would be calculated to injure public morals.

Apart from the criminal penalties for breach of such and prohibition, such material will not be protected by privilege at common law.

Absolute Privilege

Section 18 of the Defamation Act 1961 conferred a privilege which was effectively an absolute privilege on fair and accurate reports, published contemporaneously, of court proceedings held in public. The "fair and accurate" requirement was identical to that considered above in relation to common law privilege. The requirement of contemporaneity would cover reports in the next edition of a newspaper or similar publication after the report, but not a book or film made a considerable time later: such a publication may be able to avail of common law privilege.

Section 17 of the Defamation Act 2009 carries forward this "absolute privilege" and defines it as attaching to "fair and accurate" reports of statements made during the process of certain public hearings. That section contains a list of persons and bodies[12] in respect of which the reporting of such statements attracts the statutory "absolute privilege". The list includes statements made in the Houses of the Oireachtas, by members of the European Parliament in the Parliament, Oireachtas and European parliamentary committees, the courts, public hearings in the courts in Northern Ireland and any other state, tribunals established in the State, coroners' courts, publicly held government inquiries in the State or in Northern Ireland. The requirement of contemporaneity of reporting no longer appears to be necessary in respect of statements made attracting the privilege under the 2009 Act,[13] although much belated reporting might not necessarily attract this privilege

The connected question of qualified privilege is dealt with in Chapter 5 of this work.

---

[12]   Refer to s.17 of the Defamation Act 2009 in Appendix 2(b).
[13]   The 2009 Act was commenced on January 1, 2010 by S.I. No. 517 of 2009.

CHAPTER FIVE

DEFAMATION

Striking a Balance

The Constitution protects both the right to one's good name and the right to freedom of expression. Neither right is absolute, each qualifies the other. If the right to a good name were absolute, no criticism or statements of a damaging kind would be possible at all. If the right to freedom of expression were absolute, a citizen's reputation would be unprotected even against lies. Accordingly, the law seeks to strike a balance. It does this through the law of defamation.

Article 40.3.2 of the Constitution provides that:

> The State shall, in particular, by its laws protect as best it may from unjust attack and, in the case of injustice done, vindicate the life, person, good name and property rights of every citizen.

This is a strong formulation of the right to a good name, in which that right is mentioned at the same sentence as the right to life, person and property. It reflects the value which has been placed on good name or reputation, in one form or other, by law codes from ancient times to the present. There is even an example from Brehon law.

The right to freedom of expression is also provided for in the Constitution. Article 40.6.1° guarantees certain rights including:

i.   The right of the citizens to express freely their convictions and opinions.

The education of public opinion being, however, a matter of such grave import to the common good, the State shall endeavour to ensure that organs of public opinion, such as the radio, the press, the cinema, while preserving their rightful liberty of expression, including criticism of Government policy, shall not be used to undermine public order or morality or the authority of the State.

The publication or utterance of blasphemous, seditious or indecent matter is an offence which shall be punishable in accordance with law.

KEY PRINCIPLES OF THE LAW OF DEFAMATION

The key principles of the law of defamation, insofar as it affects the media, are:

- A person has a right not to have his reputation adversely affected by false publications which discredit him.
- A journalist (or anyone else) has an absolute right to publish anything which can be shown to be true or substantially true.
- In relation to matters of public interest there is broad scope for comment, even damaging comment, to be made on facts which are truly stated.
- In some circumstances there may be a right to publish a statement which turns out to be false; this arises by reason of privilege.

The whole law of defamation is about the application of these principles to the myriad of individual cases which occur.

The law of defamation is not limited to media libels but extends also to, private letters, emails, in-house journals, blogs, words written on walls, leading gestures and other physical acts.

However, no clear distinction can be made between media and non-media defamation, firstly, because the general law applies to each, and secondly, because a private defamation can easily become the source of a media defamation as when a privately circulated document falls into the hands of, or is "seen by" the media. In those circumstances quite different considerations may apply to private circulation as opposed to publication by the media to the public generally, especially if there is a sensational headline.

Because defamation by the media has far greater circulation than private defamation, damages in a media action are likely to be very much greater. One of the big growth areas for defamation cases relate to defamatory statements contained on the internet.

Remedies

The civil law of defamation has evolved in the context of the availability or otherwise of the principal remedies that the law provides for an attack on a person's reputation—damages and/or an injunction. If these remedies are available the defamation is said to be actionable, that is, the defamation is one which the law will recognise and for which it will provide a remedy unless one of the excepted defences is available.

Before January 1, 2010 the law of defamation was not fully codified but consisted in the main of the common law as it evolved over time through its application in the courts. Since the passing into law of the Defamation Act 2009 (the "2009 Act") the law is now codified for defamations occurring after January 1, 2010. The new Act contains a range of other remedies previously not available which are now accessible to a person who believes he has been defamed. For the purposes of the 2009 Act, "defamatory statement" means a statement that tends to injure a person's reputation in the eyes of reasonable members of society.

Summary Disposal

Section 34 of the 2009 Act allows for the summary disposal[1] of defamation actions. The remedy of summary disposal existed before the 2009 Act but was rarely used. The court at any stage of proceedings is entitled to consider the strength of the claim and dispose of it summarily in favour of either party. Applications are made by way of notice of motion grounded on affidavit and are to be determined by a judge sitting alone in the absence of a jury.

For a plaintiff to obtain summary relief the court must be satisfied, first, that the statement in respect of which the action was brought was defamatory, and secondly, that the defendant has no defence to the action that is reasonably likely to succeed. If the judge is satisfied that a case has been made then he may make a correction order or one prohibiting further publication of the statement to which the action relates. No damages are awarded in cases of summary disposal.

Defendants too can apply for summary disposal of the action if they can demonstrate that a statement complained of is not reasonably capable of bearing a defamatory meaning.

Declaratory Orders

A declaratory order is an order of the court declaring that the statement is false or defamatory of the plaintiff. Applications for declaratory orders are made to the Circuit Court and can be made at anytime during the course of Circuit Court proceedings. The application is

---

[1] Summary disposal in this context, means that the matter is dealt with by the court by reference to the pleadings and evidence on affidavit as opposed to a full hearing with oral testimony.

brought before the court by way of a motion on notice which is supported by an affidavit setting out the grounds upon which the application is based. Section 28(2) of the Defamation Act 2009 sets out the circumstances when a court should give an order of this nature.

A court shall make a declaratory order if it is satisfied that:

(a) the statement is defamatory of the plaintiff and the defendant has no defence to the application,

(b) the plaintiff requested the respondent to make and publish an apology, correction or retraction in relation to that statement, and

(c) the defendant failed or refused to accede to that request or, where he or she acceded to that request, failed or refused to give the apology, correction or retraction the same or similar prominence as was given by the defendant to the statement concerned.

An applicant for a declaratory order shall not be required to prove that the statement to which the application concerned relates is false. If an application is made under this section, the applicant is not entitled to bring an application for damages but he may apply to the court for a correction order.

Correction Order

Section 30 of the 2009 Act allows a plaintiff to a defamation action to apply to the court for a correction order at any time during the trial on notice to the defendant. The court may grant such an order where there is a finding that the statement in respect of which the action was brought was defamatory and the defendant has no defence to the action. The court may, upon the application of the plaintiff, make a correction order directing the defendant to publish a correction of the defamatory statement. The order may contain details as to the period of time within which the apology must be published and the form of the apology.

Order Prohibiting Publication of a Defamatory Statement

This remedy under s.33 of the 2009 Act allows the court to make a specific order to ensure that future damage to reputation does not occur. The order, if made, restrains future publications of the statement in question once the court is satisfied that it is defamatory and the defendant has no defence to the action that is reasonably likely to succeed. The remedy is not new however, as it was previously available to the court to grant an injunction to the same effect.

The 2009 Act further provides in s.34 for summary disposal of such an action. The court in a defamation action may, upon the application of the defendant, dismiss the action if it is satisfied that the statement in respect of which the action was brought is not reasonably capable of being found to have a defamatory meaning. Like the other "new remedies" referred to above, this section shall be brought by motion on notice to the other party to the action and shall be grounded on an affidavit.

A successful application for a prohibition order was made in *Watters v Independent Star Ltd*.[2] The complaint in this case related to an article carried in the *Star* referring to the plaintiff by name and address and accompanied by his photograph. The article was entitled "Larry's secret shower buddy" and purported to be an exposé of a relationship quite clearly presented to the reader as being sexual in nature between the plaintiff and one Larry Murphy, a recently released and extremely high profile convict. The judge outlined how the plaintiff's solicitor had written to the defendant company seeking an apology. No apology was forthcoming and proceedings were duly issued.

The court issued a declaratory order under s.28(1) of the Defamation Act 2009 and found that the statement in respect of which the action was brought was defamatory and that the defendant had no defence to the action. It also granted the applicant an order under s.33 of the Act prohibiting the defendant from publishing or further publishing the false and defamatory statements in respect of which the application was made.

As the parties were unable to agree the contents of an apology and the form of correction that would be published, the court made an order under this section.

Publication of a Defamatory Statement

The gist of any actionable defamation is the publication of a statement that conveys a defamatory imputation. Since the enactment of the 2009 Act, "statement" includes a statement made orally or in writing, visual images, sounds, gestures and any other method of signifying

---

[2] [2010] IECC 1.

meaning. It also includes a statement that is broadcast, published on the internet and an electronic communication.

In the law of defamation, the term "publication" means any communication to a third party, i.e. a person other than the speaker or writer on the one hand, and the person spoken about on the other. A person may say what he likes about another to that person's face, or in a private letter: there is no publication in law unless and until a third party hears or reads it. The person who communicates the material is called the publisher and this term is used whether the communication takes the form of a private conversation, a newspaper article or a television broadcast.

A printed story about some scandal may make no reference at all to the plaintiff but the inclusion of his photograph in the middle of the text may lead to the inference that the whole article refers to him. Equally, a caricature showing the plaintiff in a distorted or threatening or repulsive pose may colour the interpretation of what is said about him in a printed text. A defamation may be communicated wholly without words as where the plaintiff's photograph is published between photographs of notorious criminals or in a "chamber of horrors".[3]

Libel and Slander

Formerly a statement made in permanent form was a defamatory statement but if it was made in an impermanent form (mainly spoken) it was slander. The distinction between libel and slander has been abolished by the Defamation Act 2009.[4] From January 2010 there is one single action known as the tort of defamation. The tort of defamation now consists of the publication, by any means, of "a defamatory statement" concerning a person to one or more than one person. The requirement in most cases of alleged slander to prove special damage is now abolished. Consequently, all actions for defamation are now actionable without proof of special damage. Although slander remains a separate cause of action in respect of spoken defamations committed prior to January 1, 2010 there are few cases left to be disposed of before the courts at the time of writing.

---

[3] *Monson v Gossauds* [1894] 1 Q.B. 671.
[4] Section 2 of the Defamation Act 2009.

Who may be Sued?

Any person involved in the publication of the statement could potentially be a defendant. However, it is usually the media organisation itself that is named as the defendant as it is regarded the best "mark" for damages.

The Civil Liability Act 1964 provides that all persons who participate in the commission of a tort or civil wrong are "concurrent wrong doers". All are liable to be sued. If one is sued and the other(s) are not, the defendant can seek to join the other wrongdoers and seek "contribution or indemnity" from them. This means they can be made responsible for some or all of the damages and costs.

There is no legal reason why media defendants do not seek to use these provisions against those who misinform them. No doubt they feel that doing so would kill off sources of information or quotation. But this remedy is available, and might be considered more often, especially in the case of larger public or private bodies that court the media and seek to use it for their ends.

Multiple Publications

Section 11 of the 2009 Act permits only one action in respect of multiple publications unless the court has given leave to bring more than one action if it considers it in the interests of justice to do so. Presumably, this protects, for example, a media organisation from a multitude of actions if the story is carried in its newspaper, website and RSS feed. It is not clear whether this prohibition of multiple actions will apply if the content of the defamatory statement differs in the relevant publications.

The Internet

Many of the organisations that are involved in online publications are to some degree protected by the European Communities (Directive 2000/31/EC) Regulations 2003.[5] The Regulations implement into Irish law the terms of what is often called the E-Commerce Directive. This Directive defines the circumstances in which internet intermediaries can be held accountable for material that is "hosted", "cached" or "carried" by the providers but which material was not created by them. An internet provider is not liable for information transmitted by

---

[5] A copy of the Regulations is contained in Appendix 5 to this work.

them provided certain conditions are met. The conditions are that the information had been provided to them by an end user or if the service provider provides access to a communication network by others and the following additional requirements are satisfied:

- The service provider did not initiate the transmission.
- The provider did not select the receiver of the transmission.
- The provider did not select or modify the information.

The Regulations were interpreted quite broadly by the High Court in *Mulvaney v Sporting Exchange Ltd.*[6] Here the court concluded that the particular chat rooms involved in that case did come within the scope of the regulations. The provider in this case was exempt from liability for defamation as it did not have actual knowledge of the existence of the comments. It is important though that providers act promptly in taking down comments that are defamatory as they might otherwise be fixed with knowledge and lose the protection of the Regulations.

What is Defamatory?

In general, a defamatory statement or imputation is one which:

(a) is false; and
(b) tends to discredit a person by damaging his good name, i.e. the regard in which he is held, his reputation, in the eyes of reasonable right-thinking people.

False

Only a false statement or imputation is actionable. This is because a defence of justification (now called truth) is available to the publisher (see defences below). However, a journalist must also consider the degree to which a right to privacy might apply to the article in question. So even though the article might not be defamatory, it may well give rise to an action in damages (see the Chapter on privacy). The defence of justification may be available even though part of what is published is false, assuming the publication as a whole is substantially true. But the onus is on the defendant to prove the truth of defamatory words which he has published.

---

[6] [2009] IEHC 133.

Tending to Discredit

Over the years many forms of words have been used to describe the nature of a defamatory statement. One can regard the definition "tending to discredit" as authoritative.[7] Other formulations which have the weight of authority behind them are "tending to lower him in the estimation of others", "tending to expose him to hatred, contempt or ridicule", "tending to injure his reputation in his office, trade or profession", or "tending to injure his financial credit". Some of these relate to specific circumstances only.

The American Law Institute's *Restatement of the Law, Torts 2d* contains perhaps the best contemporary attempt at a comprehensive definition as follows:

> "A statement is defamatory if it tends to harm the reputation of another so as to lower him or her in the estimation of the community or to deter third parties from associating or dealing with him or her."

In order to be actionable, it is not necessary to prove that the words published have, in fact, damaged the plaintiff's reputation. This is because specific instances of such damage are generally impossible to prove except in an impressionistic way and the witnesses available to a plaintiff are likely to be his friends who presumably do not believe the words. In deciding whether words are defamatory the law looks to their tendency, not necessarily to their actual effect. However, if words can be proved to have a specific effect this may lead to an award of aggravated damages (see damages, below).

Although falsity is an essential aspect of an actionable defamation, it has to be borne in mind that not every untrue statement is defamatory. To be defamatory, a statement must be false and be such as to make people think the worse of the plaintiff in a moral or social sense. Thus, to say, falsely, that a professional person has retired from practice due to ill health may well cause damage but is not actionable as defamation.[8] This is because ill health is misfortune not normally causing a loss of social or moral standing in the eyes of reasonable people. It would be otherwise if the statement were that a professional person had ceased to practice after having been "struck off" for

---

[7] *Youssoupoff v Metro Golden Mayer* [1934] 50 T.L.R.

[8] It may, however, be actionable as injurious falsehood: see below.

misconduct. Furthermore, words which are false and perhaps hurtful, but which in no way reflect on a person's character or reputation are not actionable as defamation. In particular, words which only damage the feelings of the plaintiff are not defamatory. Thus, it has been held not to be defamatory to overstate a person's age although this may help hurt his feelings.[9] For practical purposes, in deciding whether a statement is defamatory the key question is "assuming this to be false, does it tend to harm the plaintiff's reputation?"

The Standard of Right Thinking People

It is not enough to show that some small quirky group of the community think the worst of the plaintiff as a result of a publication. The court must consider whether he or she has been damaged in the eyes of reasonable right thinking persons, or some significant group of them, either large or small. Furthermore, the standards to be applied are those of reasonable right thinking people in the present time and not at some former period. To say, for example, that one member of a criminal gang "peached" on the others may lower him in the eyes of criminals and their associates. But their standards are not such that a court can approve or apply, so such a statement is not actionable. To say that a person is a practising catholic may cause fanatical fundamentalists or rationalists to think the worst of him but for the same reason is not actionable.

In *Berry v Irish Times*,[10] the paper printed a photograph of a protestor's placard on which the plaintiff, a former secretary of the Department of Justice, was described as a "felon setter". This truly means one who attempts to bring criminals to justice. Both the jury and the Supreme Court on appeal declined to find the words defamatory. The Supreme Court found that though the words might injure the plaintiff in the minds of some people, their standards were not those of reasonable or right thinking members of the community. The court, then, does not approve the standards of people with antisocial or utterly irrational views. But it does acknowledge that short of this, individuals and groups are entitled to strong views, even if they are not widely shared. Particularly if the plaintiff is himself a member of such a group, their standards may be important. Thus, the views and standards of strictly observant Jews, though a tiny minority of the population, are

---

[9]   *Van Baggen v Nichol* (1963) 38 D.L.R.
[10] [1973] I.R. 365; and see "innuendo" below.

both reasonable and capable of being held by persons who are "right thinking". These standards may be highly relevant if, for example, the plaintiff is a Rabbi. Decisions as to what is and is not defamatory vary over time and with circumstances, including especially, the identity of the plaintiff and the standards of contemporary, as opposed to historic, opinion. At one time it was defamatory of a person to say that he was a Roman Catholic or a Francophile or, later, pro-German, but it is obvious that none of these is now defamatory in itself. On the other hand, it is now gravely defamatory to say of a person that he is a member, or associate, of the IRA, but this would not have been so in the Ireland of 1922.[11] Although there is no single formula for identifying a defamatory statement, experience suggests that certain types of statements are almost always defamatory. These include:

(a) False statements that a person has committed a crime. Except in the most trivial cases, these are found to be defamatory. Allegations of very serious crimes, e.g. murder, subversive activities or drug dealing attract very substantial damages. This may seem obvious, but quite a number of such allegations have been published in Ireland over the last decade. False allegations of offences that are minor (in the legal sense) may be seriously defamatory. A false allegation of drunk driving against a priest resulted in Hibernia magazine going out of business in the 1970s, and would probably be even more seriously regarded today.

(b) A false allegation reflecting on a person's behaviour or capacity in his profession or trade. If this kind of allegation is seriously damaging it can attract large damages. Allegations of professional or commercial dishonesty (whether amounting to a crime or not) are extremely risky.

(c) False allegations of sexual immorality, especially if they involve suggestions of adultery, family irresponsibility or hypocrisy. Such allegations are well established as defamatory. It has yet to be established whether it is defamatory in contemporary Ireland to state merely that a person is having a non-marital sexual relation-ship. The practice for such cases has been to settle unless there is a defence of justification available. This subject matter has increased in practical importance with the rise of the gossip column. Such allegations are often based on third hand information, which is

---

[11] *McDonagh v News Group Newspapers, Irish Times Law Reports*, December 27, 1993.

impossible to establish in evidence. Informants of these topics are notoriously elusive if asked to give evidence. The decriminalisation of homosexuality does not necessarily mean that a false allegation of homosexuality made against a person is not defamatory. Such an allegation against a married person is probably defamatory. False allegations of consorting with prostitutes are defamatory.[12] False allegations of sexual activities which amount to crimes (e.g. rape, child abuse, intercourse with an underage person) are clearly defamatory.[13]

In *Quigley v Creation Ltd,*[14] it was suggested that a false statement about a woman to the effect that she had been the victim of a rape (or, presumably, any sexual offence), might be defamatory as "exposing her to undesirable interest".

(d)   False allegations of misconduct by public officials are likely to be defamatory.

(e)   False allegations of insolvency against an individual or company and statements casting doubt on one's ability to pay one's debts as they fall due.

(f)   False allegations of commercial or professional "sharp practice", not amounting to crime, can be defamatory. Such stories have this in common with sexual ones: informants are often eager to see a story published but are most elusive and unwilling to give evidence later.

The following are examples of allegations in the mainstream media that have come to the attention of Irish lawyers in recent years:

- that the plaintiff is a mass murderer;
- that the plaintiff is a manufacturer of bombs;
- that the plaintiff is engaged in a campaign of terrorism including the murder of innocent civilians;
- that the plaintiff has bribed public officials;
- that the plaintiff is a drug dealer;
- that the plaintiff and his family suffer from AIDS;
- that the plaintiff is a prostitute or a procuress;
- that the plaintiff is unfaithful to his or her spouse;

---

[12]   *Andrews v Irish Press,* unreported, High Court, 1987.

[13]   *McDonagh v News Group Newspapers, Irish Times Law Reports,* December 27, 1993.

[14]   [1971] I.R. 269.

- that the plaintiff is insolvent;
- that the plaintiff's business is a front for criminals;
- that the plaintiff's incompetence as a professional person has needlessly caused deaths;
- that the plaintiff has deceived his clients and cheated them out of money;
- that the plaintiff is incompetent in his profession;
- that the plaintiff has defrauded a state scheme;
- that the plaintiff, a married man, is actively homosexual;
- that the plaintiff is a spy;
- that the plaintiff is a petty tyrant at his work;
- that the plaintiff, a Government Minister, had been a member of a political party financed by "special activities" including drug-running, prostitution, and forgery of currency.

Journalists as Plaintiffs

Journalists and media executives normally see themselves as potential defendants rather than plaintiffs. But, surprisingly often, the boot is on the other foot. A statement that a journalist is a "libellous journalist" is defamatory, as also are any words to the same effect. In the 1950s the well-known writer, Honor Tracey, successfully sued the *Daily Telegraph* for a retraction and apology in relation to an article written by her on this basis.[15]

Determination of Defamatory Statement

We have been considering, in general terms, the meaning of defamation. We now move from the general to the particular and ask: how does the court determine whether or not any particular publication conveys a defamatory meaning? And if it is defamatory, what precise meaning or meanings does it convey?

This question is to be answered by the application of an objective test: in what sense would the ordinary reasonable man understand the words in question? The court or jury must consider the words in their natural or ordinary meaning, including the inferences which would naturally be drawn from them. They must also, if innuendo is pleaded,

---

[15] *Tracey v Kennsley Newspapers Ltd, The Times*, April 9, 1954.

consider how the words would be interpreted by people with special knowledge of extrinsic facts. The intention of the publisher or the sense in which witnesses may have understood the words is binding on the court or jury, by reason of the objective nature of the text.

Ordinary and Natural Meanings

Often, there is no difficulty. A statement that "Smith is the biggest heroin dealer in Dublin" has a plain meaning that is plainly defamatory if false. Lawyers say it is defamatory "in its natural and ordinary meaning". These words, in their ordinary sense mean:

* Smith deals in heroin;
* he does so on a bigger scale than anyone else in Dublin;
* he is a criminal;
* he is engaged in antisocial activity of a gross kind;
* he does so for financial profit.

It is very important for a journalist to be aware that the "ordinary and natural meaning" is held to include *inferences*. In the leading English case of *Lewis v Daily Telegraph*,[16] it was said:

> "... what the ordinary man would infer without special knowledge has generally been called the natural and ordinary meaning of words. But that expression is rather misleading in that it conceals the fact that there are two elements in it. Sometimes it is not necessary to go beyond the words themselves, as where the Plaintiff has been called a thief and a murderer. But more often the sting is not so much in the words themselves as in what the ordinary man will infer from them, and that is also regarded as part of their ordinary and natural meaning."

This is of great importance in practice, because one quite often sees instances where a writer has been careful not to make any direct accusation, and thinks he has thereby avoided liability. But if a defamatory meaning is capable of being detected in the ordinary and natural meaning in the language used, it will be part of the ordinary and

---

[16]   [1964] A.C. 258.

natural meaning. Take a crude example, from a non-media case: the statement "as a result of our discussion with the company's bankers we had no option but to dismiss the General Manager" contains a clear defamatory inference although in the particular case it was held to be covered by qualified privilege.

Writing which is insinuatory or tongue-in-cheek in its tone is particularly liable to have a defamatory meaning construed by inference. This is often found in gossip magazines. In considering what ordinary readers understand or infer from words in their ordinary and natural meaning, it is important to bear in mind that the reader is not bound either by strict rules of grammar or by the rules which lawyers use to construe a legal document: a general impression damaging to the plaintiff may be present even though neither a grammarian nor a lawyer would consider it a necessary implication from the words used. In the words of a leading English case[17]:

> "the results of a columnous falsehood arise from the impression which it – all of it, including reservations, cautions, and all the rest – makes upon the minds of the readers, an impression which may be quite apart from any artificial restriction which the author of the falsehood sought to impose."

Accordingly, words may be defamatory even if they are written in interrogative form ("Smith: the biggest heroin dealer in Dublin?") or tentatively or hypothetically. Note in particular, that words conveying the imputation that the plaintiff is under suspicion ("Police probe 'drug dealer' Smith") are defamatory as they are suggesting that the person of the probe is reasonably suspected of serious crime.

Nor can a defamatory implication be conclusively concluded by putting in qualifying words before or after. If one added to the "heroin dealer" headline at the beginning of this section a sentence to the effect that Smith had not yet been convicted and should be given the benefit of the doubt, it would be for the jury to say whether that qualified the initial defamation out of existence: it is unlikely that they would find that it did, especially if the qualification was much less prominently printed.

In general, the experience of the court is that the layman's capacity for inference is much greater than that of lawyers or grammarians but that, in the words of a leading textbook: "the tendency and effect of the

---

[17] *Stubbs v Mazure* [1920] A.C. 66.

language, not its form, is the criterion and a Defendant cannot defame and escape the consequences by dexterity of style".

Here, as throughout the law of defamation, it is extremely important for a journalist or media executive to be realistic above everything. It is usually disastrous to go to court insisting on an artificially innocent meaning of words when it is very probable that a jury will opt for the more obvious defamatory meaning. See, for example, "the Roses from Rock Hudson" example under "very odd meanings" below.

Innuendo

Look again at the "Smith is the biggest heroin dealer in Dublin" headline and suppose that, though not stated in the publication, some but not all the readers know some additional facts about Smith, viz he is a teacher, a county councillor and a prominent anti-drugs campaigner.

To those who know these facts, the words have additional meanings. These include:

- Smith is a hypocrite;
- he is unfit to practice his profession;
- he has deceived those who voted for him;
- he is unworthy to be an elected representative.

Because these meanings are not apparent unless one has information not contained in the publication, they are "innuendos".

Sometimes, a statement is not defamatory at all without an innuendo. Thus, "Smith goes twice a week to No. 20 Main Street" will mean nothing to many people but to those who know that there is a brothel at that address it is clearly defamatory.

Similarly, "Mr Smith, solicitor, paid promptly for his swimming pool with a cheque drawn on his client account." To solicitors, accountants and many others, but not to the general public, this will mean that Smith has appropriated his clients' money. This is because they know that a solicitor is not entitled to use his clients' money in the client account for personal expenditure. This additional information gives rise to an "innuendo".

Whether a defamatory imputation arises from the natural and ordinary meaning of words, or from one or more innuendos, is often very important in practice. The case of *Berry v Irish Times*,[18] above, is

---

[18]   See fn.10.

an example of a situation in which failure to plead innuendo was responsible for the plaintiff losing his case. Furthermore, different rules of evidence apply when innuendo is alleged, as opposed to when the ordinary and natural meaning alone is relied on. Where innuendo is alleged, evidence can be lead as to the meaning and interpretation of the words which is not possible otherwise. This can be vital.

Nevertheless, there is often confusion as to the precise legal meaning of the term "innuendo". This is because the legal meaning is different from the meaning of the term in ordinary speech. It is therefore worth looking at the distinction in the little detail.

The word "innuendo" derives from the Latin verb *innuere* meaning "to nod", and by extension, to hint or insinuate. In ordinary speech, therefore, the word means something hinted at or insinuated. This is usually done by a form of words which gives rise to a damaging inference and is therefore, in law, part of the ordinary and natural meaning.

The legal meaning of innuendo, however, is a damaging inference conveyed by something outside the written or recorded form of words. Usually, as the examples at the beginning of this section show, this is some special knowledge which leads some or even all of the readers or listeners to interpret the words in a sense different from their ordinary meaning. For example, the information that No. 20 Main Street is a brothel enables a person who possesses it to interpret a statement that a man goes twice weekly to that address in a completely different sense.

However, "the extrinsic matter" causing or allowing a different interpretation may be much broader. In spoken or broadcast words, the extrinsic circumstances may be a tone of voice or expression which may even suggest that what is conveyed is the precise opposite of the literal meaning of words: see the Jason Donovan example later in this chapter. Slang terms, technical terms, words in a foreign language, or literary or historical references may also be used. The essence of a legal innuendo, however, is that information or the terms used require a more than ordinary general knowledge to interpret them. To say that a man is a "Judas" conveys the clear meaning even to people with very ordinary general knowledge. To say that he is an "Annias" or a "Quizling" requires the more specialist knowledge that the first was a New Testament figure struck dead for lying and dishonesty and the second was a wartime Norwegian politician who collaborated with the Nazis. In both these examples an innuendo arises.

It is possible that an innuendo may be capable of establishing that words had no defamatory meaning, or a less serious one, even though on their face they convey a very serious libel. To attribute to somebody the phrase "I'll murder him", literally means that the speaker announced an intention of killing someone but the innuendo represented by the colloquial use of the term in certain contexts, meaning merely "I'm very angry with him", wholly destroys that meaning.

Social Context

Words change in their meaning and context over time and, to some extent, from place to place. A classic example is the word "gay" whose new meaning over the last 30 or 40 years has virtually driven out the original connotation of cheerful and light hearted. The homosexual connotation of the term is now so well-established that it would be unrealistic in most contexts for a media defendant to allege that its use conveyed only the original meaning.

When, in 1971, Mr Berry took offence to the word "Felon Setter" applied to himself, he knew that the original technical meaning of the term was someone who took active steps to bring felons to justice. However, he relied on the proposition that in Ireland, for historical reasons, the term meant a person paid by the British Government in Ireland for reporting nationalist plans and who was therefore a traitor to his race. In reality, the term in both its senses had become archaic by 1971 and is even more so now. It is a classic example of a term which required an innuendo to convey any meaning at all, first, because it was archaic and secondly, because special construction even of the archaic word was required for him to make his case.

A Defamatory Statement can have Multiple Effects

In practice, all but the simplest defamatory words have multiple meanings. For example, in the case of *De Rossa v Independent Newspapers*,[19] the former Democratic Left leader and Minister for Social Welfare was libelled by a piece which, the jury found, meant that he was involved in or tolerated serious crime and that he had personally supported anti-semitism and violent communist oppression. The Supreme Court held that these allegations, being untrue, constituted the gravest and most serious defamatory statement: "it is hard to imagine a more serious one". They also felt that the defamatory statement being true would mean that the plaintiff was guilty of

---

[19]   [1999] 4 I.R. 432.

conduct, which was not only likely to bring him into disrepute with right minded people, but was such as to render him unsuitable for public office.

The latter meaning is an innuendo communicated to anyone (surely the great majority) who knew of his political office and, later, his ministerial one. A serious defamatory statement alleging criminality, dishonesty, or anything along those lines is likely to carry innuendo of the same kind: a person would surely be just as unfit for employment as, say, a teacher or a doctor on the same basis.

As will be seen in the chapter on pleadings below, each innuendo must be separately pleaded and is, in theory, a separate cause of action.

Defamation is a Matter of Fact

Despite all technical difficulties and unpredictabilities of interpretation, each form of words has, in law, only one meaning and that is the meaning which the judge or jury find that the reasonable reader, either with or without special knowledge, would attribute to it. If it is not defamatory, it does not matter that many persons may in fact have interpreted it in a defamatory sense. This is because "defamation is a question of fact, not of intention". This cuts both ways. The journalist who wrote about No.20 Main Street in the example above may not have known that the premises was a brothel. In *Capital and Counties Bank v Henty*,[20] a circular saying that a large company "will no longer receive in payment cheques drawn on any of the branches of the Capital and Counties Bank" actually caused a run on the bank but was held not to be defamatory because the interpretation which led to the run was an unreasonable one.

However, the fact that a defamatory statement may have been published in genuine ignorance of its meaning is highly relevant to the question of damages (see Chapter 7 below).

Interpretative Problems

Let us now look again at the "heroin dealer" example in various different forms. Suppose it read: "Jones says: Smith deals in heroin" or "Jones lashes 'heroin dealer' Smith".

---

[20] (1882) 7 App. Cas. 741.

These forms seek to distance the publishers from the allegation by attributing it to Jones. As a means of avoiding liability this does not work. If it did, anything could be published as long as someone somewhere was prepared to say it. It is of course true that Jones said what is reported, but if the media repeat what he says, with or without attribution, they make his statement their own. This is an important rule of general application: A defamation is no less a defamation because it is reported in indirect speech, or in the passive voice ("… is believed to …"), and whether or not the original source is mentioned.

The only exception to this is where the original remark was made in public in circumstances of absolute privilege (in the Dáil or courts or equivalent circumstances).[21]

It is important to note that a report of what Jones said may be actionable even though Jones said it in circumstances of qualified privilege.[22] Thus, for example, if Jones is the headmaster of the school where Smith works, he is entitled to tell the Board of Management, privately, what he believes about Smith. But if a newspaper reports what he said to the public, the only defence is that the statement is true.

Now consider: "Smith is suspected of heroin dealing" or "Heroin deals: police suspect Smith".

These are not statements in indirect speech that Smith is a heroin dealer. They are statements that some people (identified as the police in the second example) suspect him of heroin dealing. The plaintiff's lawyers would argue that in each case (and certainly the second) the natural implication is that there are reasonable and substantial grounds for suspicion which has caused people who know the facts to suspect him. This is defamatory in itself because it tends to make "reasonable right thinking" people suspicious of him. Would you employ or vote for someone whom the police reasonably suspect of drug dealing?

The same effect is created by a statement like: "Police sources were yesterday naming Smith as the subject of their investigations in the heroin dealing case."

Even assuming that the police were indeed doing this "off the record", that fact is not necessarily a defence of any headline worded in the way mentioned above. More fundamentally, if Smith sues it will be necessary for the defendant to prove that police sources were naming Smith, and told the journalist so. But the policeman perhaps should not have been talking to the reporter in the first place and probably

---

[21]   See Chapter 6 on "Defences".
[22]   See Chapter 6 on "Defences".

will not give evidence or allow the journalist to name him. The plaintiff may then suggest that the whole story is malicious invention and this may be difficult to contradict.

No short-cuts based on attributing defamatory sentiments to others work. If the "Smith" story is to be written at all, it has to be on the basis of finding out the facts which led to the suspicions and printing those facts, if they stand up.

Meanings and Delivery

A well-known personality once sued a magazine for alleging that he was homosexual. He won, and recovered large damages. For several weeks after this a television program referred to X. at every opportunity. In particular, it said over and over "X" is certainly not homosexual. What did this mean? The tone, expressions and repetition all suggested it meant exactly the opposite of what it ostensibly stated. Especially in the case of broadcast material, words can convey the opposite of what they state on paper. Or, they may make a strong negative statement, which nonetheless conveys a positive.

Consider: "Friends and political associates strongly denounced suggestions that Mr Smith was involved in heroin dealing."

This may be a perfectly fair report; for example, if the "suggestions" have already received wide publicity. But if no such suggestions have been made publicly so that this is the first the readers knew of them, a court or jury may well view the publication as constituting a statement that Smith was, or was suspected of being, involved in heroin dealing. This view may be particularly attractive if the media cannot or will not identify the source of the "suggestions".

Every school child learns at an early stage that a phrase like "that's really great", can convey anything from genuine delight to "you've really screwed up" to "we're in trouble now", and "it couldn't be worse". Not surprisingly, the law also takes account of the great variety of meanings possible for words and phrases, especially where ambiguity is deliberately sought (as by whoever arranged that "tired and emotional" should mean "drunk").

There is no easy formula for the interpretation of oblique phrases, but one usually knows exactly what is conveyed. Some years ago an Irish publication said that a prominent person in his youth had been given roses by Rock Hudson. The written defence denied any defamatory suggestion, but the case was settled on the morning of the hearing. There can be little doubt what view the jury would have taken.

Identification

When words are proved to be defamatory, and to have been published in the media, there is still another test to be met before the plaintiff can rest his case. He must show that the words have been published "of and concerning" him—not someone else, or a vague group of people, or a fictitious person, or an unidentifiable person, but himself. That is, he must bring evidence to show that he is capable of being identified, and has in fact been identified as the subject of the defamatory words.

Two main points arise:

1. The plaintiff must be named or otherwise identified so as to convey to reasonable readers, or some section of them, that the publication is about him.

2. If it is conveyed in any way that the publication relates to the plaintiff then it is irrelevant to the question of libel that the defendant did not intend to refer to the plaintiff. But the defence has other options.[23]

The most common form of identification is by name, and here there is usually no problem for the plaintiff. But identification can take place in other ways as well. In one case,[24] a newspaper carried a front-page report of a notorious criminal case, which involved serious allegations against the defendant. Beside this, it carried a photograph of a completely uninvolved person, claiming he was the defendant leaving court. The subject of the photograph sued, claiming he was identified as the defendant. The paper settled. Again, a photograph of someone appearing at the centre of an article which describes some defamatory behaviour, but does not name him or her, may be seen as linking him or her to the text, especially if no explanation is forthcoming.[25]

Identification from Extrinsic Facts

In most of the cases that cause difficulty however, the plaintiff is not identified by name or by photograph or other likeness. He may be referred to by a nickname, initials, forename or surname only, a

---

[23] See Chapter 6 on "Defences".
[24] *O'Kelly v Irish Press Newspapers, Irish Times*, May 23–28, 1992.
[25] *Cooney v Sunday World, Irish Times*, November 8, 1978.

pseudonym or by blanks and asterisks. Or, he/she may not be directly referred to at all, as in *Morgan v Odhams Press*,[26] where a statement that a person was illegitimate (a term now in disuse) was held to be sufficient identification of his mother, as the subject of a defamation.

Often, identification takes place by the application of extrinsic facts, in a process similar to that applicable to innuendos (see above). Such a statement gives enough information to allow people with special knowledge to identify the plaintiff or, perhaps, to make enquiries which leads to his identification.

Thus, a statement such as "if competent medical care had been available Mr. Smith would not have died" is defamatory of Smith's doctor to those who knew that Smith was under his care in the period prior to his death. A statement making serious allegations about the conduct of an organisation such as a company or government department may, depending on the circumstances, be defamatory of those known to be in charge of it.

Where a newspaper makes allegations against an unidentified person but later identifies him in another edition, that identification may allow an action based on the first publication.[27] Although, this very point will shortly be clarified in a case pending before the Supreme Court. A similar position applies where an organ of the media identifies no one as the subject of its strictures but refers to other publications which contain such identification.

Words That Could Refer to Two or More People

Because "defamation is a question of fact, not of intention", a form of words which is equally referable to two or more people is actionable by either or all of them. Thus, it would be an unwise newspaper which published a report that "Patrick Murphy of Rathmines" had been convicted of a crime, because of the high likelihood that this description, without more detail, could apply to a significant number of persons. In *Newstead v London Express*,[28] the headline was "Harold Newstead, 30 year old Camberwell man, who was jailed for 9 months, liked having two wives at a time". This was held to be defamatory of a completely innocent Harold Newstead of Camberwell, although the

---

[26] [1971] 1 W.L.R. 1243.
[27] *Hayward v Thompson* [1982] Q.B. 47.
[28] [1940] 1 K.B. 377.

damages were derisory. This situation is now covered by the defence of unintentional defamation.[29]

The Danger of Using a Fictitious Name

Fictitious names are naturally used in fiction and, less frequently, in news stories. If, however, a fictitious name is used in a news story there is a risk that it will coincide with that of a real person. If, in addition, some details of the fictitious character also correspond, there is a real danger of identification of the real person as the subject of the story. Since the usual reason for the use of false names is the sensitive nature of the story, there is a clear risk of defamation.

This was illustrated in *Browne v Independent Newspapers*.[30] A front page story spoke of complaints by builders of bribes they were forced to pay by corrupt planning officials. A box in this story referred readers to a "News Analysis" feature inside, about a builder who described what went on. This article, several thousand words long, began "Builder John Browne knew the score", and went on to say how he was forced to pay increasing bribes in brown paper bags which he could no longer afford to pay. He then went to the authorities, it was said.

The plaintiff was John Browne, builder. He—and he alone—was thus described in the Dublin phone book. Many respectable witnesses, whose truthfulness was not challenged, swore that they believed the article referred to him. The paper pointed out that, at the very end of the article, thousands of words and several columns away from the references to Browne, there was a statement in italics that all names were fictitious. Most witnesses had simply not read that far, and those who had thought it was a device inserted for legal reasons.

The judge (Carney J.) refused to hold with the paper's submission that a person who read part only of a long article was not a "reasonable" person in law. He said it was for the jury to find whether the addendum, having regard to its contents and position, negatived the references to Browne.

The paper called no evidence whatever and therefore gave no explanation of why Browne's name was used, whether they had looked up the phone book, or who they were, in fact, referring to. The jury awarded Browne damages of £75,000.

---

[29] See Chapter 6 on "Defences".
[30] *Irish Times*, November 19, 1991.

Criminal Libel Now Abolished

The old offence of criminal libel has now been abolished. Prior to the Defamation Act 2009, the publication of a serious libel was at common law regarded as a crime as well as a civil wrong. Prosecutions for criminal libel in a non-media context occasionally occurred. An example of the sort of case was where an identifiable person repeatedly made grossly offensive statements about another in public places. In a media context, however, criminal libel was rare. Section 8 of the Defamation Act 1961 provided that no criminal prosecution could be commenced against any proprietor, publisher, editor or other person responsible for the publication of a newspaper in respect of any libel without an order of the High Court after a hearing in camera. This protection did not extend to publications other than newspapers within the meaning of the Act. In the case of *Hilliard v Penfield Enterprises,*[31] the relatives of a deceased gentleman were outraged by the publication of an alleged libel on him in the immediate aftermath of his death. In that case, leave to prosecute for criminal libel was refused even though the judge was plainly sympathetic to the application—going so far as to observe that it was difficult to believe that the individual defendants could stoop so low as to publish the libel complained of, but he nevertheless refused leave to initiate a prosecution.

Blasphemy

Section 35 of the 2009 Act abolished criminal libel but introduced a new offence of publishing or uttering a blasphemous matter. Such a person is liable upon conviction on indictment to a fine not exceeding €25,000. The Act specifies that for the purposes of this section, a person publishes or utters blasphemous matter if he publishes or utters a matter that is grossly abusive or insulting in relation to matters held sacred by any religion, thereby causing outrage among a substantial number of the adherents of that religion, and he or she intends by the publication or utterance of the matter concerned to cause such outrage.

The 2009 Act goes on to provide that it is a defence to proceedings for an offence of this kind for the defendant to prove that a reasonable person would find genuine literary, artistic, political, scientific or academic value in the matter to which the offence relates.

---

[31] [1991] I.R. 138.

It also provides that religion does not include an organisation or cult the principal object of which is the making of profit, or that employs oppressive psychological manipulation of its followers, or for the purpose of gaining new followers.[32]

The 2009 Act provides that where a person is convicted of an offence under s.36 the court may issue a warrant authorising members of the Garda Síochána to enter any premises and seize and remove all copies of the statement to which the offence related that are in the possession of any person, and to dispose of same following final judgment in the matter. As stated above, prosecutions for criminal libel were few and far between and it remains to be seen how this section will be interpreted in the future.

---

[32]   Section 36 of the Defamation Act 2009.

CHAPTER SIX

DEFENCES TO DEFAMATION

Prior to the enactment of the Defamation Act 2009 (the "2009 Act") there were many defences which might in practice be available in a libel action. Frequently, two or more of them could be used in combination. They vary considerably in their nature and effect. Some defences exempt the defendant from liability altogether. Others merely mitigate it or reduce the damages. Some are strong positive defences, while others merely consist of denying that the plaintiff has established the elements of a prima facie case.

Section 15 of the 2009 Act expressly abolishes the old defences with respect to causes of action arising after January 1, 2010[1] with some exceptions. Although, some of the "new" defences in the 2009 Act appear to reincarnate some of the old ones, it is not necessarily the case that the common law (court-based) interpretations of the "old" defences will apply to the "new" defences. Nevertheless, it is considered worthwhile to have some regard to the manner in which the courts have interpreted the pre-2010 positive defences due to the striking resemblance that they bear to their predecessors. The principal defences prior to the introduction of the Defamation Act 2009 applying to publications before January 1, 2010 were:

1. Justification
2. Fair comment
3. Privilege
4. Consent

These defences are still applicable in relation to defamations occurring prior to January 1, 2010.[2] For defamations occurring after that date a new scheme of defences exists.

---

[1] Subject to ss.17 and 18 preserving the old defences of qualified and absolute privilege.
[2] Section 3(1) of the Defamation Act 2009.

DEFENCES UNDER THE DEFAMATION ACT 2009

Defence of Truth

Section 16(1) provides:

> It shall be a defence (to be known and in this Act referred to as
> the "defence of truth") to a defamation action for the defendant
> to prove that the statement in respect of which the action was
> brought is true in all material respects.

This is the most fundamental of all defences. It is a claim that the
words complained of are true "in all material respects". The truth is a
complete defence to an action for defamation. Once established, it
protects the publication no matter how unfair, gratuitous, or intrusive
it may be, subject of course to the possibility of the plaintiff seeking
damages for breach of his right to privacy (see Chapter 11).

And so, if a publication contains two or more defamatory allegations
against the plaintiff, the defence shall not fail by reason only that the
truth of every statement is not proved, if the words not proved to be
true do not materially injure the plaintiff's reputation having regard to
the truth of the remaining allegations.[3] A plea of truth will not fail
because of minor inaccuracies in detail so long as the gist or substance
of the story is correct. Thus, an allegation that a person has been
convicted of shoplifting on 12 occasions can be justified by proof that
he has been convicted 11 times. But any statement which alters the
character of the main allegation or adds to its gravity must be proved
to be true or the defence will fail.

The principal difficulty with the defence of truth is not a legal one
at all. The burden of proof of the truth of a story is on the person who
published it. This means, in practice, that a journalist must ask himself
or herself not whether he or she believes the story to be true but whether
he or she can prove that it is true on the balance of probabilities.

The process of legal proof may be quite different to the process
whereby the journalist researches the story in the first place. In
particular, where a story arises from information from a third party, the
journalist must consider his informant's means of knowledge. Can the
informant himself prove the truth of what he says? Is he willing to do
so? If the information, as often happens, is known to the informant

---

[3]   Section 16(2) of the Defamation Act 2009.

only at second-hand, who are the persons who can prove it by direct evidence, and are they willing to testify?

These questions are of particular relevance in commercial and gossip column-type stories. In these cases in particular, informants are often, for their own reasons, extremely anxious that a particular story damaging to someone else should be published. But the story may be false or incapable of proof. The informant may be malicious or unwilling to be seen to assist the media. Such a person will whisper scandal to a journalist on the promise of anonymity, but won't stand up in public to stand over it

A further specific difficulty is posed by leaks from official sources. Again, the leaker may be anxious, for reasons of his or her own, to have a story published but be absolutely unwilling to support it afterwards. In many such cases, the official source should not be speaking to the press in the first place, under the rules of his or her occupation.

In circumstances such as these, a prudent journalist will simply regard the informant as alerting him to the story and will then make his own inquiries to see if the facts can be established in an admissible way. Surprisingly often, no attempt is made to do this because the journalist puts too high a premium on early publication. If there is an action, the media is in a position of trying to research the story after the event, which is usually much more difficult.

There will be circumstances in which a journalist will recognise that a story is quite unprovable but still wishes to publish. He may think that the story is undoubtedly true and the injured party will not sue. This is a risk which cannot usually be recommended.

Another technique sometimes employed in these circumstances is to put the story to the person who is the subject of it and publish it in the form of reporting that person's denial. In these circumstances it is hoped that any action by the injured party can be defended on the basis of consent (see below). A well-informed or well-advised person will rarely make any comment in answer to an unattributed allegation of this kind and a reaction of "no comment" will not, of course, justify the publication of the allegation about which that person has declined to comment. A decision to plead truth is a serious one because if it is unsuccessfully pleaded it will almost certainly increase the damages and costs and may assist the plaintiff in seeking aggravated or punitive damages.

On the other hand, once truth is pleaded it puts the truth of the matters alleged in the forefront of the issues to be tried and entitles the defendant to discovery against the plaintiff in relation to that issue.

Discovery is dealt with in more detail elsewhere but for present purposes it means that the defendant is entitled to seek from the plaintiff a list of all documents in his possession or power which bears on the issue of truth and, subject to any claim of privilege, is later entitled to demand their production.

Discovery is of most use in commercial cases which, of their very nature, tend to generate documents. If a defendant seeks discovery from a plaintiff, the plaintiff will be likely to seek a "cross order" for discovery against the defendant. This may reveal that the defendant has no documents at all to support the story.

When a media defendant pleads truth, it is expected that the plaintiff is entitled to full and detailed "particulars" of the plea. The pleadings in the case of *Cooney v Browne*[4] contained a "rolled up" plea that the statements of fact were not defamatory by reason of justification and that the expression of opinion was fair comment. The case supports the plaintiff's right to be told: (a) which part of the story will be alleged to be fact, as opposed to comment; and (b) each and every fact which the defendant proposes to prove to establish the plea of justification. The plaintiff, however, is not entitled to be told the evidence (*Leech* case) whereby these facts will be proved. The effect of this decision is that before the pleadings close, and therefore before the defendant can usually get discovery, he must pin his colours firmly to the mast by stating that he will prove truth, and the facts which he intends to prove in order to do so. The affidavit of verification previously referred to must also focus his mind considerably before raising this defence.

The plaintiff may think that it is unfair that the defence can be used to justify the publication of intimate personal, sexual or family matters even though the evidence may have been obtained very intrusively. This may be countered by an action for damages for breach of privacy rights. Previously, media defendants may also have considered that the defence of justification was unfair as the onus of proof rested on them. Prior to the 2009 Act, a politician or other prominent figure could simply remain dumb and decline to comment on allegations that they believed to be true. This criticism is now resolved in the 2009 Act because of the requirement imposed in the Act on both parties to swear affidavits verifying their pleadings containing assertions and allegations of fact no later than two months after service of the relevant pleadings. The swearing of a false or misleading statement in such an

---

4   [1985] I.R. 185 at 190.

affidavit is an offence. The onus on each party to swear an affidavit verifying what is contained in the pleadings is an important new dimension of the defamation proceedings.

One of the features contained in the 2009 Act is a reiteration of a section in the 1961 Act whereby a defendant succeeds if the publication contains a number of allegations capable of being separated, some of which are found to be true and some of which are not, and if those allegations which are proved are sufficiently significant and stain the plaintiff's reputation, then the unproved more minor allegations are seen to have no appreciable impact on the plaintiff's reputation.

In *Irving v Penguin*,[5] the defence of justification succeeded as the unjustified allegations were considered more minor and not to have caused any material harm to the plaintiff's reputation. In *Cooper Flynn v RTÉ*,[6] the defendant failed in demonstrating that the broadcast leading to the initiation of proceedings was true in respect of the person specifically identified in that broadcast but was able to show that the same allegation was true of others.

Finally, as with the old defence of justification, truth is a complete defence to an action for defamation. Malice or the absence of belief in the truth of the statement is irrelevant to the applicability of this defence. A statement may be true though the writer did not know that at the time

Honest Opinion

This is a new defence under the 2009 Act and is not too dissimilar to the defence of fair comment under the old regime.

The Act[7] sets out that the defence is available where the following criteria apply:

(a) at the time of the publication of the statement, the defendant believed in the truth of the opinion or, where the defendant is not the author of the opinion, believed that the author believed it to be true,

(b) (i) the opinion was based on allegations of fact—

(I) specified in the statement containing the opinion, or

---

[5] [2000] EWHC Q.B. 115.
[6] [2004] 2 I.R. 72.
[7] Section 20 of the Defamation Act 2009.

(II) referred to in that statement, that were known, or might reasonably be expected to have been known, by the persons to whom the statement was published,

or

(ii) the opinion was based on allegations of fact to which—

(I) the defence of absolute privilege, or

(II) the defence of qualified privilege,

would apply if a defamation action were brought in respect of such allegations,

and

(c) the opinion related to a matter of public interest.

Where the opinion is based on allegations of fact, a defendant cannot rely on honest opinion unless either:

(a) he proved the truth of all the allegations; or

(b) where some allegations are proved and some not, the defendant's opinion is honestly held in light of the allegations of fact which have been proved.

The defendant is now required to show that he or she believed in the veracity of the opinion, or alternatively, that he or she believed that the author believed it to be true. This defence therefore appears to place an additional burden on the defendant to show, at least to a certain extent, that there was no malice on their part in the publication of the statement. Arguably, this places a heavier onus on the defendant, as previously under the fair comment defence the courts considered the defence established if a hypothetical commentator could express the views in question honestly.[8]

Quite frequently, it may be difficult to distinguish between fact and opinion. However, it is important to distinguish them because the scope for defending an opinion is much greater than that available in defending the publication of defamatory fact which must be shown to be true. If there is ambiguity as to whether a particular publication is an opinion or a fact, it is likely to be regarded as fact because, in the words of a leading case, "comment in order to be justifiable as fair comment must appear as comment and must not be so mixed up with the facts that the reader cannot distinguish between what is report and what is comment".[9]

---

[8] *Benson v Bower* [2002] Q.B. 737.

[9] *Hunt v Star* [1908] 2 K.B. 319.

Sometimes, indeed the same form of words may be either fact or opinion depending on its context. If a writer says that "the minister is taking bribes and is therefore unfit to hold office", the first statement is clearly one of fact and the second is an opinion based on it. But if he merely says, "the minister is unfit to hold office" without making it clear what facts this is based on, the statement can only be regarded as a statement of fact which must be justified as the truth. Equally, what appears to be a statement of fact may be capable of defence as an opinion if it is accompanied by other facts and is a deduction or conclusion come to by the writer from those other facts.

The defence of honest opinion is also available to a defendant if the opinion was based on allegations of fact to which either the defence of qualified or absolute privilege attaches, but provided the opinion relates to a matter of public interest.

The following things have been expressly held to be matters of public interest in case law before the 2009 Act:

(a) political and governmental matters;

(b) ecclesiastical matters;

(c) the administration of justice;

(d) the management of publicly funded or supported companies, bodies or institutions;

(e) artistic works offered to the public such as books, paintings, films and musical performances;

(f) newspapers and media productions publicly disseminated;

(g) local government matters;

(h) public enquiries;

(i) the public conduct of a person who holds public office, or a candidate.

This list is not, and cannot be, complete because anything which may fairly be said to invite comment and which is brought before the public by the person who later becomes the plaintiff may be commented upon. The scope of "matters of public interest" is extremely wide and expanding.

However, the mere fact that a person has invited public attention in some way, e.g. by standing for election or publishing a book does not mean that he is open to every kind of criticism. It is not open to a writer under the guise, e.g. of a book review, to attack the private character of the author or to libel him in some way which is only tenuously connected to the work in respect of which he invited public attention.

Once again it will be necessary for each party to an action to swear an affidavit of verification and clearly this will put an onus on the defendant to set out details as to the honesty of the opinion which he holds.

Privilege

Privilege is based on recognition by the law that there are circumstances in which a person should be allowed to communicate material even though it later transpires to be false. Occasions of privilege occur where the law recognises that the public or social interest in freedom of speech takes precedence over an individual's right to have his or her reputation protected. Privilege may be absolute or qualified. In the case of absolute privilege, applying for example to a deputy in the Dáil, the person protected by that may say absolutely anything he likes and still be absolutely protected: neither falsity nor malice nor carelessness deprives him of the protection. In the case of qualified privilege, as the term suggests, the privilege is qualified in the sense that certain conditions apply to it.

Absolute Privilege under the 2009 Act

This is dealt with in s.17 of the 2009 Act which in terms harks back to the previous law. Section 17(1) provides as follows:

> It shall be a defence to a defamation action for the defendant to prove that the statement in respect of which the action was brought would, if it had been made immediately before the commencement of this section, have been considered under the law in force immediately before such commencement as having been made on an occasion of absolute privilege.

Section 17(2) of the 2009 Act provides an extensive though not exhaustive list of specific examples of statements which will attract privilege under the 2009 Act. It is important for a working journalist to be familiar with the types of proceedings that are covered by absolute privilege:

… it shall be a defence to a defamation action for a defendant to prove that the statement in respect of which the action was brought was—

(a) made in either House of the Oireachtas by a member of either House of the Oireachtas,

(b) contained in a report of a statement, to which paragraph (a) applies, produced by or on the authority of either such House,

(c) made in the European Parliament by a member of that Parliament,

(d) contained in a report of a statement, to which paragraph (c) applies, produced by or on the authority of the European Parliament,

(e) contained in a judgment of a court established by law in the State,

(f) made by a judge, or other person, performing a judicial function,

(g) made by a party, witness, legal representative or juror in the course of proceedings presided over by a judge, or other person, performing a judicial function,

(h) made in the course of proceedings involving the exercise of limited functions and powers of a judicial nature in accordance with Article 37 of the Constitution, where the statement is connected with those proceedings,

(i) a fair and accurate report of proceedings publicly heard before, or decision made public by, any court—

  (i) established by law in the State, or
  (ii) established under the law of Northern Ireland,

(j) a fair and accurate report of proceedings to which a relevant enactment referred to in section 40 of the Civil Liability and Courts Act 2004 applies,

(k) a fair and accurate report of proceedings publicly heard before, or decision made public by, any court or arbitral tribunal established by an international agreement to which the State is a party including the Court of Justice of the European Communities, the Court of First Instance of the European Communities, the European Court of Human Rights and the International Court of Justice,

(l) made in proceedings before a committee appointed by either House of the Oireachtas or jointly by both Houses of the Oireachtas,

(m) made in proceedings before a committee of the European Parliament,

(n) made in the course of proceedings before a tribunal established under the Tribunals of Inquiry (Evidence) Acts 1921 to 2004, where the statement is connected with those proceedings,

(o) contained in a report of any such tribunal,

(p) made in the course of proceedings before a commission of investigation established under the Commissions of Investigation Act 2004, where the statement is connected with those proceedings,

(q) contained in a report of any such commission,

(r) made in the course of an inquest by a coroner or contained in a decision made or verdict given at or during such inquest,

(s) made in the course of an inquiry conducted on the authority of a Minister of the Government, the Government, the Oireachtas, either House of the Oireachtas or a court established by law in the State,

(t) made in the course of an inquiry conducted in Northern Ireland on the authority of a person or body corresponding to a person or body referred to in paragraph (s),

(u) contained in a report of an inquiry referred to in paragraph (s) or (t),

(v) made in the course of proceedings before an arbitral tribunal where the statement is connected with those proceedings,

(w) made pursuant to and in accordance with an order of a court established by law in the State.

Two leading practitioners, Mr Hugh Mohan SC and Mr Eoin McCullough SC have drawn attention to the fact that certain examples listed include the proviso " where the statement is connected to those proceedings", while most examples do not.[10] Absolute privilege is a complete defence to a defamation action and is not defeated by malice. This remains the position under the 2009 Act.

Qualified Privilege

Qualified privilege is a defence of very broad scope but its application to media libels is a limited one. The reason for this lies in the nature of the defence itself. However, the occasions where qualified privilege

---

[10] Contrast proceedings before a Tribunal of Inquiry with that of an inquest.

does apply to the media are important and, in addition, there are specific statutory occasions of qualified privilege created specifically for the benefit of the media.

The law recognises that there are some circumstances in which a person is entitled to say what he thinks even though it is defamatory and turns out to be untrue or at least unprovable. It defines these circumstances by reference to a concept of duties: the speaker must have a duty or interest in saying what he does and the person or body to whom he addresses himself must have a reciprocal duty or interest to hear it.

The nature of these duties and interests are not narrowly defined or limited. They may be legal, social or moral duties, and may arise in very disparate circumstances. Thus, for example, a person is entitled to tell the Gardaí about a suspicion that another person has committed a crime even though it transpires the other person is completely innocent. A parent is entitled to warn a child about one of his companions. A banker or an employer is entitled to give their actual opinions when asked for a reference even though that opinion may be mistaken.

It will be seen that the foregoing examples all relate to private communications. A person is entitled to tell the Gardaí privately about their suspicions of a particular person but is not entitled to publish them in the newspapers. The parent can tell his or her child of his reservations about a particular companion but cannot broadcast it to the world at large. This is because the person to whom it is addressed must have a duty and/or interest in receiving it which is special to him or her. If, however, an allegation is published in the newspaper it will necessarily be read by a large number of people who have no special duty or interest in hearing it and therefore the privilege will usually be lost.

Qualified Privilege under the 2009 Act

This is dealt with by s.18 of the 2009 Act. As a preliminary point, unlike the abolition of other defences, the defence of qualified privilege at common law is preserved:

> Subject to section 17, it shall be a defence to a defamation action for the defendant to prove that the statement in respect of which the action was brought would, if it had been made immediately before the commencement of this section, have been considered by the law (other than the Act of 1961) in force immediately

before such commencement as having been made on an occasion of qualified privilege.

From this it is clear that the law on qualified privilege as set out in the second edition of this work, and other works on defamation, still applies. But the section goes on to provide:

> Without prejudice to the generality of subsection (1), it shall ... be a defence ... for the defendant to prove that—
> (a) the statement was published to a person or persons who—
>   (i) had a duty to receive, or interest in receiving, the information contained in the statement, or
>   (ii) the defendant believed upon reasonable grounds that the said person or persons had such a duty or interest, and
> (b) the defendant had a corresponding duty to communicate, or interest in communicating, the information to such person or persons.

This perfectly restates the scope of qualified privilege as it has existed for centuries.

It is further provided by s.19 that the defence of qualified privilege shall fail if the plaintiff proves that the defendant acted with malice, or if the statement is published to a person who is not a person with an interest in receiving it, because the publisher mistook such person for an interested person.

Section 18(3) refers to the First Schedule to the 2009 Act.[11] Statements which are within Pt 1 of the First Schedule are privileged, but subject to a defendant's obligation, on request, to publish a reasonable statement by way of explanation or contradiction. This sort of statement will not attract qualified privilege if the defendant ignores such a request. The general law of qualified privilege applies, with a right to call for explanation or contradiction, to the other statements. The contents of the First Schedule to the 2009 Act are set out in Appendix 2(b) to this work.

Newspapers and Privileged Communications

It frequently happens that a newspaper becomes aware of a defamatory allegation made privately, whether through a leak or otherwise.

---

[11] See Appendix 2(b).

Consider Mr Smith, a suspected heroin dealer who is a teacher. If a person who has grounds to suspect him of heroin dealing communicates this suspicion without malice to his headmaster or the school's board of management, this communication attracts qualified privilege. It does so because the headmaster or board of management has both a duty and an interest to consider the facts of the case so as to determine whether Mr Smith should be allowed to continue teaching in their school. But if the private communication comes to the attention of a newspaper, there will be no privilege in its publication there because it will come to the attention of many thousands of people with no legal interest in the matter. If the allegation is untrue it will obviously constitute an appalling injustice to Mr Smith. It is for this reason that the defence of qualified privilege is of limited utility for the media.

It is not possible to give a comprehensive statement of the circumstances in which qualified privilege may arise because everything depends on the detailed circumstances. Usually, they feature a person who is either acting under legal, social or moral duty, seeking redress for a grievance, or replying to an attack. In the last example, replying to an attack, especially, privilege may attach to a newspaper publication. Section 18 of the 2009 Act reiterates this principle that the categories of qualified privilege are not closed.

The person whose character is attacked is entitled to defend himself and, to that end, he is entitled to make relevant defamatory statements about the person who attacked him. If the attack is made in public, the response may also be public. Accordingly, where the attack was printed or broadcast in the mass media the response may be published there as well, with privilege for any relevant defamatory statements.

In an Irish case in 1938[12] it was stated that, "where a person publishes in a public newspaper statements reflecting on the conduct or character of another, the aggrieved party is entitled to have recourse to the public press for his defence and vindication". The privilege of the attacked person then attaches not only to him but to the newspaper or other organ which publishes his response.

There are however two significant qualifications. The first is that a public and defamatory response to an attack which was made only to a small number of people will not attract privilege. The second is that the privilege applies only to material which is a bona fide defence to an attack: it does not extend to an unconnected defamation which is irrelevant to the attack which is rebutted.

---

[12] *Willis v Irish Press* (1938) 72 I.L.T.R. 238.

Consent

Section 25 of the 2009 Act puts the common law defence of consent onto a statutory footing. It is based on a very simple proposition which applies to all areas of the law: if the plaintiff has expressly, by implication or by conduct, consented or agreed to the publication of the words complained of, there is a good defence. This is based on the legal principle expressed in Latin as *volenti non fit injuria*. This means that the plaintiff's consent (*volenti*) prevents the publication from constituting an actionable wrong (*injuria*) even though there may be actual damage (*damnum*). The defendant must show consent to the actual statement before it can be upheld. Precisely how this "consent" is evidenced is a matter that is yet to be focused on.

Can the Court Imply Consent or must it be Expressed?

In a media context the defence of consent is likely to arise in one of two ways. The plaintiff may actively consent to the publication of his own words or someone else's. Thus, where the plaintiff gives an on-the-record interview to a journalist in which he refers to or answers allegations defamatory of him he is probably consenting to publication of the whole interview. This is because he knows he is speaking to a journalist and must be taken to consent to the publication. The position is different if he declines to comment on allegations or, of course, if he deals with them "off-the-record".

The second instance is where a person agrees in advance to the publication of the findings of a tribunal, whatever those findings may be. This usually occurs when a person joins an association (for example, horse racing regulatory bodies) whose rules provide that complaints will be decided by a committee and the results will be published.

In all cases, evidence of consent must be clear and unequivocal and the consent must be to the publication of what was actually published, and not merely to something along the same lines.

Challenges to Repeat

It sometimes happens that the person who is aggrieved by what someone else has said has no cause of action because, for example, the words were spoken under absolute privilege or he cannot prove publication to a third party. In these circumstances he may challenge the other party to "repeat those words outside", or "in front of witnesses". While this sort of challenge has the appearance of consent to the repetition, it appears that, at least if he makes it clear that he is seeking the repetition so that he can sue, the repetition will be actionable. In those circumstances a newspaper which carried the repetition would appear to be liable.

Fair and Reasonable Publication and the Matter of Public Interest under the 2009 Act

Many commentators believe that this is the most important element of the new Defamation Act. It is designed to facilitate public discussion where there is public benefit in such discussion and would appear to give a statutory basis to a defence not dissimilar to that developed by the House of Lords in *Reynolds v Times Newspapers*.[13] This common law defence was created to protect the media in circumstances where they act "responsibly" in dealing with a matter of public interest and also with a view to ensuring that the right to freedom of expression was not unduly restricted.

The *Reynolds* defence of responsible publication on matters of public interest has been considered in two cases before the High Court in Ireland. In *Hunter v Duckworth*,[14] O'Keeffe J. stated that:

> "The flexible approach adopted in Reynolds v. Times Newspaper Ltd. is the best way in which the Courts, in the absence of legislative reform in this area can protect the constitutional rights of parties coming before the Court where the rights such as those at issue in these proceedings are at issue."

Again in the case of *Leech v Independent Newspapers (Ireland) Ltd*,[15] Charleton J. expressly adopted the *Reynolds* defence into Irish law, stating that the publication considered as a whole was a matter of public interest, and that the question as to whether a newspaper or a television channel or a radio channel on the evidence behaved fairly and responsibly in gathering and publishing the information would potentially take into account some of the tests set out by Lord Nichols in the *Reynolds* case; in particular, whether the article contained the gist of the plaintiff's side of the story and whether the plaintiff was contacted for comment.

Charleton J. held that a publisher seeking to rely on this defence, that is the public interest defence, had to show:

---

[13] [1999] 4 All E.R. 609; [2001] 2 A.C. 127.
[14] [2003] IEHC 81.
[15] [2007] IEHC 223.

(1) that the subject matter of the publication was a matter of public interest; and

(2) that she/he acted responsibly in accordance with proper standards of journalism.

Section 26(1) of the 2009 Act deals with this defence and it states that it shall be a defence to a defamation action for the defendant to prove that:

- (a) the statement in respect of which the action was brought was published—
    - (i) in good faith, and
    - (ii) in the course of, or for the purpose of, the discussion of a subject of public interest, the discussion of which was for the public benefit,
- (b) in all of the circumstances of the case, the manner and extent of publication of the statement did not exceed that which was reasonably sufficient, and
- (c) in all of the circumstances of the case, it was fair and reasonable to publish the statement.

It then goes on to deal with the factors that a court and/or jury should take into account when considering whether it was fair and reasonable to publish the statement concerned. These include any or all of the following of which list is not exhaustive:

- (a) the extent to which the statement concerned refers to the performance by the person of his or her public functions;
- (b) the seriousness of any allegations made in the statement;
- (c) the context and content (including the language used) of the statement;
- (d) the extent to which the statement drew a distinction between suspicions, allegations and facts;
- (e) the extent to which there were exceptional circumstances that necessitated the publication of the statement on the date of publication;
- (f) in the case of a statement published in a periodical by a person who, at the time of publication, was a member of the Press Council, the extent to which the person adhered to the code of standards of the Press Council and abided by determinations of the Press Ombudsman and determinations of the Press Council;

(g) in the case of a statement published in a periodical by a person who, at the time of publication, was not a member of the Press Council, the extent to which the publisher of the periodical adhered to standards equivalent to the standards specified in paragraph (f);

(h) the extent to which the plaintiff's version of events was represented in the publication concerned and given the same or similar prominence as was given to the statement concerned;

(i) if the plaintiff's version of events was not so represented, the extent to which a reasonable attempt was made by the publisher to obtain and publish a response from that person; and

(j) the attempts made, and the means used, by the defendant to verify the assertions and allegations concerning the plaintiff in the statement.

Another important principle in the Act is that, if the plaintiff fails to respond to attempts by the defendant to get the plaintiff's version of events that will not imply consent to publication or entitle the court and/or the jury to draw any inferences from the failure to respond.

The fact that we now have a specific public interest defence in Irish law would suggest that the principles set out in *Leech* and *Hunter* are no longer directly applicable except for defamations occurring before January 1, 2010. The view of some leading practitioners is that the issue needs to be clarified by the courts.

Offer to Make Amends under the 2009 Act

The person who has published a statement that is alleged to be defamatory of another person, after January 1, 2010, may make an offer to make amends. Under s.22 an offer to make amends shall:

(2)(a) be in writing,

(b) state that it is an offer to make amends for the purposes of this section, and

(c) state whether the offer is in respect of the entire of the statement or an offer (in this Act referred to as a "qualified offer") in respect of

(i) part only of the statement, or

(ii) a particular defamatory meaning only.

(3) An offer to make amends shall not be made after the delivery of the defence in the defamation action concerned.

(4) An offer to make amends may be withdrawn before it is accepted and where such an offer is withdrawn a new offer to make amends may be made.

The defendant is required:

(a) to make a suitable correction of the statement concerned and a sufficient apology to the person to whom the statement refers or is alleged to refer,

(b) to publish that correction and apology in such manner as is reasonable and practicable in the circumstances, and

(c) to pay to the person such sum in compensation or damages (if any), and such costs, as may be agreed by them or as may be determined to be payable.[16]

When an offer to make amends is made, that is the *only defence* that can be pleaded. If the parties cannot agree on the terms then the amount of damages or the extent of the apology will be determined by the court in which the action has been initiated.

Apology

The 2009 Act restates the law that a defendant may give evidence in mitigation of damages that he or she has made or offered to make and published or offered to publish an apology. An apology is not a defence to the claim but rather a defence to an award of compensation

The apology must be published in such a manner as to ensure that the apology was given the same or similar prominence as was given to the defamatory statement. The offer to publish an apology in this way should be made as soon as practicable after the plaintiff makes a complaint to the defendant.

An important element of the new regime relating to apologies is contained in s.24(4) of the 2009 Act which states that evidence of an apology made by or on behalf of a person in respect of the statement to which the action relates is not admissible in any civil proceedings as evidence of liability of the defendant. In practical terms this represents

---

[16] Section 22(5) of the Defamation Act 2009.

a major change in the manner in which court actions were run as the plaintiff often relied on the fact that an apology was proffered as indicating the weaknesses of the defendant's side.

Defence of Innocent Publication under the 2009 Act

The question of innocent publication has been a serious issue for publishing houses for many years. Such houses were just as guilty as any other defendant even though they merely facilitated publication of the defamatory words as opposed to having written them. Section 27 of the 2009 Act creates a defence of innocent publication for a defendant who is not the author/editor/publisher of the statement and who:

(a) ... took reasonable care in relation to its publication, and
(b) he or she did not know, and had no reason to believe, that what he or she did caused or contributed to the publication of the statement that would give rise to a cause of action and defamation.[17]

In determining whether reasonable care was taken the court will take into account: (a) the extent of the person's responsibility for the content of the statement or the decision to publish it; (b) the nature or circumstances of the publication; and (c) the previous conduct or character of the person.

The section also states that a person should not be considered the author/editor/publisher of a statement if:

(a) in relation to the printed material containing the statement, he or she was responsible for the printing, production, distribution or selling only of the printed material,
(b) in relation to a film or sound recording containing the statement, he or she was responsible for the processing, copying, distribution, exhibition or selling only of the film or sound recording,
(c) in relation to any electronic medium on which the statement is recorded or stored, he or she was responsible for the processing, copying, distribution or selling only of the electronic medium or was responsible for the operation or provision

---

[17] Section 27(1)(b) and (c) of the Defamation Act 2009.

only of any equipment system or service by means of which the statement would be capable of being retrieved, copied, distributed or made available.

Dr Neville Cox in his publication, *Defamation Law*,[18] draws attention to the fact that despite the degree of similarity between the Irish and the English legislation, there is no replication of the section in the English Act whereby "the broadcaster of a live programme containing the statement in circumstances in which he has no effective control over the maker of the statement" is expressly deemed to come within those categories of publishers who can avail of the defence. This protection would be of obvious importance to radio companies and television companies who broadcast live talk shows or reality television shows.

Time Bar

The Statute of Limitations 1957 provides that any action must be brought within a specified time. The precise period of time varies from one cause of action to another. Prior to January 1, 2010, in libel cases the limitation period was six years.

In the case of an infant plaintiff, i.e. a person who was under the age of 18 when the libel was published, the period does not begin to run until he or she has attained the age of 18.

Important Changes to Limitation Period under the 2009 Act

In the past the limitation period would not normally be a major feature of a media libel because publication, being a public act, would usually come to the attention of the potential plaintiff quite rapidly. The 2009 Act, while abolishing the distinction between libel and slander and creating a new tort of defamation, deems it to be actionable within the limitation period of one year, although there is discretion to extend the period to two years in the interests of justice.[19] A plaintiff who wishes to sue under the new regime will have to act much more quickly than before. The importance of the limitation period of one year with respect to defamatory statements after January 1, 2010 cannot be over-emphasised.

---

[18]　N. Cox, *Defamation Law* (Dublin: First Law, 2007) *www.firstlaw.ie*.
[19]　Section 38(1) of the Defamation Act 2009.

NEGATIVE DEFENCES

In this section we consider defences which consist of negativing one or more of the essential elements of the plaintiff's claim. For practical purposes these consist of allegations:

1. That the defendant did not publish the words complained of.
2. That the words complained of do not, or have not been shown to, refer to the plaintiff.
3. The words complained of have no defamatory meaning.

Non-publication

In the case of a media libel, it is usually plain to demonstrate what was published and by whom. A newspaper speaks for itself in this regard and the plaintiff can easily get a tape of a broadcast. But this fact is not conclusive of the liability of any particular defendant. As we have seen earlier, a plaintiff may bring an action against any person who participated in or brought about the publication of a defamatory statement. This includes, amongst others, the proprietor, editor, writer, printer and distributor of a written statement. It also includes a person who causes the defamatory statement to be printed, e.g. a person who supplied the material of the defamation to the newspaper hoping or requesting that it would be published, or a person who publishes a defamatory advertisement, or forces the publication of a defamatory apology.

In these cases, any individual defendant may be able to show that it did not publish the statement in question. For example, a journalist whose by-line appears may be able to claim that he did not publish a defamatory headline or sub-head. A person who supplied the story may be able to claim that the story printed deviated from what he gave the newspaper, although the deviation would have to be substantial to end his liability. The person sued as editor may not in fact have that position or a corporate defendant may not actually be the publisher of the newspaper: this happens in many cases where a publishing company has a number of subsidiary companies which publish individual titles. Finally, of course, there may be the case where the defamatory statement pleaded in the plaintiff's statement of claim simply does not correspond to what was printed or broadcast.

No Identification of the Plaintiff

A plaintiff must prove that the defamatory statement published was in fact referring to him. There is frequently dispute about this issue where the article complained of does not name any particular individual. This sort of dispute arises in two main situations. The first is where it is clear that one person is referred to, but the problem being, that that person is not named. The second is where a group of people, e.g. "the Gardaí" are mentioned and the plaintiff claims that the circumstances are such as to lead people with special knowledge to identify him as the subject of the defamation.

The "non-identification" defence has been successful as in cases such as *Gallagher and Shatter v Independent Newspapers*,[20] but experience shows that it is a dangerous defence for the media defendant. If apparently honest witnesses give evidence of having identified the plaintiff on some reasonable ground, it is difficult to shake this evidence. Moreover, if the non-identification defence is persisted with throughout the hearing, and a jury find against it, they may regard it as evidence of a pettifogging attitude on the part of the newspaper. Serious thought should be given to the employment of this defence and only in the rarest circumstances should it be relied on as the sole defence.

The significance of this defence is that the media is often inclined to try to sanitise a story which it knows to be defamatory by removing references to individuals. This may work if the story is of a general kind, for example, about the practices of lawyers as a class. The more specific the story, however, the more likely it is that a reasonable reader may infer the identity of a particular person. Much depends on how much other detail there is in the story. The more detail, the more risk there is of the identity being deduced. Furthermore, if a media defendant has to go into evidence it may be difficult to maintain that the story does not relate to the plaintiff unless the defence is prepared to say to whom it does relate. The guiding principle is that it does not matter how much the plaintiff's identity is disguised so long as it can be deduced by some section of the readers.

No Defamatory Meaning

Very frequently, a defendant will see nothing defamatory in what he has published whereas the plaintiff, perhaps relying on innuendos, will

---

[20]   *Irish Times*, May 10, 1980.

see a clear defamation. In these circumstances it will be for the judge to say whether the words are capable of a defamatory meaning; where there is a jury it will be for the latter to say whether they are in fact defamatory.

In the case of *Conlon v Times Newspapers*,[21] the defendant published a review of the film "In the Name of the Father" in which it alleged that Gerry Conlon, one of the Guildford Four, had implicated his father in a statement to the English police thereby causing his father to be imprisoned for the Guildford bombings. Mr Conlon Senior, it said, had been thrown into prison on the word of his "churlish son". It further stated that the father had never forgiven his son. The defendant sought to have the action struck out on a number of grounds. One of these was that, since the review had made it clear that Gerry Conlon's statement to the English police had been a "forced confession", no rational person could think the worse of him in respect of the admittedly untrue publication. The defendants failed in a preliminary application to satisfy the High Court that a reasonable jury could not find these words defamatory and the court refused to strike out the action.

In considering whether to plead no defamatory meaning, a media defendant should endeavour to be realistic. There is no point in advancing a purely academic argument if the publication is such that, on a common sense construction, a defamatory meaning will almost inevitably be found. A good example is the instance given in a previous chapter about the allegation that a man had, when much younger, received "roses from Rock Hudson". While it is perfectly possible to argue that this has no defamatory meaning on a literal construction, it is most unlikely that either a judge or a jury would adopt such a literal construction. Apart from anything else, it is difficult to see why the fact would be sufficiently interesting to merit publication years later if a literal meaning was all that was intended.

---

[21] [1995] 2 I.L.R.M. 76.

CHAPTER SEVEN

DAMAGES IN DEFAMATION SUITS

The principal remedy the law provides for a person who has been defamed is an award of damages.

> "The plaintiff is entitled to recover, as general compensatory damages such sum as will compensate him for the wrong which he has suffered and that sum must compensate him for the damage to his reputation, vindicate his good name and take account of the distress, hurt and humiliation which the defamatory publication has caused. Such sum should, however, be fair and reasonable and not disproportionate to the wrong suffered by the plaintiff."[1]

The above quotation is taken from a case in which the Supreme Court upheld an award of £300,000 to Mr Proinsias de Rossa TD, the former Democratic Left leader and Minister for Social Welfare. The case was the occasion for a major review of the law concerning damages in defamation actions by the Supreme Court, and must be regarded as the authoritative statement of Irish law on this topic. In two very recent cases, juries have awarded much higher amounts. Over €1.8 million was awarded to Monica Leech in her action against the *Evening Herald* over false suggestions that she had received government contracts because she had an affair with a Minister. A most unusual feature of the case was that the libel was much repeated by the original publisher even after the plaintiff had complained. This makes it hard to compare with other cases.

The highest award ever given by an Irish jury in a defamation case was the award of €10 million to Donal Kinsella in his action against the company of which he was a director, Kenmare Resources Ltd[2]. This was not a media case. Both cases are under appeal, as is an award of €900,000 to Martin Mc Donagh against the *Sunday World* for alleging he was involved in the drug trade.

---

[1] *De Rossa v Independent Newspapers* [1999] 4 I.R. 432 at 470, per Hamilton C.J.
[2] Unreported, December 2010. The jury found that the plaintiff had been defamed by the contents of a press release issued by the defendant concerning an incident abroad in which the plaintiff had sleepwalked to a female colleague's bedroom.

The Defamation Act 2009 provides for directions on damages to be given to juries and sets out a range of matters which they should take into account in assessing damages. It also allows the Supreme Court, on appeal, to substitute an amount it considers appropriate for any amount of damages awarded. These provisions will not affect these appeals as the cases all predate the 2009 Act.

De Rossa Case

It is important to stress, however, that the *De Rossa* case was a most unusual one in which the false allegations were of the gravest sort. Furthermore and separately, "the plaintiff was subjected to immensely prolonged and hostile cross-examination by Counsel for the newspaper".[3] Throughout the trial, as well as in the article, the newspaper had sought to damage the plaintiff by association and had made no effort at any time to withdraw or apologise for the allegation made.

In this case the plaintiff, a leading Irish political figure claimed he had been defamed—and seriously so—by an opinion piece in the *Sunday Independent* newspaper written by a well-known journalist. The article in question was a commentary on an ongoing political story concerning the relationship between a political party with whom the plaintiff had connections and socialist groups in Russia. Mr De Rossa sued for defamation claiming the words meant that he was either involved in or tolerated serious crime and supported anti-semitism and violent communist oppression. After two failed libel trials in which no verdict could be reached, a third jury found that there had been a libel and awarded the plaintiff £300,000 in compensation (with no reference being made to any award for punitive damages).[4]

The case must, therefore, be regarded as an extremely serious one. Both the nature of the allegations made and the subsequent conduct of the media defendant placed it at the highest end of the scale of permissible damages. Nevertheless, the case contains a good deal of general guidance on the topic of damages and their assessment.

---

[3]   *De Rossa v Independent Newspapers* [1994] 4 I.R. 432 at 469, per Hamilton C.J.
[4]   See Cox, *Defamation Law* (Dublin: First Law, 2007), p.368.

MATTERS TO BE TAKEN INTO ACCOUNT IN THE AWARD OF DAMAGES

The Gravity of the Libel

The Supreme Court cited with approval the English case of *John v MGN Ltd*[5] in which the English Court of Appeal stated that:

"The most important factor is the gravity of the libel; the more closely it touches the plaintiff's personal integrity, professional reputation, honour, courage, loyalty and the core attributes of his personality, the more serious it is likely to be."

In *De Rossa*, the Supreme Court held that:

"To publish of any person words meaning that he or she was involved in or tolerated serious crime and personally supported anti-Semitism and violent Communist oppression would, if untrue, constitute the gravest and most serious libel: it is hard to imagine a more serious one."

It is noteworthy that in *De Rossa*, the Supreme Court took into account in assessing the gravity of the libel, that it was published at a time when the plaintiff was engaged, to the newspaper's knowledge, in negotiations which might have led to his participation in government: this feature was said to "render such publication more serious and grave, particularly when they might have interfered with his chances of participation in government". By extension, this means that any defamatory statement which has a tendency to affect the plaintiff's lawful advancement in his profession or business, particularly at a crucial stage, will be seriously regarded.

Extent of Publication

The Supreme Court in the same case also adopted the following statement: "The extent of publication is also very relevant. A libel published to millions has a greater potential to cause damage than a libel published to a handful of people." The identity of the plaintiff must also be considered. The allegation that a plaintiff had prostituted

---

5   [1997] Q.B. 586 at 607.

herself for commercial gain may be most serious of a married woman with a young family.

The Supreme Court noted that the *Sunday Independent* was read each Sunday by over a million people and that, consequently, the publication of the defamatory matter "was widespread and extensive and that is a factor which the jury was entitled to take into account".

Vindication of the Plaintiff

The Supreme Court clearly took the view that an award of damages must be sufficient to vindicate the character of the plaintiff. This indeed is the constitutional obligation on the State contained in Art.40.3.1 of the Constitution, by its laws to, "protect as best it may from unjust attack and, in the case of injustice done, vindicate the life, person, good name, and property rights of every citizen".

This factor is, in practice, a most important one, especially in the case of a very grave defamatory statement. It is also a factor which differentiates defamation actions from other claims for compensation for civil wrongs, the most common being for negligently caused personal injuries. The court cited with approval the judgment of Lord Hailsham L.C. in *Cassel & Co. Ltd v Broome*,[6] where the following was said in relation to the plaintiff in a libel action:

> "Not merely can he recover the estimated sum of his past and future losses, but, in case the libel, driven underground, emerges from its lurking place at some future date, he must be able to point to a sum awarded by a jury, *sufficient to convince a bystander of the baselessness of the charge*." (Emphasis added)

The Conduct of the Defendant

This is closely linked in many ways with the need to vindicate the plaintiff. In the *John v MGN Ltd* case cited above, it was said:

> "A successful plaintiff may properly look to an award of damages to vindicate his reputation; but the significance of this is much greater than a case where the defendant asserts the truth of the libel and refuses any retraction or apology than in a case where the defendant acknowledges the falsity of what was published

---

[6] [1972] 1 All E.R. 801.

and publicly expresses regret that the libellous publication took place."

The Supreme Court in the *De Rossa* case held that:

"A jury is also entitled to take into account the whole conduct of the [newspaper] from the time when the libel was published down to the very moment of their verdict. They may take account of the conduct of the appellant before action, after action, and in court at the trial of the action and the fact that no apology, retraction or withdrawal was made ...".

In that particular case, not only was there no apology, but the entire conduct of the defendant's case was to attack the plaintiff's credibility and truthfulness and his bona fides. The Chief Justice in his judgment cited a considerable number of examples of this from the transcript of the High Court hearing, and another judge in the course of the appeal asked whether there was any point to certain questions put to the plaintiff except to wound and humiliate him.

This case should serve to emphasise the well-known fact that an unsuccessful defence of justification, and an aggressive manner of conducting a cross-examination can serve greatly to aggravate damages. Every feature of the defendant's conduct can be taken into account from publication down to verdict.

However, it is also necessary to bear in mind that the plaintiff's conduct too can affect damages adversely: if he is found to have provoked the defamatory statement or have responded to it by a defamatory statement of his own (neither of which were features of the *De Rossa* case), damages may be correspondingly reduced. It also emphasises the importance of pretrial correspondence. Any summary dismissal of the plaintiff's claim may sound very bad when read out in court.

Effect on the Plaintiff

Although a plaintiff cannot sue (as is possible in the United States) purely for emotional distress, once a defamation is established, he is entitled to have the emotional stress *caused to him* taken into account. Indeed, as Chief Justice Hamilton said in the *De Rossa* case: "One of the most important factors in the assessment of damages is the effect of the libel on the plaintiff's feelings."

The feelings in question here are *both* "distress, hurt and humiliation" caused to him by the libel and any "additional injury caused to the plaintiff's feelings by the defendant's conduct of the action as when he persists in an unfounded assertion that the publication was true, or refuses to apologise, or cross-examines the plaintiff in a wounding or insulting way".[7] To this may be added the important fact that the plaintiff will often suffer great emotional distress arising out of the uncertainties, expense and publicity of the litigation itself. He may be a poor man up against a media giant with a turnover of half a billion euros; he may be acutely aware that failure in the case will ruin him and that the newspaper, in their conduct of the case, may seek to punish him for suing them in the first place.

Mental suffering or distress, or even illness which is caused not to the plaintiff but to others, usually his wife and family, cannot be the basis of an award of damages to the plaintiff. But he can give evidence of the effect of a wife's or child's distress on him as part of the evidence of damage to his own feelings. Note that the wife or child themselves could not sue under the law as it stands. They suffered only mental distress and were not personally defamed.

Assessment of Damages

In an action tried by a jury—and the great majority of High Court defamation actions are so tried—the assessment of damages is a matter for the jury and their judgment in this matter is treated with great deference by the Supreme Court. In *Barrett v Independent Newspapers*,[8] Finlay C.J. had this to say:

> "With regard to the appeal against the amount of the damages, certain principles of law are applicable. Firstly, while the assessment by a jury of damages for defamation is not sacrosanct in the sense that it can never be disturbed on appeal, it has a very unusual and emphatic sanctity in that the decisions clearly establish that appellate courts have been extremely slow to interfere with such assessments, either on the basis of excess or of inadequacy."

---

[7] *John v MGN* [1997] Q.B. 586.

[8] [1986] I.R. 19.

In England, where the practice as to the guidance or directions which a judge can give a jury as to damages is different to that here,[9] the Court of Appeal nevertheless stated in the *John* case[10]:

> "The jury must, of course, make up their own mind and must be directed to do so. They will not be bound by the submission of Counsel or the indication of the judge. If the jury make an award outside the upper or lower bands of any bracket indicated and such award is the subject of appeal, real weight must be given to the possibility that their judgment is to be preferred to that of the judge."

The reason for the near inviolability of the verdict of a jury as to damages arises from the nature of the tort of defamation. Media defamation is published to the public at large and not merely to a restricted group such as judges or lawyers, who may be case-hardened, inclined to discount emotional or other special factors, or simply out of touch with the broader reaches of public opinion. The jury is meant to represent the public generally, with whom, presumably, the plaintiff will have day to day dealings, and to be representative of their views and opinions. From a defendant's point of view, a jury may be expected to represent the ordinary reader of a newspaper or a viewer of television, to value the information which the media provide them with and, perhaps, to be less sensitive to the wounded feelings especially of people in a prominent position in society. Certainly, many plaintiffs feel that the verdict of a jury in their favour is a more thorough and emphatic vindication in many cases than the verdict of a judge alone. The media sometimes hint that a case was taken in the Circuit Court to avoid a jury. (When the full impact of the Defamation Act 2009 is felt it is likely that many more cases will be tried in the Circuit Court.)

A jury, however, gives its verdict having heard, not merely the submissions of the parties, but the guidance on matters of law which the judge must give them. Prior to the Defamation Act 2009 judges have given only general guidance on the topic of damages and, in particular, have not indicated either specific sums or general brackets within which, in the judge's view, the damages (if any) should be awarded. The *Sunday Independent's* submissions to the Supreme Court

---

[9] Now changed by s.31 of the Defamation Act 2009 for defamations occurring after January 1, 2010.

[10] *John v MGN* [1997] Q.B. 586.

on the appeal in the *De Rossa* case were a root and branch challenge to this practice. They argued, in fact, that the existing practice was unconstitutional and contrary to the European Convention on Human Rights and that proper practice would require the judge to refer, not only to the purchasing power of an award and to the income which such an award would produce, but to make comparisons with previous libel awards and to make a comparison with personal injury awards, and to indicate a level of award which it would consider appropriate.

In conformity with the existing practice, the trial judge in the *De Rossa* case, Carney J. told the jury that they were "entitled to award damages for loss of reputation as well as for the hurt, anxiety, trouble and bother to which the plaintiff had been put". He told them that the award of damages must be assessed "entirely on the facts found by you" and that they were entitled to consider "… the nature of the libel, the standing of the plaintiff, the extent of the publication, the conduct of the defendant at all stages of the case, and any other matter which bears on the extent of damages."

In so doing, the trial judge was closely following the judgment of the Supreme Court in *Barrett v Independent Newspapers Ltd*.[11]

In conformity with that judgment, he also directed the jury to consider the nature of the defamation and to "fit the allegation into its appropriate place in the scale of defamatory remarks to which the plaintiff could be subjected".

Barrett was an example of a fairly trivial defamation: the allegation was that a politician, in a moment of triumphal exuberance, had "tweaked" the beard of a hostile journalist. Contrasting that allegation in *Barrett* with those in *De Rossa* the trial judge said:

> "It would not surprise me, members of the jury, if you went to the opposite end of the scale and even apart from Mr. Justice Henchy's helpful observations, I think there can be no question in this case but that if you are awarding damages you are talking about substantial damages."

The *Sunday Independent* did not criticise that form of guidance as being a departure from the practice established by the authorities, but claimed that the practice itself was wrong and unconstitutional.

The Supreme Court rejected these submissions and held that there was no appropriate comparison to be made between awards for libel

---

[11] [1986] I.R. 13.

and those for personal injuries because many factors in a libel action which were entirely absent from a personal injuries action, e.g. the necessity to vindicate the plaintiff's character, the necessity to reflect the conduct of both the plaintiff and the defendant from the time of publication onwards; the fact that "… compensation here is a solatium rather than money recompense for harm measurable in money".

The Supreme Court also rejected the view that either Counsel or the trial judge would make any suggestion to the jury as to what an appropriate award would be, on the basis that this would be "an unjustifiable invasion of the province or domain of the jury" and that utter confusion would be caused by a direction which "buried the jury in figures", and at the same time told them that they were not bound by such figures and would have to make up their own minds.

In this respect, the *De Rossa* case must be regarded as a strong reaffirmation of the traditional position after the case for the contrary had been fully and thoroughly argued.

It is worth noting that the reason why the *Sunday Independent* submitted that comparisons should be made with figures in personal injuries cases was that a series of decisions in those cases has established an upper level of general damages for personal injuries. This figure presently stands at approximately €300,000 and is, of course, exclusive of the "special damage" for loss of earnings, cost of professional care, etc. which make up so large a proportion of the substantial, multi-million pound, personal injuries settlement. The newspaper, however, was anxious to establish that in no circumstances could an award of damages for libel exceed the maximum amount for *general* damages for personal injuries. The Supreme Court, however, entirely rejected the analogy.

Independent Newspapers' Failed Challenge

Independent Newspapers claimed that the award of damages made in this case breached the European Convention on Human Rights and brought a case to the European Court of Human Rights. That court had ruled earlier, in the case of *Tolstoy Miloslavsky v United Kingdom*,[12] that an award of £1.5 million in damages awarded against Mr Miloslavsky was excessive and in breach of his rights under art.10 of

---

[12]   (1995) 20 E.H.R.R. 442.

the Convention. The court in that case considered there were no adequate safeguards within the judicial system in the United Kingdom against disproportionate awards.

Independent Newspapers v Ireland (the De Rossa Case)[13]

At the European Court of Human Rights the paper questioned whether the appellate review system in Ireland provided adequate protection against an excessive award of damages by juries. The court rejected the newspaper's argument and found that the Irish appellate system in respect of jury verdicts on damages in this case did not amount to a violation of art.10.

O'Brien v Mirror Group Newspaper Ltd

The matter of assessment of damages was again considered by the Supreme Court in an appeal bought by the defendants against an award to Denis O'Brien of IR£250,000 in *O'Brien v Mirror Group Irish Newspaper Ltd*.[14] The court was invited by the defendants in this case to reconsider its decision in *De Rossa* having regard to the jurisprudence of the court as to the extent to which it is free to depart from its previous decisions. The Chief Justice, with whom the majority of the court agreed, took the view that the case had to be decided on the basis of the law as stated in *De Rossa*. The court went on to consider, in the light of the *De Rossa* and *Barrett* judgments, whether the award should be set aside as being disproportionately high. The Chief Justice and the majority of the court took the view that it was, and sent the matter back for retrial.

Among the factors which were taken into account were:

- That the libel, although serious and justifying an award of substantial damages, could not be regarded as coming within the category which the Chief Justice described as the grossest and most serious libel to have come before the courts.
- The fact that *The Mirror* was read by 130,000 people as opposed to the *Sunday Independent* which was read by over a million people.

---

[13] Application No. 55120/00 [2005] E.C.H.R. 402.
[14] [2001] 1 I.R. 4.

- The fact that Mr De Rossa as a plaintiff was better known than Mr O'Brien, and the fact that Mr De Rossa had to go through three protracted High Court actions in front of a jury before his reputation was finally vindicated by the jury and was subjected to prolonged and hostile cross-examination.

Interestingly when the case came on for rehearing in the High Court the jury awarded substantially more damages than the Supreme Court thought were excessive. Mr O'Brien was awarded €750,000 by the jury.[15] The case subsequently settled.

The Impact of the 2009 Act on Awards of Damages

Submissions and Directions on Damages

For the first time in Irish defamation law, parties to the action may make submissions to the court in relation to matters of damages. The trial judge will be obliged to give directions to the jury on the question of damages, whereas prior to this, judges had largely avoided such directions following the cases of *De Rossa v Independent Newspapers*[16] and *O'Brien v Mirror Group Newspapers Ltd*.[17]

The 2009 Act sets out, in s.31(4), 11 factors which the jury must have regard to in assessing damages in respect of defamation occurring after January 1, 2010. These factors are:

(a) the nature and gravity of any allegation in the defamatory statement concerned,

(b) the means of publication of the defamatory statement including the enduring nature of those means,

(c) the extent to which the defamatory statement was circulated,

(d) the offering or making of any apology, correction or retraction by the defendant to the plaintiff in respect of the defamatory statement,

(e) the making of any offer to make amends under s.22 by the defendant, whether or not the making of that offer was pleaded as a defence,

(f) the importance to the plaintiff of his or her reputation in the eyes of particular or all recipients of the defamatory statement,

---

[15] Unreported, November 2006.
[16] [1999] 4 I.R. 432.
[17] [2001] 1 I.R. 1.

(g) the extent (if at all) to which the plaintiff called or contributed to, or acquiesced in, the publication of the defamatory statement,

(h) evidence given concerning the reputation of the plaintiff,

(i) if the defence of truth is pleaded and the defendant pleads the truth of part but not the whole of the defamatory statement, the extent to which that defence is successfully pleaded in relation to the statement,

(j) if the defence of qualified privilege is pleaded, the extent to which the defendant has acceded to the request of the plaintiff to publish a reasonable statement by way of explanation or contradiction, and

(k) any order made under section 33, or any order under that section or correction order that the court proposes to make, or, where the action is tried by the High Court sitting with the jury, would propose to make in the event of there being a finding of defamation.

A defendant may give evidence in mitigation of damage of any matter having a bearing on the plaintiff's reputation which is related to the defamatory statement or of an award of damages to the plaintiff in another action taken in respect of a statement which contained substantially the same allegations as are contained in the defamatory statement published by the defendant.

Role of Supreme Court in Relation to Damages

The 2009 Act also provides that the Supreme Court on appeal may substitute for any amount of damages awarded to the plaintiff such amount as it considers appropriate.

Other Forms of Damages

In addition to general damages, a court may award aggravated or punitive damages. Such damages are awarded to a plaintiff in exceptional circumstances not to compensate the plaintiff but to punish the defendant. These can be awarded in addition to general and special damages. Such cases are rare and confined to circumstances of oppressive conduct, deliberate falsity or publication with an express view to financial gain. In the recent case of *Donal Kinsella v Kenmare Resources*, €1 million of the €10 million awarded to him was in respect of punitive damages.

Special damages are those amounts which are capable of precise calculation in advance of the hearing, e.g. medical expenses.

Nominal damages on the other hand are awarded where the plaintiff has succeeded but has sustained no, or virtually no, loss.

Contemptuous damages can be awarded where it is thought necessary to express contempt for the plaintiff's conduct by a very small award.

Mitigation of Damages

We now turn to matters which, though they do not provide a full defence, may be used by a defendant to mitigate its liability to the plaintiff. These are:

1. The plaintiff's bad reputation.
2. Offering an apology.

The Plaintiff's Bad Reputation

It is open to the defendant, whether or not they plead justification, to rely on evidence of the plaintiff's general bad reputation in an area of the plaintiff's character which is relevant to the defamation. Thus, for example, if the statement alleges financial dishonesty, evidence of a reputation for loose sexual morals would not be relevant, or vice versa.

The rationale underlying the admission of evidence of bad reputation in mitigation of damages relates to the nature of the libel itself. It is an action intended to protect the plaintiff's reputation or good name, to use the constitutional phrase, from unjust attack. If the fact that the plaintiff has no character in the relevant area, even prior to publication of the libel, it is "most material that the jury who have to award those damages should know if the fact that he is a man of no reputation".[18] This is because "the damage ... which he sustained must depend almost entirely on the estimation in which he was previously held".[19]

It is not usually possible to prove in evidence specific acts that led to this general reputation. The reasoning behind this limitation is that, if evidence of specific acts were admissible, a defamation case would be virtually unlimited in its scope, as the defendant tries to allege and the plaintiff to rebut, numerous specific matters. Accordingly, it is open to

---

[18]   *Scott v Samson* [1882] QBD 481.
[19]   *Scott v Samson* [1882] QBD 481.

a defendant only to call evidence to the effect that the plaintiff has a poor reputation in the relevant area.

In *Browne v Tribune Newspapers Plc*,[20] Keane C.J. questioned the whole logic of the rule against admitting evidence of previous acts of misconduct, commenting that:

> "… clearly, it would be wrong in principle for a jury to be asked to assess damages in respect of an admittedly untrue statement that the plaintiff had stolen money from his employer on a particular occasion without being informed that he had stolen money from a number of other employers in the past. As it has been pithily put in a number of cases the plaintiff should not be allowed to recover damages for injury to a reputation that is not his."

In *Cooper Flynn v Radio Telifís Eireann*,[21] Keane C.J. again stated:

> "… since the purpose of the law of defamation is to compensate a plaintiff for damage to his or her reputation it would be singularly unsatisfactory if a jury were obliged to award anything other than nominal or contemptuous damages to a plaintiff whom they had found in effect not to be entitled to any reputation in the relevant area."

Defamation Act 2009

For actions commenced after January 1, 2010, s.31(6) permits a defendant in a defamation action, for the purpose of mitigating damages, to give evidence:

(a) with the leave of the court on any matter that would have a bearing upon the reputation of the plaintiff provided it relates to matters connected with the defamatory statement;
(b) that the plaintiff has already in another defamation action been awarded damages in respect of a defamatory statement that contains substantially the same allegations as are contained in the defamatory statement to which the first mentioned defamation action relates.

---

[20] [2001] 1 I.R. 521.
[21] [2004] 2 I.R. 72.

Section 31(4)(h) of the 2009 Act is also relevant. This subsection requires the court in a defamation action to have regard to the evidence given concerning the reputation of the plaintiff when making an award of general damages.

Apology

The 2009 Act restates the law that a defendant may give evidence in mitigation of damages that he or she has made or offered to make, and published or offered to publish, an apology. The apology must be published in such a manner as to ensure that the apology was given the same or similar prominence as was given to that statement, or offer to publish an apology in such a manner as soon as practicable after the plaintiff makes a complaint to the defendant concerning the utterance to which the apology relates or after the bringing of the action whichever is earlier.

An important element of the regime relating to apologies is contained in s.24(4) of the 2009 Act, which states that evidence of an apology made by or on behalf of a person in respect of a statement to which the action relates is not admissible in any civil proceedings as evidence of *liability* on the party of the defendant. In practical terms, this represents a major change in the manner in which court actions are likely to be run. Under the old legislation the plaintiff often relied on the fact that an apology was proffered as indicating the weaknesses of the defendant's case.

Offer to make Amends (sections 22 and 23 of the Defamation Act 2009)

As already stated these sections of the Defamation Act 2009 are likely to have a big impact, not only on how cases are approached, but also on how such an offer may affect the level of damages. In the UK the Court of Appeal in the case of *Nail v News Group Newspapers*[22] upheld the view of the lower court that, if an earlier and unqualified offer of amends is accepted, there is bound to be substantial mitigation in the amount of the award. In that case a discount of 50 per cent was upheld.

---

[22] [2005] 1 All E.R. 1040.

CHAPTER EIGHT

ASPECTS OF PROCEDURAL TACTICS

Is there a Prima Facie Case?

The foregoing chapter provides a simple checklist to address the question—is there a prima facie case of defamation or not? A prima facie case means simply a set of facts which, if uncontradicted by other evidence or challenged in their legal effect by technical argument, would entitle the plaintiff to judgment. If you swear you saw me break the window of your car and take out your radio that is a prima facie case of larceny and of malicious damage against me. I may be able to answer it in any number of ways, but unless I do I will be convicted.

Before an action for defamation is intimated, the plaintiff's lawyers will have considered whether there is a prima facie case or not. But the mere fact that they have decided to proceed does not mean that there is in fact a prima facie case. The plaintiff's legal advice may be wrong, or more likely, the lawyer may hope that the media defendant will be intimidated, or give in to save costs, even though there is no case, or only a doubtful one.

Preliminary Letters

A claim may be initiated by letter, usually from a solicitor asserting that the plaintiff has been defamed and seeking some form of redress. Alternatively, legal proceedings may be started without correspondence by the issue of a "plenary summons", which is the originating document in a High Court defamation action. If the proceedings are in the Circuit Court then a civil bill is issued. It is likely with its increased jurisdiction (up to €50,000) and the availability of new remedies to it that the Circuit Court will see an increase in activity for defamations occurring after January 2010.

A summons or civil bill very rarely issues without preliminary correspondence. Where this does happen, the plaintiff is signalling that the defamation, in his view, is so serious and deliberate that there is no point in corresponding.

However, in most cases, there is correspondence. It is extremely important for a media defendant to read and assess the first letter properly and, if appropriate, to take steps to redress the wrong without delay. If that is not possible, preparations to fight are best made immediately.

First Question

A media defendant's first questions, once an action is intimated, are not technical ones. They are: "Are we, as of today, quite happy with the publication? Are the facts true? How do we know? Does the solicitor's letter raise any issues of fact or meaning which we didn't consider before? Have we made any mistake?"

Mistake or Uneasy Feeling

If you have made a mistake, or have an uneasy feeling, ask: Can this case be settled right away? Except in the most serious cases and, where for some reason, either the plaintiff or the media defendant is determined to go to court, the first few days (sometimes hours) after publication is the best and cheapest time to settle and make an apology and offer to make amends. This is because the plaintiff is just beginning to suffer damage. The calls and questions from family, friends and associates are just starting. The gossipy embellishments may not yet have begun. If he can secure, right away, an apology/clarification he may feel (correctly in many cases) that the trouble is nipped in the bud.

On the other hand, even a few days' delay may change everything. He may have been "called in" by superiors or some other formal or informal regulatory body. He may have seen a look of incredulity greet his explanations to friends and associates. To prevent further damage or to add force to his denials, he may have said, "I'm suing, of course". Also, especially if the defamation is of such a kind as causes hurt to spouses or children, the iron may enter his soul. Such a plaintiff feels that nothing that will happen later can be as bad as what he has already suffered, and will be determined to proceed.

Immediate Action

If there is any feeling of uneasiness at all, explore whether immediate settlement is available for an apology and an offer to make amends. In a serious case, damages may be inevitable even at an early stage. Settlement now may cost one-tenth or even less of the value (including both sides' costs) of the same case after a hearing.

The Defamation Act 2009 (the "2009 Act") makes it much easier to progress matters at this stage. The new defence of "offer to make amends"[1] contained in s.22 of the 2009 Act is similar to that contained

---

[1]   See Chapter 6 on "Defences".

in the equivalent English legislation. In *Milne v Express Newspapers*,[2] Eady J. said that:

> "… the main purpose of the statutory regime is to provide an exit route for journalists who have made a mistake and are willing to put their hands up and make amends."

As already stated, the offer must be in writing and must state that it is an offer to make amends under s.22. An offer to make amends cannot be made after the delivery of the defence. It should also be noted that a defendant can also make a qualified offer to make amends in respect of part only of the statement complained of or only in respect of a specified meaning.

Mechanism for the Offer to Make Amends

If the offer is made after the issue of proceedings and the plaintiff is not accepting the manner of the apology or its content, the defendant can ask the court to rule on the matter by formally making a correction and apology by means of a statement before the court. It is then for the court to consider and approve the offer, in which case the defendant will also have to give an undertaking to the court as to the manner of publication of the apology.

If the parties do not agree as to the damages or costs that should be paid by the person who made the offer, those matters can also be determined by the High Court or, where a defamation action has already been brought, in the court in which the action was brought. In those circumstances, the court can determine damages in the normal way. The new provisions, however, require the court to take into account the adequacy of any measures already taken to ensure compliance with the terms of the offer by the person who made the offer in its assessment of damages. This procedure could prove to be a considerably beneficial tactic for media defendants and will almost certainly truncate the length of the proceedings and reduce costs.

Negotiation

Negotiations for a settlement are best undertaken by lawyers, for reasons to do with the complex operation of the "without prejudice" rule.[3] This states that everything said or written by either side in the

---

[2] [2003] 1 W.L.R. 927.
[3] See Chapter 6 on "Defences".

course of a genuine attempt to bring about settlement is without prejudice and may not be referred to in court.

If the plaintiff approaches the media himself, and the defendant is fairly clear there has been an error and wants to settle, it may be worth negotiating a conclusion there and then. If the defendant does this, remember that all that is said that is not part of any offer to settle is *not* protected from disclosure and may be proved in court. Thus, it is very foolish to say "I have to admit we've been sloppy" or anything of that sort, unless, of course, it is obvious.

Assessment of the Case and Balancing the Risks

All of the above is based on the assumption that, at first blush, the case is a doubtful one from the point of view of the media defendant— there has been a mistake or the story just does not stand up on examination. Surprisingly often, a newspaper or broadcaster and its advisers come to this conclusion, but two to three years after the publication, and on the eve of a court hearing. By that time both sides have incurred large costs and the settlement value of the case has greatly increased. Still worse, a lapse of time may have made impossible the investigation of a fighting defence which should have been undertaken years before.

When this happens, it is because the media defendant has put the case on the long finger. It has done a holding reply to the first letter, and then passed the file to its solicitors. They too have temporised and the plaintiff has issued proceedings. These take on a life of their own which, mainly, the lawyers deal with. Then, after years of ignoring it, the journalist is asked to attend a pretrial consultation because the case is listed in court.

This sorry tale repeats itself often and there is one good reason— about 50 per cent of defamation actions just go away. From a defendant's point of view, the problem is trying to identify which 50 per cent is this particular case in?

Defamation cases go away for many reasons: the person has a skeleton in the cupboard which the media may know nothing about; he cannot afford the risks; his life has changed and the case is history; he fears the media will take revenge; his family cannot take the pressure; he is frightened of the costs; he cannot face further publicity, and so on.

If a plaintiff's case goes dormant, it is rarely in the interests of the media defendant to revive it. But this policy of masterly inactivity— quite appropriate in 50 per cent of cases—is often applied by default to the other 50 per cent. This means that media defendants lose or settle more cases than they should, and pay large multiples of the minimum costs and damages by settling late instead of earlier where settlement is appropriate.

What the Plaintiff Wants

Sometimes it may transpire almost immediately that the parties are so far apart that no settlement is possible. But even if this happens, assuming that all discussions have been kept without prejudice, no-one is any worse off for having tried.

If settlement is reached, the plaintiff almost always wants some printed statement. He or she may or may not insist on the word "apology". Sometimes a "statement" or "clarification" will do.

At a very early stage, the plaintiff is surprisingly undemanding about where and in what form a statement is published. This is because, at this stage, he or she is still focused on the people he or she knows personally to have read the defamatory statement, and he or she intends to show the retraction to them personally. Later, he or she will begin to register emotionally that thousands of people whom he or she will never know also read it and will be much more demanding about prominence, print size, boxing and so on.

Equally, the contents of the statement will vary a good deal with the stage at which it is offered and the quality and experience of the plaintiff's legal advisers. A fairly bland statement correcting some error and regretting any inconvenience could suffice. Many readers, however, see this as just a bit of legalese, a mere hedge against litigation. A good lawyer, especially in a serious case, will require prominence, the use of the term "apology" and some explanation of how the defamation came to be printed (usually human error) and some reference to costs, damages or a contribution to charity. Any or all of these may be negotiable in a particular case and, sometimes, the client is so eager for an immediate statement that he will settle for less than his lawyers tell him should be available. If after negotiations a settlement is not achieved, the defendant may still make an offer to make amends at any time up to the delivery of his defence (see above).

Costs

In a very early settlement a defendant will usually pay the plaintiff reasonable costs. A specific sum may be agreed. The amount varies greatly with the gravity and complexity of the case. Whatever the outcome of the settlement, it is wise to have it translated into an offer to make amends under s.22 under the 2009 Act, thus ensuring that the defendant has the statutory advantages under that Act should anything go wrong with the implementation of the settlement.

Damages

In a debatable case, or one where the whole sting can be removed by apology, it may be possible to settle early without paying damages. In a very bad case from the point of view of the media defendant, a huge saving can still be made by making a realistic offer or an offer to amend very early. Even the most aggrieved and best positioned plaintiff will usually be prepared to settle early at a relatively conservative valuation, and much less in costs, than would be the case after a hearing. It is important to note that under the new defamation legislation a court can assess the extent to which an offer of amends goes to mitigate damages.

Other Relevant Matters to be Taken into Account for Defamations Occurring after January 1, 2010

Verifying Affidavits

Under the 2009 Act there is a new requirement now to file a verifying affidavit in support of any pleading of fact. Section 8 of the Defamation Act 2009 requires a party to a defamation action to swear an affidavit verifying any facts or assertions made in the statement of claim or the defence not later than two months after serving the pleading. Knowingly making a false or misleading statement will be a criminal offence and will attract a fine of up to €50,000 or five years' imprisonment or both, and the parties may be cross-examined on their affidavits. A sample of a verifying affidavit is contained in Appendix 1. This new requirement will focus parties on the finer points of their respective cases at a much earlier stage than heretofore. Great care is needed in these affidavits. Having to admit a serious error in the affidavit may well be catastrophic.

Summary Disposal

It is likely that parties to defamation actions in the future will see an increase in applications for summary disposal under s.34 of the 2009 Act.[4] This is a tactic which plaintiffs and defendants will have to

---

[4]   See Chapter 5, p.43.

consider as soon as proceedings issue. It can be used by a plaintiff or a defendant. If a plaintiff is successful the court can issue a declaratory order as seen in the case of *Watters v Independent Star Ltd*.[5]

Lodgements

If negotiations fail and an offer of amends is not made, a defendant may choose to make a lodgement in court of the sum of money which in his or her opinion is the appropriate amount of damages that the plaintiff should receive. If the plaintiff is awarded a lesser sum in damages, then it is likely the court will order the plaintiff to pay the defendant's costs from the time of the lodgement. Previously, the making of a lodgement was not permitted in a libel action without an admission of liability. Since January 1, 2010, it is now permissible to lodge a sum of money without admission of liability. This will also be a factor which plaintiffs and defendants will have to take into account when reviewing tactics. Lodgements are much more likely to be frequently used since the coming into operation of the 2009 Act, not least because the Act removes the uncertainty of setting an action in circumstances where, because of multiple publications, the plaintiff previously could issue a number of different actions.

In conclusion therefore:

- Review each case early and often (i.e. every month to three months thereafter).
- If the decision is to defend, it should be a positive decision, not a default decision.
- If there's an obvious error or serious uneasiness try to settle right away—within days, even hours. If the defamatory statement was made after January 1, 2010 use some of the new procedures now available, e.g. offer to make amends, an apology or a correction order—within days, even hours.
- In such a case, be prepared to be generous in the terms of a statement/apology, but avoid offering damages except in serious cases (multiple small settlements encourage claims).
- Remember inadequacy of the offered statement/apology is the single most common reason for failures in early settlement talks. The differences rarely seem important in retrospect.

---

[5] [2010] IECC 1.

- If your first review, confirmed by legal advice, suggests that the case can and should be fought, start right away (see below).

At all stages, make sure you know, not just what your lawyers think, but why they have made the recommendations to you. Put your view of the case, including a full statement of facts and evidence, in writing and get theirs in writing too. Focus a meeting on the issues causing problems, determined in advance.

First Review

At the first review:

- Divide the publication complained of into FACT and COMMENT.

- Is each statement of fact true or false? How do you know? Can you prove it? How?

- List the witnesses required. Get someone to get a statement from each.

- Be clear as to what each witness can and can't prove.

- Go through the article/story with the writer(s). Ascertain the source for each statement. Get and keep copies of all notes, drafts, proofs, tapes, etc. See to preservation of originals.

- Approach all sources, whether usable as witnesses or not. Tell them of the case to stop memories fading. See if they can find out more if necessary. Make sure the writer keeps in touch with them. A turn in a case can make a peripheral witness central.

- List the comments in the article. List the facts on which they are based. Are these facts stated or indicated in the article? If merely indicated, where are they fully stated? Are they true? Perform the same exercise as for the Statement of Fact.

- If the piece complained of consists of, or includes, statements by the plaintiff himself, whether to the writer of the piece or to someone else, get the notes of the interviewer on the occasion the statements were made. If possible, get the author of the notes to do a full statement on everything to do with the occasion in question.

- Once these exercises have been done, the media defendant can address the question of which defence, or mix of defences, will be used.

CHAPTER NINE

PLEADINGS, DISCOVERY AND INJUNCTIONS

The term "pleading" refers to the system of formal written documents exchanged between the parties before a case comes to court. The principal pleadings are the plaintiff's summons and statement of claim, the defendant's defence and where necessary, the plaintiff's reply. Either party can seek "further and better" particulars of the other's claim or defence. Allied to these is a system of discovery, notices to admit facts, and interrogatories which may or may not feature in any particular case.

Pleadings are, perhaps, of more importance in a defamation action than in any other type of proceeding. Cases can be won or lost at the pleading stage. Proper attention to pleadings will define the issues to be tried and force a plaintiff or defendant to think out his case in a realistic way. Discovery, notices to admit facts and interrogatories, together with the power to summon witnesses, can be essential in the all-important process of evidence gathering.[1]

It is therefore important for a journalist or media executive to have a sound knowledge of these matters, which are too often cloaked in mystery.

Preliminary Correspondence

The great bulk of libel actions begin with a letter of complaint from a solicitor acting for an aggrieved person. This will usually demand some form of redress either in general or specific terms. Far too often this preliminary letter elicits no reply at all. This is rarely a sound tactic: it will usually have the effect of propelling the plaintiff further towards issuing proceedings. On other occasions, the preliminary letter elicits merely a civil service style holding letter, which may or may not be followed by a more substantive reply.

It is particularly undesirable to reply to an initiating letter with a statement that time is needed to investigate the complaint. Such a reply may be used at trial to suggest that the story complained of was

---

[1] See Appendix 1.

insufficiently researched before it was published. Every preliminary letter should be examined carefully and quickly along the lines indicated elsewhere in this book. If there has been a mistake or injustice, or if the letter seems to indicate a significant claim, the question of providing some redress satisfactory to the plaintiff should be considered immediately.

Offer to Make Amends

Since the Defamation Act 2009 (the "2009 Act") a new formal step in the litigation called an "offer to make amends" may be made.[2] This offer can be with respect to part or all of the statement concerned but must be made before the delivery of the defence (see Chapter 6). An offer to make amends is an offer to make a suitable correction of the statement concerned, a sufficient apology to the person to whom the statement refers and an offer to publish the correction. The offer to make amends under the 2009 Act must also set out the parts of the statement that are to be corrected and mention the fact that the offer is made under s.22 of that Act. It must also offer to make a suitable correction, publish the correction and pay a sum of compensation that is either agreed between the parties or as may be determined by the court to be payable.

If the offer to make amends is accepted, then it is enforceable in court if it is not implemented. The court has further powers then to assess the damages under the offer or make directions as to the manner of correction if there is no agreement on these issues.[3]

If no accommodation is possible at an early stage and it is not intended to deliver an offer to make amends, considerable attention should be paid to correspondence. The preliminary letters and replies thereto will almost certainly be read out in court and all open correspondence[4] should be composed with a view to that possibility. Those dealing with a complaint should have firmly in mind the distinction between open correspondence and correspondence which is "without prejudice". This term refers to correspondence which is written in an attempt to settle the case and is privileged from disclosure in court, unless this privilege is waived. All correspondence from a potential plaintiff should normally be handed to a solicitor at an early stage and its contents discussed.

---

[2]   Section 22 of the Defamation Act 2009.
[3]   Section 23 of the Defamation Act 2009.
[4]   Correspondence which has not been marked as being sent on a "without prejudice" basis.

Particular attention should be paid to correspondence which requires an apology, especially if the form of the proposed apology is included in the letter. It frequently happens that a media defendant is prepared to publish some form of apology or clarification, but not that required by the plaintiff. A court or jury will naturally compare and contrast the form of apology sought by the plaintiff with any apology actually published by the media defendant.

If the plaintiff demands an apology or retraction without specifying the form, consideration should be given to some form of publication acceptable to the media defendant which can, of course, be published with or without the plaintiff's consent. This may be central in mitigation of damages and may have the effect of prevailing on the plaintiff not to issue proceedings.

Plenary Summons

If the plaintiff proceeds to litigation, his first step would be the service of a plenary summons. In the United Kingdom this is referred to as a "writ" and that terminology is sometimes (incorrectly) used here. The plenary summons is purely an initiating document, and is usually very simple in form. The date of its service may be crucial because it is the date on which the statute of limitations ceases to run against the plaintiff.

The plenary summons is a formal document issued out of the Central Office of the High Court under the authority of the Chief Justice. It is titled with the name of the parties so that the defendant knows who precisely is being sued. It contains a request to the defendant to enter an "appearance" in the Central Office of the High Court within a specified number of days.

The plenary summons also contains a "general endorsement of claim". This states in very broad terms the nature of the plaintiff's claim and will often be as simple as "the plaintiff claims for damages for libel". Other claims may also be intimated such as a claim for an injunction or other causes of action, such as malicious falsehood or breach of copyright. This endorsement of claim will normally be signed by the plaintiff's counsel.

Finally, the plenary summons will contain a form identifying the plaintiff and his address and the name and place of business of his solicitor. It is of course possible for a plaintiff or a defendant to issue a plenary summons and take all the other steps in an action personally. A solicitor is, however, employed in the huge majority of cases.

Appearance

Once a plenary summons has been issued and served on the defendant, the defendant is required to enter an appearance. If this is not done, the plaintiff can deliver a statement of claim and seek judgment together with an order that the damages be assessed by a judge or jury. An appearance is simply a statement that the defendant intends to defend the action and identifying the solicitor retained on his behalf.

Statement of Claim

Once the appearance is entered, the plaintiff becomes obliged to deliver a statement of claim, if he has not done so already. This is the plaintiff's principal pleading in which he sets out his case. The statement of claim is a document divided into numbered paragraphs in which the plaintiff states in detail what his case is.

It would usually commence with an identification of the plaintiff by name, address and occupation, and similar particulars in relation to the defendant. If a number of defendants are sued it will normally identify their respective roles in relation to the publication, e.g. proprietor, editor, etc.

The substantial part of the statement of claim will then recite the publication complained of, identifying it by date. It must allege that the publication was "of and concerning" the plaintiff. If the plaintiff has not been named in the publication, it may give particulars of the way in which it is claimed he is to be identified as the subject of it.

The statement of claim will then allege that the words complained of are defamatory of the plaintiff. It will often do so by using a form of words such as, "are grossly defamatory of the plaintiff and damaged him in his credit and reputation and exposed him to odium ridicule, contempt and distress". The statement of claim will very frequently set out the meanings which the words complained of are alleged to bear. It will often say: "said words in their ordinary and natural meaning, further or in the alternative by innuendo, meant and were understood to mean". There will then follow a list of the meanings alleged.

This aspect of the statement of claim is most important. A defendant's lawyer will look to see whether innuendo is in fact pleaded. If it is not, the plaintiff is confined to the "natural and ordinary" meaning of the words and will normally be precluded from calling evidence from witnesses who will say how they understood them. In a number of cases, the failure of the plea of innuendo has confined the plaintiff to the natural and ordinary meaning, which has then been held not to be defamatory. In the case of *Berry v Irish Times*,[5] a failure to plead innuendo in relation to the term "felon setter" led to the plaintiffs losing the action when the courts held that the word was not defamatory in its natural and ordinary meaning.[6]

If innuendo is pleaded, it should be followed by a statement of the "facts extrinsic to the words complained of" as a result of which the innuendo arises. A statement of claim may go into detail about the loss, damage and distress allegedly suffered by the plaintiff. A statement of claim will usually allege that the words complained of were published "falsely and maliciously". This form of words may not indicate a claim of actual malice. Where actual malice is relied on details of it may be given in the statement of claim, e.g. that the words were published knowing them to be false or reckless as to whether they were true or false. Other circumstances may be relied on to support the claim of actual malice.

The statement of claim may also allege that the words were published for profit, to increase the sales of the newspaper or for some other specified motive. The statement of claim will end with a claim for damages. The defendant's lawyers will be anxious to see whether the claim includes aggravated or punitive damages in addition to general damages. The statement of claim will normally be signed by the plaintiff's counsel and will be delivered by his solicitor.

Affidavit of Verification

A new provision contained in the Defamation Act 2009[7] requires the plaintiff and defendant to verify on affidavit all assertions of fact contained in any pleading. These affidavits are extremely important documents as they have the effect of transforming the pleadings into sworn evidence by the plaintiff and defendant.

Service

The plenary summons must of course be served before the case is properly pleaded. Most initiating letters will invite the defendant to nominate a solicitor to accept service and proceedings, and this is usually done. Thereafter, all documents can be served on the solicitors on record unless and until there is notice that their retainer has been terminated.

---

[5] [1973] I.R. 368.
[6] See "Innuendo" in Chapter 4.
[7] Section 8 of the Defamation Act 2009.

Service often gives rise to difficult problems for a plaintiff. In media cases, however, the identity and whereabouts of the defendant publisher and those employed by him is usually well-known or easily ascertainable and problems rarely arise. Provision has been made for the service of documents on European defendants under European Council Regulation (EC) No. 1348/2000. A summons intended to be served under these provisions requires a special endorsement and usually only a notice of the proceedings (a summary) as opposed to the full summons must be served. This procedure is quite frequently employed because a significant number of defamation actions are against foreign, usually English, defendants without an office in Ireland.

A summons can also be issued in Ireland for service out of the jurisdiction to countries outside the European Union that are signatories to the Hague Convention on the Service Abroad of Judicial and Extrajudicial Documents in Civil or Commercial Matters. This requires an application to the Court under the terms of the rules of the relevant court in which the proceedings are issued.[8]

Defence

The defence is the defendant's principal document—in which he answers the plaintiff's statement of claim and denies any fact on the statement of claim which he or it intends to dispute: matters not denied will be taken to be admitted. The defence must contain one or more of the recognised defences to a defamation action: truth, fair comment on a matter of public interest, privilege, no defamatory meaning, and so on. Since the Defamation Act 2009, only those defences that are contained in that Act may be used with respect to statements made after the coming into effect of the relevant provisions. It is perfectly possible to plead most defences in the alternative. Furthermore, they can be pleaded in the alternative so that the fact that one fails does not prejudice another. The defences must be pleaded in legally recognised form. Thus, for instance, the usual form of a plea of truth is that "the words complained of are true in all material respects". If it is desired to plead fair comment, the usual form is:

> "... the words complained of in so far as they consist of statements of fact, are true in substance and in fact and in so far as they consist of comment are fair comment made without malice on a matter of public interest."

---

[8]   Order 11E of the Rules of the Superior Courts.

Since the enactment of the Defamation Act 2009, this plea is more likely to read:

> "The words complained of were published in good faith and in the course of the discussion of a subject of public interest, which was for the public benefit namely … and, in respect of which it was fair and reasonable to publish the words complained of."

It is important to note that the plea of fair comment on a matter of public interest, if it stands alone, will not be construed as including a plea of truth, which must be separately pleaded.[9]

Very frequently, a defence is filed merely as a holding measure, without any serious thought about whether there is a defence and, if so, what it is. It is always unwise to put in a defence merely as a holding device. Such defence will have to plead all possible defences. It can be highly prejudicial, particularly, to plead truth and then be forced to abandon it. By way of example, the plaintiff will usually have identified the true meanings which he or she says attach to the publication complained of in the statement of claim to the proceedings. A full denial by the defendant "that the words complained of bore, or were capable of bearing the meaning set out at paragraph [X] on the statement of claim, or any meaning defamatory of the plaintiff" may well be a proper pleading, if it is in fact intended to dispute all of the meanings alleged.

But there is a great need for the defendant to be realistic: he should admit any meanings which the words plainly bear and, if appropriate, plead another defence such as justification in respect of them. For example, if the article alleged that the plaintiff had engaged in shop lifting, it would be unrealistic to deny that the words meant that the plaintiff had committed a criminal offence and was dishonest. Those meanings would have to be defended by a plea of justification or possibly privilege, or not at all. But it might be entirely reasonable to deny that the words meant that he was unfit for his occupation as a school teacher or some other extended meaning.

In general, a defendant who is contemplating denying any particular meaning should ask himself whether he will be quite comfortable standing over the denial in evidence. Or, on the contrary, would the denial put him into an artificial position, undermining his credibility with a court or jury?

---

[9] *Burke v Central Independent Television Plc* [1994] 2 I.R. 61.

Reply

Depending on the nature of the defence, the plaintiff may wish to deliver a rejoinder to it, known as a reply. Especially where malice is denied, or privilege pleaded, this may be necessary. In the first case, the rejoinder is necessary to make it perfectly clear that express malice is being contended for by the plaintiff. Where privilege is pleaded, the plaintiff will be required to put on the record the factual basis upon which he says that the occasion was not one of privilege or the reasons why the privilege has been lost, e.g. by excessive publication.

Notice for Particulars

It is open to either party to seek "further and better particulars" of the plaintiff's claim or of the defendant's defence. This is usually done first by the defendant after receipt of the statement of claim, and later by the plaintiff after receipt of the defendant's defence. The particulars relate to the *nature* of the claim or defence: neither party is entitled to particulars of the *evidence* which its opponent proposes to need.

Particulars can be of great importance in defamation cases. Ideally, they should bring about a situation in which neither party will be surprised by the nature of the case made by the other at the trial.

Particulars consist of a series of questions about the claim or defence, which are first asked by letter. If there is no reply or only an unsatisfactory reply, proper answers can be compelled by motion to the court.

Of particular importance is the plaintiff's right to raise particulars of a defendant's plea of justification of fair comment. Following the case of *Cooney v Browne*,[10] it has been established that the plaintiff is entitled, when these matters are pleaded, to knowledge of "the full factual range" of the defence. Thus, he is entitled:

(a) to ask the defendant to state what portion of the words complained of is alleged to be fact and what portion is comment; and

(b) in relation to the facts, to particulars of the facts which the defendant proposes to prove in order to establish the truth of the factual components of the words.

On the other hand, the defendant is entitled to rely on the statutory provision relating to partial justification, and is not obliged to give

---

[10] [1985] I.R. 185.

particulars in advance of what portions of the article or programme he suspects he will not be able to prove to be true. Where the plaintiff pleads actual damage, the defendant is entitled to full and detailed particulars of such damage.

Where innuendo is pleaded, the defendant is entitled (if not already detailed in the statement of claim) to particulars of the extrinsic facts, as a result of which the plaintiff claims that some or all of the defamatory meanings arise. If the plaintiff is not identified by name, he is entitled to particulars of the extrinsic facts which he relies on to illustrate that some or all of the persons to whom the article is published would identify him.

A reading of the English textbooks on libel and procedure indicate a practice in the UK, especially relating to particulars, which is somewhat stricter than that obtaining here. However, the trend of decisions here shows a tendency to approach the English level of strictness. A party is well advised to give particulars which are as complete as possible. However, if it is felt that the other side's particulars are sparse, and that this may put them at some disadvantage at trial, it is prudent to write to them significantly in advance of the hearing requesting further and better particulars, and stating that an omission to provide these will be relied upon at the trial, as the basis of objection to evidence of the relevant kind.

Discovery

Discovery is a procedure of great and growing importance in all civil litigation and in defamation cases in particular.

The law proceeds on the assumption that the court, through each party, is entitled to all available evidence, whether the oral evidence of witnesses or documentary evidence. The latter term now comprises all forms of recording of information, including traditional ones such as correspondence, diaries and receipts, the result of technical processes such as x-rays, scans and analyses, or electronically stored information, on disc or otherwise.

In principle, either party is entitled to an order for discovery against the other, requiring him to make a list, authenticated on oath, of all documents in his "possession or power"[11] which are relevant to the matters in issue. Furthermore, since 1986, a person is entitled to discovery against a person, company or institution not involved in the litigation, if he can show that it is likely that that party has documents

---

[11] Order 31 r.20(3) of the Rules of the Superior Courts.

relevant to the case, and is prepared to pay their costs of making discovery.

The procedure envisages that the party from whom discovery is sought will make a list of all such documents authenticated on oath with respect to the specific categories of documents nominated by the person seeking discovery. The list provided will typically divide the documents into those same categories and will also specify, most relevantly, those which he is prepared to disclose or produce, and those in respect of which he claims privilege. The idea of this is to give a full picture of the documents available so that the other party can, if so advised, challenge the claim of privilege.

An order for discovery in itself merely entitles the party to the list of the other party's documents, sub-divided into those which he is prepared to produce, if necessary, and those which he objects to produce usually on the basis of privilege. A party making discovery must also list those relevant documents which he once had, but which are no longer available, and in this case he must say what has become of them.

It is obvious that discovery can be a most potent weapon in litigation. Its uses are both positive and negative. Documents in the possession of another party, or a third party, may be of the greatest assistance to either a plaintiff or a defendant in making their case, that is in establishing in evidence what they need to establish to support their claims. Over and above this, it gives an insight into the armoury of the other side, prevents a party from being taken by surprise by a document suddenly produced at trial and allows preparations to be made. Furthermore, the absence of a document in the affidavit of discovery can be just as significant as its presence. For example, a plaintiff reading a media defendant's affidavit of discovery and seeing that there is no mention of journalist's notes, will be aware that the journalist either took no notes or if he did they have been lost since. Indeed, a plaintiff's initiating letter to a media defendant will often contain a paragraph requiring that all notes and drafts be preserved.

It is generally of great importance that each party to a defamation action should seek discovery. Even if nothing positive is gained, it is a great insurance against surprise at the trial. The only circumstance in which discovery should not be sought is where a party does not himself wish to make discovery. If a plaintiff seeks discovery, it is almost inevitable that the defendant will seek and obtain a "cross-order" whereby the plaintiff has to make discovery in turn. Sometimes, of course, neither party will seek discovery for tactical reasons. For example, the plaintiff may not wish to disclose his accounts in a commercial defamation case, either because they do not support the case he is making or because they would supply ammunition for embarrassing cross-examination. But the media defendant may be embarrassed by the record of its investigation and may conclude that it too has more to lose than to gain from discovery. Other than in wholly exceptional circumstances, each side in a substantial defamation action will be well advised to seek discovery.

What is Discoverable?

A court will only order a party to make discovery if it is satisfied that it is in possession or has access to documents which are relevant to the proceedings and are necessary for fairly disposing of the matter or for saving costs.[12] Morris J. in *Mc Kenna v Best Travel Ltd*[13] held that it is only documents which would support or defeat an issue which arises in an existing action which are relevant and required to be discovered. Discovery applications are normally dealt with by the Master of the High Court. There is a right of appeal from the decisions of the Master to the High Court.

The phrase "possession or power" is an important one. It refers not only to documents of which the party has actual possession but to those to which he is entitled, or of which he can in fact get possession. Thus, a document in the possession of a person's agent, whether a spouse, relative, solicitor, accountant or other agent, is within his "possession or power". Similarly, a document in the possession of a media defendant's associated company, even if that company is out of the jurisdiction, is within its possession or power to obtain.

A copy or electronic document is liable to be discovered in the same way as any other document. In the case of correspondence, the copy will normally be in the writer's possession while the original will have left his possession and is presumably in the possession of the addressee. Original correspondence of which no copy was kept would fall to be discovered in the category of documents which the party once had, but is no longer in possession of.

Where it is sought to obtain a discovery order against a non-party, it is necessary to prove that the non-party is "likely to have, or to have had in his possession, custody or power, any documents which are relevant to an issue arising or likely to arise" in the case, or "is likely to be in a position to give evidence relevant to any such issue". In relation

---

[12] Order 31 r.12 of the Rules of the Superior Courts.
[13] [1995] 1 I.R. 577.

to third parties, the court has a discretion to allow or disallow discovery: for example, a non-party might object to making discovery on the basis that it was simply too onerous to ask it to search its records for a long period of time. It is a requirement of obtaining discovery against a non-party that the person seeking it "shall indemnify such person in respect of all costs thereby reasonably incurred". These costs can be substantial. A non-party may incur considerable man hours in searching records over a long period of time and may also require legal advice in relation to whether documents are relevant to the action in which they are sought, and whether any privilege can be claimed in respect of them.

In many cases, the parties will agree to make discovery as between themselves without the necessity of applying for a court order.

Production

When a party has obtained an affidavit of discovery and the accompanying list of documents, a number of situations may arise. He will normally wish to inspect some or all of the documents and to do this he can serve a notice under the Rules of Court requiring the other party to produce the relevant documents for his inspection and to permit copies of them to be taken. If this notice is not complied with, the party who has obtained discovery may apply to the court for an order that the documents be produced for inspection. The Rules of Court provide that an order of this sort "shall not be made … if and so far as the court shall be of opinion that it is not necessary either for the purpose of disposing fairly of the cause or matter, or for saving costs".

Applications under this provision are the procedure whereby many important disputes in relation to documents in defamation actions are resolved.

In *Beverly Cooper Flynn v RTÉ and Others*, the plaintiff was com - plaining about broadcasts suggesting that she advised or encouraged a particular person and other unnamed people to participate in an investment scheme which had as its purpose the evasion of tax. The defence was justification, both in relation to the named persons and the other unnamed persons. RTÉ sought non-party discovery against the bank and obtained discovery and, subsequently inspection, of some 65 client files from which, however, the names and addresses of the clients had been deleted. Having read these files in that form, they sought inspection of the entire files, including the names, personal data or identifying numbers of the clients in question.

It was clear that this information was relevant to the defence which RTÉ and the other defendants proposed to make, but equally clear was that it involved a considerable attack on the undoubted confidentiality which dealings between banker and customer normally attract. The court balanced the competing interests in this way. It first held that the burden of proof lay on the party seeking discovery to show that it was "necessary for the fair disposal of the action". If necessary, the court will itself inspect the documents to see whether they fall into this category. Disclosure will be regarded as necessary if:

1. It will give "litigious advantage" to the party seeking inspection.
2. The information sought is not otherwise available to that party.
3. The order for disclosure would not be oppressive, for example because of the sheer volume of documentation.

The phrase "litigious advantage" apparently means that it will be of real use in supporting a plea which the party seeking inspection has already made in the action.

Applying those standards, RTÉ were successful in seeking inspection, though the persons to whom the documents could be shown were somewhat restricted.

In the case of *National Irish Bank Ltd v Radio Telefís Éireann*,[14] the defendant had in its possession information about the operations of the plaintiff which had been disclosed to it by former employees of the bank, and which was confidential. The court nevertheless declined to give an injunction restraining its publication because "a defence allowing publication where there was an overriding public interest in such a publication existed in cases of breach of confidence". While this is not an authority directly on the question of discovery, it obviously has significant scope for media defendants in cases where they can allege such a public interest as a factor tending to outweigh confidentiality.

It is, of course, important to bear in mind that in almost every case, the pleadings will have to be completed and the defendant's case adequately particularised before discovery will be granted. It is not possible (unless the plaintiff is very poorly advised) simply to put a plea of justification on the record and then to seek disclosure in general terms in an attempt to support it. A study of the judgment in the *Cooper Flynn* case demonstrates just how detailed the defendant's particulars of justification were, and apparently needed to be, before it could get discovery of the type sought.

---

[14] [1998] 2 I.R. 465.

Use of Discovered Documents

It is extremely important to note that documents obtained as a result of discovery and inspection can only be used for the purpose of the action. No matter how interesting they may be from other points of view, or even from the point of view of similar stories of exactly the same kind, they cannot be used for any such purpose. Even if they are read out in court, they cannot be the subject of further separate journalistic stories. In *Ambiorix Ltd v Minister for the Environment (No. 1)*,[15] Chief Justice Finlay said:

> "As a matter of general principle, of course, a party obtaining the production of documents by discovery in an action is prohibited by law from making any use of any description of such documents, or the information contained in them otherwise than for the purpose of the action. To go outside that prohibition is to commit contempt of court."

In practice, the courts will take various steps to mitigate the risk of other use being made of documents. For example, in the *Cooper Flynn* case, only solicitors, counsel and named members of the defendant's legal department—all lawyers—were permitted to inspect the documents.

Notice to Admit and Interrogatories

It is open to a party to set out certain factual propositions and invite the other side to agree that they are true. This is done by a notice to admit facts, and its purpose is to save time and costs at the trial. Thus, for example, a party who has obtained a very large bulk of documents may call on the other party to admit that the documents are authentic.

A party is never bound to make such an admission. If he does not, the only sanction is that his opponent may fix him with the costs of proving the matters whose admission was sought, regardless of the outcome of the trial as a whole.

Sometimes, however, a party will find it difficult to plan the presentation of his case at trial unless he knows precisely what he can and cannot prove in advance. In these circumstances he may ask the court to permit him to deliver "interrogatories" to the other side. These are a series of questions generally of a sort that can be answered yes or no. A common instance of their employment is where a party to a road traffic accident suffers amnesia after the accident and lacks other

---

[15]   [1992] 1 I.R. 277.

witnesses. In these circumstances he may ask the other party such basic questions as whether he was driving a particular car, whether it was involved in an accident at a particular time, and so on.

In *Mercantile Credit Company v Heelan and others*,[16] a number of points have been established in relation to interrogatories. The first is that something exceptional must be shown before they can be administered: the general rule is that trials proceed on oral evidence. Where something rather mechanical is the only matter at issue such as the admission of the authenticity of documents, interrogatories will usually be ordered. Interrogatories will not, however, be ordered as to the evidence in a party's possession. All applications for interrogatories, and indeed for discovery, must be shown to be relevant.

In the case of *Conlon v Times Newspapers*,[17] the defendant published an article that referred to the plaintiff's relationship with his father following a forced and false confession made while in police custody.[18] The plaintiff brought proceedings for defamation for the content of the article. During the case an issue arose as to the appropriateness of interrogatories sought by the defendant. The interrogatories sought the plaintiff to answer a number of questions that related to the content of those discredited confessions. The tactic of asking interrogatories of the plaintiff concerning the content of statements he had made during those false and forced confessions would have presumably avoided the need for the defendant to bring witnesses from the UK to give evidence of these facts. Lynch J. in the Supreme Court decided that as it would be virtually impossible to secure the attendance in court in Ireland of the UK police officers who took statements from the respondent the interrogations were appropriate. Even if this were not so, as substantial costs would be incurred in attempting to obtain their attendance in the Irish courts, he decided that relevant questions posed by way of interrogatory ought to be allowed.

Third Party Discovery

Since 1986, it has been possible for a party to proceedings to seek discovery against a person who is not a party to those proceedings. This procedure is more properly known as "non-party discovery" but the description above has gained acceptability.

---

[16] [1998] 1 I.R. 81.

[17] [1995] 2 I.L.R.M. 76.

[18] Mr Conlon was one of the "Guilford Four" who were freed from prison as a result of a miscarriage of justice in the UK.

This procedure provides a weapon of far reaching scope. It allows a party who can show that it is *likely* that a person or company who is not itself a party to the action nevertheless has documents in its possession or power which are relevant to the matters at issue. Once this is shown, an order can be granted against the non-party ordering discovery. The party seeking such discovery must pay the third party's costs and expenses immediately, and such sums then become part of his costs in the action.

In *Holloway v Belenos Publications*,[19] the former secretary of the Department of Energy, Mr Holloway, was suing the proprietors of *Business and Finance* arising from an article which the latter had published relating to the Bula/Tara Mines saga. The article, he claimed, defamed him in relation to his discharge of his functions as secretary.

The defendant sought third party discovery against the Minister himself seeking discovery of documents relevant to the matters at issue. This was at first refused on the basis that it had not been shown the Department were likely to have such documents. On reapplication on somewhat changed facts, the Department sought to make the far reaching claim that the rule permitting third party discovery was invalid and ultra vires (beyond the power of) the rule-making authority. This contention was rejected. The State appealed to the Supreme Court but withdrew the appeal on the day of the hearing. The action was subsequently settled.

It will be seen that scope of these various applications, notably for discovery and third party discovery, is very broad and can be of great assistance to a party and particularly, perhaps, to a defendant. However, the whole area of discovery in particular is highly technical and often raises difficult legal and tactical issues. It is essential to take advice in the context of the facts of any particular case.

Injunctions

An injunction is an order of the court directing the defendant to do or (more commonly) to refrain from doing a particular thing. Injunctions may be granted after a full hearing in which case they are usually "perpetual". More commonly, they are granted shortly after proceedings are commenced for the purpose of preserving the position until the full hearing can take place. These injunctions are known as "interlocutory". Finally, an injunction may sometimes be granted for a very short

---

[19]   [1988] I.R. 49.

period, in order to preserve the position that the defendant can be heard on the question of whether there should be an interlocutory injunction. These injunctions are applied for ex parte (in the absence of the other side) and are referred to as "interim" injunctions.

A plaintiff who has successfully established that he has been defamed and who has been awarded damages will usually get a perpetual injunction restraining repetition of the defamation. In fact, such injunctions are rarely sought because there is seldom any reason to believe that a media defendant will repeat something that has been conclusively proved to be an indefensible defamation. Perpetual injunctions in these circumstances are common where the defendant is an individual.

More recently, s.33 of the Defamation Act 2009 permits the court to make an order prohibiting the publication or further publication of the statement concerned if the court considers that the statement is defamatory and the defendant has no defence to the action.

The area of interim interlocutory injunctions is of more practical interest. If a person learns in advance that it is intended to publish something defamatory of him, it is much more useful for him to prevent the publication taking place at all than to sue for damages after the event. Alternatively, where the defamatory statement is contained in a book or magazine he may see it shortly after publication and think of trying to prevent further sales.

The court undoubtedly always had power to grant an injunction restraining the publication or the republication of a libel.[20] Prior to the 2009 Act, however, there had been considerable doubt as to the terms of which such an injunction would be granted, and even as to whether there was a power to grant an injunction restraining a publication. Although this power is now established, the conditions for the grant of an interim injunction in cases of alleged defamation are different and much more onerous on a plaintiff, than those applying in the case of any other civil wrong.

A person applying for an injunction to restrain publication of a defamation must show:

1. a prima facie case of defamation;

2. evidence that the defendant is likely to publish the defamatory statement, or publish it further than has already been done; and

3. that such publication will inflict on the plaintiff an injury which cannot be fully compensated in damages.

---

[20] *Sinclair v Gogarty* [1937] I.R. 377.

Even when these matters have been established, the court has a considerable discretion. In *Sinclair v Gogarty*, it was observed that the jurisdiction was "of a delicate nature". In practice a pretrial injunction will not be granted if *either* there is any doubt that the words are defamatory *or* if the defendant swears that he intends to plead justification or any other recognised defence, unless such defence is plainly unstateable. In other words, the plaintiff has to show, at a very early stage, that it is most unlikely that the defendant will succeed.

The reason for these unusually onerous requirements is that the injunction restraining the publication of a defamatory statement involves interfering with the defendant's constitutional right to freedom of expression.

Unlike the UK where so-called super-injunctions have been granted, the result of this approach on the part of the courts has been that very few applications for interlocutory injunctions restraining publication of libel have been made, and fewer still have succeeded. The rationale underlining the court's attitude was well set out in the judgment of Carroll J. in *Attorney General for England and Wales v Brandon Books*.[21] This was not a defamation case but an application to restrain publication of a book by a lady who had been employed in the British Secret Service many years before. The book, it was alleged, represented a breach of her obligation of confidentiality. Carroll J. refused to grant the injunction, relying on the defendant's constitutional right to publish and pointing out that it was a right to publish "immediately", and not at some unascertained future date after the case had been disposed of. This attitude also underlies the judicial approach in Ireland to defamation injunctions.

Nevertheless, injunctions have been given in suitable cases. *Sinclair v Gogarty* was one such situation, where it turned out there was a real attempt at justification. The defendant defended himself by contending that the plaintiffs were not identified, and that the words were not defamatory. The High Court and Supreme Court each took the view that the words were beyond argument, defamatory, and there was ample evidence that they referred to the plaintiff. In these circumstances the injunction was granted. It may be that the attitude of the court was influenced by the fact that the libel was regarded as a particularly foul one.

Injunctions were also granted in the case of *Trainor v Independent Newspapers*.[22] This was a most unusual case in that the plaintiff sought

---

[21]   [1988] I.R. 597.
[22]   Unreported, High Court, Barron J., 1996.

an injunction on the basis that he had been told by a journalist writing for the defendant that she was going to publish a story about him which she acknowledged to be false. Some two weeks after the initial application came out the journalist in question was shot and died without having put in an affidavit. No other affidavit was filed on behalf of the defendant. The allegations proposed to be published were of a very serious nature. In these circumstances the court granted an injunction.

Kelly J. in *Foley v Sunday Newspapers*[23] indicated that the right to a free press and freedom of expression enshrined in the Constitution is an important right "which the courts must be extremely circumspect about curtailing particularly at the interlocutory stage of a proceeding."

Before such an injunction would be granted:

"… the plaintiff would have to demonstrate by proper evidence a convincing case to bring about a curtailment of the freedom of expression of the press.

This is particularly so having regard to the strongly expressed guarantees in the Constitution in favour of freedom of expression. The Irish (and indeed the English courts in the absence of a written constitution) have always shown a marked reluctance to exercise their jurisdiction in a manner which would entrench the freedom of expression enjoyed by the press and the media generally. A good example of this is to be found in the judgment of O'Hanlon J in *MM v Drury & Ors* [1994] 2 IR 8.

This approach is also justified having regard to the provisions of Article 10 of the European convention on Human Rights and the jurisprudence which has built up on foot of it."

A person may also seek an injunction to prevent publication on the grounds that the publication will breach his privacy rights.[24] This issue arose in *Cogley v RTÉ*.[25] Clarke J. again emphasised the importance of public debate on matters of public interest.

"Thus the reluctance of the courts in this jurisdiction (and the European Court of Human Rights) to justify prior restraint save in unusual circumstances and after careful scrutiny. Similar considerations also apply to a situation where a party may contend that there has been a breach of his right to privacy but where

---

[23] [2005] 1 I.R. 88.

[24] See Chapter 11 for a consideration of privacy rights and the press.

[25] [2005] 4 I.R. 79.

there are competing and significant public interest values at stake. It is for that reason that I have distinguished between a right to privacy which subsists in the underlying information which it is sought to disclose on the one hand and information which legitimately be the subject of public debate on an issue of public importance (albeit private to some extent) but where there may be a question as to the methods used to obtain that information on the other hand. I would wish to emphasise that the balancing exercise which I have found that the court must engage in is not one which would arise at all in circumstances where the under-lying information sought to be disclosed was of a significantly private nature and where there was no, or no significant, legitimate public interest in its disclosure. In such a case (for example where the information intended to be disclosed concerned the private life of a public individual in circumstances where there was no significant public interest of a legitimate variety in the material involved), it would seem to me that the normal criteria for the grant of an interlocutory injunction should be applied. In such cases it is likely that the balance of convenience would favour the grant of an interlocutory injunction on the basis that the information, once published, cannot be unpublished. It is also likely in such cases, that damages would not be an adequate means of vindicating the right to privacy of the individual."

In *Murray v Newsgroup Newspapers*,[26] the approach of Irvine J. to an interlocutory injunction grounded on a breach of privacy rights was similar to the approach of Kelly J. in *Foley v Sunday Newspapers*. She considered that the plaintiff must demonstrate at an interlocutory application that he is likely to establish at the trial of the action that the publication complained of should not be allowed. This means that the person seeking the injunction must at the interlocutory stage adduce "proper evidence" that would justify prohibition of the publication at the trial proper. In that case, Irvine J. refused the application for the injunction as she considered that she had not been furnished with:

"… proper or cogent evidence to demonstrate [the plaintiff] is likely to prove that any potential infringement of his right to life or that any interference with his rights to privacy cannot be justified in the public interest."

---

[26]   [2010] IEHC 248.

It would appear, therefore, that if a plaintiff is to succeed in obtaining an injunction against the publication of a statement on the grounds of an infringement of privacy rights, in a matter where the public have an interest, it will be necessary for him or her to adduce sufficient evidence by way of affidavit at this early stage that he or she is likely to succeed in his or her action when it eventually comes to trial.

CHAPTER TEN

CONTEMPT OF COURT

The Types of Contempt

All of the laws and rules which constitute the law of contempt exist to protect the administration of justice and to frustrate those who obstruct it or interfere with it. The mischiefs that the law is concerned to prevent are many. Some are of more interest to journalists than others. The subjects of the law of contempt vary from physical interference with court hearings themselves to prejudicing proceedings by publicity; "scandalising" the courts; interfering with or pressurising litigants, judges or jurors; to interfering with persons under the protection of the courts. These things, broadly speaking, constitute criminal contempt and expose those who commit them (called contemnors) to criminal penalties. The law of contempt also has a civil aspect, which usually arises where there is disobedience to an order of the court by a party to proceedings.

Criminal contempt is a common law misdemeanour punishable by fine and imprisonment at the discretion of the court. The objective of this branch of the law of contempt, like the criminal law in general, is punitive and deterrent. In civil contempt, on the other hand, the purpose of the law is not punitive but "coercive": its objective is to compel the party to comply with the order of the court.[1] In the case of criminal contempt, the person accused of the contempt is entitled to a trial by jury. In civil contempt, it is the court itself that decides if the person is in breach of a court order and takes action against that person so as to ensure that this position is reversed.

CRIMINAL CONTEMPT

The recognised forms of criminal contempt are:

1. Contempt in the face of the court.
2. Scandalising the courts.
3. Prejudging the proceedings (breach of the *sub judice* rule).

---

[1] See *Keegan v de Burca* [1973] I.R. 223.

Contempt in the Face of the Court

This aspect of contempt relates to unlawful acts committed physically in a courtroom, in its immediate vicinity, or in a way which is so immediately and intimately connected with a court hearing that the court will take personal knowledge of it. The eminent English judge, Lord Denning, expressed the significance of this kind of contempt in the following words:

> "The phrase contempt in the face of the courts has a quaint old-fashioned ring about it; but the importance of it is this: of all the places where law and order must be maintained it is here in these courts. The course of justice must not be deflected or interfered with. Those who strike at it strike at the very foundations of our society. To maintain law and order the judges have, and must have, power at once to deal with those who offend against it. It is a great power – a power instantly to imprison a person without trial – but it is a necessary power."

The most obvious form of contempt in the face of the court is an assault on a judge sitting as such in court. A juror is equally protected. Assaults, threats or intimidation of other people connected with the proceedings in court or going to and from court is similarly contempt in the face of the court. Thus, threats to parties, witnesses, barristers or solicitors in or going to or from court, have been held to be contempt. Typical of this sort of thing is an Australian case where one party said to another in an elevator in a court building: "You know what's going to happen to you, you bastard."

Similarly, disorderly behaviour in court, whether by way of making some form of protest or by insulting those concerned in the case is contempt in the face of the court. Examples of this vary and include stripping in court, lighting a cigarette there, shouting slogans, singing songs and other forms of disorderly behaviour.

Recording of court proceedings, whether by tape, photography or video recording is a matter within the discretion of the court. In Ireland, the general tendency has been not to permit such things. There have been exceptions: the Supreme Court allowed itself to be filmed for a few moments at the sitting of the court before the hearing of a very important constitutional case and, where the parties can afford it, proceedings have been allowed to be contemporaneously recorded by a computer-linked apparatus which, seconds later, produced a transcript on screens used by the lawyers. There is no statutory law in this area and it is entirely a matter for the discretion of the individual judge or judges. Although there has been discussion about the idea of televising court proceedings there is no move imminent on the matter. It is widely believed that the experience of the O.J. Simpson criminal trial has lessened enthusiasm for the notion. Breach of the court's rules on this subject can constitute contempt.

Contempt by Particular Persons

Advocates   An advocate can commit contempt of court if he or she behaves in such a manner as to obstruct the court's proceedings or insult it gratuitously. This is a difficult area because a lawyer is often called upon to represent his client quite robustly and to complain in strong terms if necessary about an apparent injustice being done to him. In discharging this function the advocate is entitled to be forceful, to insist on his client's case being properly put, and to protest against any step which prevents this occurring. But he cannot disobey a direct order of the court, or persist with an argument when directly ordered not to do so. Such things are best dealt with on appeal or by judicial review. Nor should an advocate be gratuitously insulting to the individual judge or the court system. It is a contempt of court to represent oneself falsely as a barrister or solicitor for the purpose of representing a party in court.

Witnesses   It is obvious that all of the types of contempt set out above may also be committed by a witness. However, there are considerations peculiar to persons called as witnesses which can be of direct relevance to journalists. In general, a witness who, without lawful excuse refuses to be sworn, disobeys an order of the court (e.g. for witnesses to remain outside until they give evidence) or refuses to answer a relevant question commits contempt. A witness, other than the defendant in a criminal case, has a privilege against self-incrimination. If he invokes this it is for the judge to decide whether there are, in fact, reasonable grounds for him to fear that he will become the subject of criminal charges.

The most sensitive area in relation to contempt by witnesses is that of refusing to answer proper questions. Various categories of persons have claimed a privilege to refuse to answer particular questions. Lawyers are entitled in certain circumstances to claim legal professional privilege. There is also a restricted recognition of a sacerdotal privilege as between priest and confessor. It is possible that a person, including a lawyer, may be able to assert that a confidence was imparted to him for the purpose of bringing about a settlement of the proceedings. In such circumstances, it would appear to be open to claim the privilege attaching to "without prejudice" communications, though this privilege would presumably be the privilege of the litigant rather than the person confided in.

Journalists' Sources

Journalists have claimed the right to refuse to reveal confidences or to disclose sources of confidential information. In *Re O'Kelly*,[2] an RTÉ journalist was called as a prosecution witness in a trial before the Special Criminal Court. Mr Seán McStíofán was charged with membership of an unlawful organisation. The journalist gave evidence that he had held an interview with a man and had tape-recorded the interview. He identified the tape in court. He was then asked to state who was the man he interviewed but refused to answer on the grounds that to do so would be a breach of confidence:

> "… between me and a client which I feel, were I to breach that confidence, I would not only be putting my own exercise as a journalist into jeopardy, I would be making it very difficult adequately for any journalist all over Ireland to promote the public good by fostering the free exchange of public opinion."

The journalist was sentenced to three months' imprisonment for contempt of court. He was, in fact, released on bail pending appeal, and the appeal was confined to sentence only. In the event he did not have to serve the balance of the sentence. However, the case constitutes a strong assertion by the Court of Criminal Appeal that, "insofar as the administration of justice is concerned, the public has a right to every man's evidence, except for those persons protected by a constitutional or other established and recognised privilege".

The judgment does, however, recognise that:

> "There may be occasions when different aspects of the public interest may require a resolution of a conflict of interests which may become involved in the disclosure or non-disclosure of evidence, but if there be such a conflict, then the sole power of

---

[2] (1974) 63 I.L.T.R. 97.

resolving it resides in the courts. The judgement or the wishes of the witness shall not prevail. This is the law which governs claims for privilege made by the executive organs of the State or by their officials or servants, and journalists cannot claim any greater privilege."

It should be noted that the *O'Kelly* case was not in fact a strong one for the exercise of a claim to journalistic privilege because there was no element of confidentiality in the giving of the original interview. In addition, since the *O'Kelly* case, the European Convention on Human Rights was incorporated into Irish law in 2003. Article 10 of that Convention provides that:

1. Everyone has the right to freedom of expression. This right shall include freedom to hold opinions and to receive and impart information and ideas without interference by public authority and regardless of frontiers. This article shall not prevent States from requiring the licensing of broadcasting, television or cinema enterprises.
2. The exercise of these freedoms, since it carries with it duties and responsibilities, may be subject to such formalities, conditions, restrictions or penalties as are prescribed by law and are necessary in a democratic society, in the interests of national security, territorial integrity or public safety, for the prevention of disorder or crime, for the protection of health or morals, for the protection of the reputation or rights of others, for preventing the disclosure of information received in confidence, or for maintaining the authority and impartiality of the judiciary.

A number of decisions of the European Court of Human Rights (ECtHR) have made clear that the protection of a journalist's sources is an essential element of the freedom of the press.[3] The importance of this freedom is also reinforced in the Council of Europe's Committee of Ministers Recommendation No. R (2000) 7 on the right of journalists not to disclose their sources of information.

Although it is a case of civil contempt, in *Goodwin v United Kingdom*,[4] the European Court of Human Rights ruled in a majority judgment of 11 to 7, that an attempt to compel a journalist to reveal

---

[3] Application No. 64752/01, 22 November 2007 at para.65.
[4] Judgment of March 27, 1996, (1996) 22 E.H.R.R. 123.

his source for a story was contrary to art.10. It was claimed that there had been a theft of confidential documents which could result in the applicant company suffering serious commercial damage. The House of Lords directed disclosure of the source and the journalist was held in contempt for refusing to comply with the terms of the order. The journalist then brought an application before the ECtHR maintaining that the order was in breach of his article 10 rights. The court upheld this claim and stated:

> "Without such protection, sources may be deterred from assisting the press in informing the public on matters of public interest. As a result the vital public watchdog role of the press may be undermined and the ability of the press to provide accurate and reliable information may be adversely affected. Having regard to the importance of the protection of journalistic sources for press freedom in a democratic society and the potentially chilling effect an order of source disclosure has on the exercise of that freedom, such a measure cannot be compatible with Article 10 (art. 10) of the Convention unless it is justified by an overriding requirement in the public interest."

The Supreme Court in *Mahon v Keena and Kennedy*[5] reflected on the circumstances that would justify an order compelling a journalist to reveal his sources and made a statement which clearly echoes the *Goodwin* test referred to above:

> "According to the reasoning of the European Court in *Goodwin*, an order compelling the appellants to answer questions for the purpose of identifying their source could only be *'justified by an overriding requirement in the public interest'*."[6]

The law, therefore, does not permit an absolute privilege in favour of non-disclosure of a journalist's source but rather requires that a balancing exercise be undertaken. The decision is ultimately left to the discretion of the court in each case. This balancing exercise will consider the important interest and right to the protection of a journalist's source on the one hand, and the public interest in the actual disclosure of the information on the other. If the journalist's source

---

[5] [2009] IESC 64.
[6] [2009] IESC 64, per Fennelly J. at para.69.

delivered the information in confidence and the information relates to a matter that is of significant public interest, it is likely that the court will be slow to compel disclosure of the journalist's source.

Refusal to Answer a Question

At present, refusal to answer a question is treated as a criminal contempt. As with all criminal contempts, it is punishable by imprisonment for a fixed period. This contrasts with imprisonment for civil contempt, which may be indefinite, since it is to last until the defendant complies with the court's order.

Interruptions

There have been cases of constant interruption of the proceedings so that it is impossible for them to continue. In such instances, apart from proceedings for contempt, the court has power to remove the offending party from a courtroom. Where this has happened in recent times, defendants in criminal cases have been brought to a room with an audio-link to the court so that they can hear, but not directly participate in, the proceedings.

Outbursts by defendants quite frequently occur in criminal cases after conviction or sentence. Although such things are clearly capable of constituting a contempt of court, they are usually ignored by the presiding judge. Apart from anything else, if a significant sentence of imprisonment is being imposed in any event, there is little point in adding to it the relatively short sentence which contempt normally attracts. Similarly, outbursts by relatives of defendants or victims and their relations may simply be ignored when not persistent. In this area the discretion of the court is paramount.

Jurors

Jurors may also commit contempt in any of the ways mentioned above. Proceedings against jurors for contempt are rare. However, the Juries Act 1976 contains a provision for a variety of summary offences which can be committed in connection with jury service.

Scandalising the Court

The risk of contempt by scandalising the court is one to which journalists and publishers are particularly, but not uniquely, liable. The offence of contempt of court by scandalising the court is committed by publishing material calculated to bring a court or a judge of a court into contempt, or to lower his authority, thereby endangering public confidence in the court and thus obstructing and interfering with the administration of justice. The offence is not committed by mere criticism or disagreement, however emphatic, with what has been decided by a court.

In practice, the Irish cases show that the offence will not be committed unless there is an attribution to the court of corrupt, dishonest or unlawful behaviour or total and unreasoned arbitrariness. Furthermore, the attack must be on a judge in his official capacity because: "In his personal character a judge receives no more protection from the law than any other member of the community at large."[7] It is obvious from the foregoing brief summary that the line between contempt and legitimate criticism may be difficult to decide in borderline cases. The reported judgments provide some guidance as to what the courts have regarded as contempt.

In *Attorney General v O'Ryan and Boyd*,[8] a letter was published in a newspaper attacking a judge who had jailed rioters despite a plea for leniency by a local priest. The judge was a Protestant and the letter suggested, amongst other things, that the result would have been different if the plea for leniency had "come from the local lodge of the Grand Orient and embossed with a square and compass". The High Court held that:

> "It is unnecessary … to point out how offensive such a statement was and how the suggestion, that the judge could be so swayed, was calculated to injure him and his court in the eyes of the public."

In *Re Kennedy and McCann*,[9] a tabloid newspaper published a "biased and inaccurate" account of child custody proceedings in the High Court which had led to custody being awarded to their father. This, in any event, was a contempt of court since it identified the children by name, contrary to statutory provisions providing for privacy of such proceedings. However, it also contained gross misstatements as to the reasons for the decision and concluded that: "It seems that money and the lifestyle it could buy was regarded by the courts as by far the most

---

[7] *R. v McHugh* [1902] 2 I.R. 82.
[8] [1946] I.R. 70.
[9] [1976] I.R. 382.

important consideration." It also suggested that justice could not be obtained in Irish courts and, accordingly, that Ireland was a "sick society".
The Supreme Court held that:

> "... in this instance there has been a contempt of a serious nature. Not only was the article written in breach of an order prohibiting publication but it was a distortion of the facts and was calculated to scandalise the members of the court ... for it imputed to them base and unworthy motives which, if substantiated, would render them unfit for their office."

It was also held that:

> "... the offence of contempt by scandalising the court is committed when, as here, a false publication is made which intentionally or recklessly imputes base or improper motives and conduct to a judge or judges in question. Here, the publication bears on its face, if not an intent, at least the stamp of recklessness."

In this case, the offence of contempt was admitted and apologies tendered. The court imposed substantial fines. Similar principles were applied in two cases where the integrity of the Special Criminal Court was attacked. In *Attorney General v Connolly*,[10] comment was made in a Sinn Féin publication about the likely outcome of the trial of one Henry White for the murder of a Garda. The defendant was described as "fast approaching martyrdom", and it was stated that he "awaits his death, which sentence will inevitably be passed on him after his mockery of a trial before the Special Criminal Court is over".

In *Re Hibernian National Review Ltd*,[11] the periodical *Hibernia* published letters about the conviction of Noel and Marie Murray for the murder of a Garda. In one, the word "trial" was printed in inverted commas and it was stated that "they were tried without a jury and virtually without evidence". Another letter suggested that, "many defendants are presumed guilty until they can prove their innocence against the belief of the gardaí. In the ordinary course of events this mixture of special justice and bias towards the police is a reversal of justice". This letter also misstated the extent of the evidence against the two defendants.

---

[10]   [1947] I.R. 213.
[11]   [1976] I.R. 388.

This case is of particular interest because the Director of Public Prosecution's initial application for a conditional order of attachment for contempt was refused by the President of the High Court. However, the DPP successfully appealed to the Supreme Court where it was held that the words meant:

> "... that the members of the Special Criminal Court conducted a travesty of a trial, that they did not give the benefit of the doubt to the accused, and that they were involved in an effort by the government and the gardaí to produce a false verdict of guilty, and that the only evidence against the accused was their own statements."

The Supreme Court, however, emphasised that criticisms of the existence of a Special Criminal Court, or of the retention at the time of a death sentence, were not in themselves a contempt of court. "These are matters which may validly be debated in public even if the comments made are expressed in strong language or are uniformed or foolish." Sometime later, the Association for Legal Justice issued a press statement commenting on the Special Criminal Court's trial and conviction in the same case. Speaking of the death sentence imposed, the Association said that it was:

> "... particularly reprehensible because it was passed by the Special Criminal Court, a court composed of government appointed judges having no judicial independence which sat without a jury and which so abused the rules of evidence as to make the court akin to a sentencing tribunal."

If, however, a publication lacks the element of attributing base, corrupt, dishonest or arbitrary motives to a judge, criticism of a judgment is entirely permissible. In *Weeland v RTÉ*,[12] the High Court considered a suggestion that RTÉ had committed a contempt of court in a portion of a programme about certain land dealings in Cork. The relevant part of the programme dealt with the circumstances in which an action for fraud in the sale of land had been dismissed in the Circuit Court. The programme was found to have been unbalanced in its report of the Circuit Court proceedings because it made "no attempt to deal, however briefly, with the Circuit judge's analysis of the evidence, the

---

[12]   [1987] I.R. 662.

view he took and the weight he attached to certain items of evidence in reaching his verdict".

Despite this, the programme was held not to constitute contempt. The judge held:

> "I do not see why a judgment cannot be criticised, providing it is not done in a manner calculated to bring the court or the judge into contempt. If that element is not present there is no reason why judgment should not be criticised. Nor does the criticism have to be confined to scholarly articles in legal journals. The mass media are entitled to have their say as well. The public take a great interest in court cases and it is only nature that discussion should concentrate on the result of cases. So criticism which does not subvert justice should be allowed. Even though this programme was in my opinion unbalanced in relation to the judgment on the Circuit judge, it did not pass over the boundary of acceptable limits."

In *Desmond v Glackin (No. 1)*,[13] a Government Minister (Mr Des O'Malley) made a comment about High Court proceedings instituted by one of those involved in a Companies Act inspectorship relating to the purchase by Telecom Éireann of premises at Ballsbridge, Co. Dublin. The proceedings had had the effect of delaying the inquiry by the inspector, who had been appointed by the Minister. Mr O'Malley, in the course of a radio interview, commented that the proceedings "certainly facilitated (a particular person) in blocking the inquiry". Although it was suggested that this was a contempt of court the High Court found otherwise, regarding the comment as a reference to delays in the court system. This finding was despite the fact that the judge plainly did not agree with Mr O'Malley's views.

The case of *McCann v An Taoiseach*[14] is a most interesting one in illustrating the present attitude of the courts and the appropriate course of action for journalists who have unwittingly strayed into this form of contempt. In the course of the campaign in relation to the referendum to approve the Maastricht Treaty, the plaintiff sought a court order to prevent a broadcast by the Taoiseach. RTÉ published a report of the case which, they subsequently admitted, was seriously inaccurate in that it attributed remarks to the judge which he had not

---

[13]   [1992] I.L.R.M. 490.
[14]   Unreported, High Court, Carney J., June 23, 1992.

made. Mr Justice Carney held that this constituted a serious contempt but that no action was required because: (a) the error had not been intentional or malicious, and (b) it had been immediately and fully repaired.

Contempt is an area uniquely for the discretion of the court and, in particular, it should be noted that it is open to a judge to take no action even though contempt is clearly established. This was done on the case just quoted. It was also the course adopted by the courts in relation to the editor of the newspaper which published the letter in question in *Attorney General v O' Ryan and Boyd*.[15] The writer of the letter, who was a County Councillor, had read the offending letter at a meeting of the County Council, which had then passed a motion critical of the judge. When contempt proceedings were taken against him, the editor of the newspaper who had printed the letter by way of a report on the County Council proceedings was also accused of contempt. The editor gave evidence that he regarded the letter as wrong-headed and unfair and considered that publishing it would indicate to a fair-minded reader that the County Council's resolution had been passed in circumstances of bias and hysteria. He therefore claimed the publication was for the public benefit.

While the court was divided on the merits of this defence in the particular circumstances, all three judges agreed that no action should be taken against the editor. Mr Justice Gavan Duffy said:

> "It must never be forgotten to an editor that his task in having to decide, often at short notice, whether or not to publish offensive material concerning a topic of the day, may be arduous to a high degree, and I should have much sympathy here with Mr Boyd if in the peculiar circumstances he had made an error of judgment; and I should be very slow indeed to hold that, having no personal interest in the unsavoury episode, he had by a very understandable mistake incurred the penalties of contempt of court."

Although this case is over 60 years old, the approach taken to the position of the editor is consistent with the approach of the courts in more recent cases and appears to suggest that the position of a journalist who merely reports remarks, in circumstances of haste, may be more favourably regarded than that of the person who originates them.

---

[15] [1946] I.R. 70.

Two other points require to be made. First, the Law Reform Commission has recommended the retention of contempt by scandalising, where the alleged contempt consists of attributing corrupt conduct to a judge or court, or of publishing a false account of legal proceedings. They recommend that it should be necessary to prove intention or recklessness, and a substantial risk to the administration of justice or the judiciary being brought into serious disrepute.

Secondly, it should be noted that many remarks capable of constituting this form of contempt would also constitute a defamation of the judge or judges referred to, and such an action might be pursued regardless of whether or not contempt proceedings were taken.

Once an issue of contempt arises, it is unlikely that there will be any opportunity for humour, but in one reported occasion, a well-known solicitor in Northern Ireland was being reprimanded by a Magistrate who asked the solicitor: "Are you trying to show contempt for this Court?", to which the response was, "No your worship, I'm trying to conceal it!"

Defences

Mens rea Most serious criminal offences require the proof of mens rea, that is, a guilty mind, in the sense of an intention to commit the crime in question. Curiously, it is unclear from the case law whether this requirement applies in the case of contempt by scandalising. The better view, on the basis of *Re Kennedy and McCann*,[16] appears to be that intention or recklessness is required. The point is probably more of academic than practical interest because in many cases the words will have an unequivocal meaning and their tendency will be clear, as it was in the case just cited.

Justification Again, there is little direct authority on this point, partly because in many of the cases the publications were admitted to be false by the time contempt proceedings came for hearing. However, the Supreme Court judgment in *Director of Public Prosecutions v Walsh*[17] included the words "baseless" in the judicial definition of the offence of contempt by scandalising and noted that it was admitted that the words complained of would amount to a criminal contempt "if untrue and baseless". It, therefore, appears that truth would constitute a

---

[16] [1976] I.R. 382.
[17] [1981] I.R. 412.

defence to an allegation of contempt by scandalising. There is, however, no recorded Irish case where this has been successfully pleaded.

Fair comment   It follows from the definition of the offence itself that a comment which is fair, in the sense in which that term is used in the law of defamation, does not constitute a contempt of court. It is probable that the jurisprudence relating to this defence in defamation would be applied with the necessary adaptations to a defence of fair comment to contempt by scandalising.

Public benefit Although it has been suggested that there may be a separate defence to the effect that publication was for the public benefit, it is probable that this is merely an aspect which, together with other features of a particular case, might prevent a publication from being contempt at all. In the case of *Attorney General v O'Ryan and Boyd*,[18] the member of the court who considered that the publication had in fact been for the public benefit gave his reasons in a form which suggests that he did not regard the publication as constituting contempt. The publication, he held, had in its context merely demonstrated the baselessness of the allegations contained in the letter which was the subject of the proceedings.

Prejudging the Proceedings of the *Sub Judice* Rule

In all forms of proceedings, there is necessarily a delay between the commission of the acts complained of, the institution of legal proceedings and the eventual verdict or judgment. Publicity during these periods can radically alter the context in which the trial takes place. For example, if the guilt or the innocence of a criminal defendant is constantly proclaimed by the media, or if selective portions of the evidence are given wide publicity, that may seriously affect the rights of the prosecution or defence, as the case may be, to a fair trial. If unrestricted comment on these matters were permitted, as it is in parts of the United States, we would also have the American phenomenon of both prosecution and defence conducting PR campaigns, leaking evidence, and generally seeking trial by media in advance of the actual hearing. Indeed, American experience has been a major factor in strengthening traditional concerns in this area.

---

[18]   [1946] I.R. 70.

This is possibly the most common form of contempt alleged and found against media defendants. It has been given a particular topicality by the recent upsurge in investigative reporting of criminal matters, including, notably, the publication of information alleged to come from "garda sources" but not otherwise proved.

This heading of contempt is not limited to prejudging proceedings. It may also consist of interfering with parties or witnesses by making it difficult or impossible for them to give evidence, or prosecute their cases by public pressure, or by disclosure of private legal information. The area also features the phenomenon of gagging writs, whereby proceedings, notably for defamation, are instituted more for the purpose of stifling comment than being prosecuted to finality.

General Principle

The Constitution provides that no person shall be tried for a criminal offence except in due course of law. This involves a trial on legally admissible evidence before a jury or other tribunal which is in fact impartial and is seen to be so. Therefore, in the words of a leading English textbook[19]:

> "Publications which directly or indirectly prejudge the merits of a trial and particularly those which impute the guilt or innocence of the accused are classical examples of trial by newspaper. Such publications obviously have the tendency to prejudice the fair trial of an accused, since they could clearly trade bias in the minds of those who actually have to try the case. It is therefore contempt to impute directly or indirectly the guilt or innocence of an accused before he has been tried."

Hardiman J., in *DPP v Independent Newspapers and others*,[20] referred to the unfairness associated with early and incomplete reporting:

> "Although the law of contempt has become encrusted with technicalities over the years, especially in the absence of statutory reform, it is not in any sense a purely technical area. On the contrary, the law which prohibits prejudicial comment one way or the other in a pending criminal trial protects a very basic

---

[19]   *Borrie and Lowe's Law of Contempt.*
[20]   [2009] IESC 20.

human and civil right: the right to have the guilt or innocence of persons accused of crime assessed by the proper tribunal, untroubled by outside pressures or by public assertions, express or implied, to the effect that the defendant is or is not guilty or should or should not be convicted.

Many Irish people will remember how strange and how utterly unfair it seemed, 30 years ago, when the media in another jurisdiction appeared, with impunity, to assume the guilt of certain Irish people facing criminal charges. It is no less inappropriate in this jurisdiction. In relation to almost every sort of criminal charge there are some persons who will be gratified or advantaged if the alleged criminals are "led out in handcuffs". But such persons, especially if they are newspaper editors or others who are powerful or influential in the shaping of public opinion, must take care not to pollute the fountain of justice by expressing, or seeming to express, a view as to the guilt or innocence of accused persons, especially in lurid or vivid terms. Apart from anything else, such views are rarely based on an examination of the evidence which will eventually come before the trial court."

Prejudging in Favour May Also be Contempt

It is important to note that contempt may be committed by prejudging the issues in favour of an accused in a criminal case, as well as against him. Indeed, the same publication may have both effects simultaneously on different readers. Thus, in the case of *Attorney General v Hibernian National Review Ltd,*[21] it was held that the description of a person awaiting trial as "a political prisoner" by a well-known and responsible journalist, who held himself out as knowing the facts, might tend to prejudice a potential juror in favour of the accused, or against him, according to the juror's political views.

Examples of Contempt

The *sub judice* rule, in the context of criminal proceedings, may be offended against in a huge variety of ways which range from the blatant to the subtle. In the 1940s, the *Daily Mirror* commenting on the arrest of a person on a charge of murder did so under the heading, "The Vampire Will Suck no More". Little knowledge or sensitivity is

---

[21] Unreported, High Court, May 16, 1972.

required to discern the contempt in this. Most contempts, however, are less dramatic and have consisted of such things as asserting that an accused's alleged statement of admission had been extracted by torture; stating that a defendant in a current trial was a relation of a well-known criminal; referring to a person pejoratively in an article on organised crime published the day before the person was due to go on trial; giving details of an accused's previous convictions prior to his trial; and making one-sided or inaccurate revelations of what was said to be the evidence for one side or another prior to the trial.

Proximity to Trial

A very important question for journalists is when the risk of contempt by prejudgment starts to apply. There is English and Northern Ireland authority for the proposition that it may apply when criminal proceedings are "imminent", though not actually commenced. However, this does not appear to be the law in Ireland, on the basis of *State (DPP) v Independent Newspapers Ltd.*[22] In that case, the defendant had reported that the Gardaí were about to bring charges for sexual offences against a local authority member. Two days later such proceedings were in fact commenced. The Director of Public Prosecutions sought attachment for contempt in these circumstances but O'Hanlon J. declined to make an order. He said:

> "As the courts must always have regard to the countervailing importance of preserving the freedom of the press, I do not consider that the facts disclosed in the affidavit grounding the present application are of such a character as would justify me in extending the law as to contempt of court in the manner now sought by the Director of Public Prosecutions."

However, it is clear from the report that the judge's attention was not drawn to authorities which support the proposition that the test is one of imminence, not the actual commencement of proceedings.

Fade Factor not Relevant in Contempt Motion

The issue of contempt is not to be confused with the need for an adjournment or prohibition of a criminal trial because of adverse

---

[22] [1995] I.L.R.M. 183.

publicity. While one might follow the other, a trial may have to be adjourned for a period of time. The trial will be adjourned so as to allow for the fading of the published information from the minds of the general public and whichever jury is eventually empanelled. While the trial may ultimately proceed after a period of time, the issue of any contempt arising is not affected by the passage of time. The *Independent Newspapers* case referred to above confirmed that the question of whether or not a party was guilty of *sub judice* contempt ought to be determined at the time of the publication and so, the "fade factor" was not a relevant consideration in a contempt motion.

After Trial: Appeal Pending

This situation was fully explored in the very important case of *Cullen v Magill Publications (Holdings) Ltd.*[23] In this case Cullen had been convicted of a notorious crime. He had an appeal pending to the Court of Criminal Appeal. Before the appeal came up, *Magill* magazine proposed to publish an article based on the exclusive story of the principal prosecution witness, a woman accomplice. Cullen sought an injunction to restrain publication. He was successful in the High Court, where Barrington J. decided that there was a risk of prejudice, even though the appeal would be heard before three judges, rather than jurors. The defendants contended that this obviated the possibility of prejudice since judges were trained to exclude irrelevant material from consideration. The judge held that: "In my view it is absurd to suggest that judges' minds could not be affected by prejudice."

The Supreme Court, however, found for the defendants, thereby permitting publication. The Supreme Court regarded the argument that judges might be affected in their consideration of legal arguments by publicity as "unsustainable".

This view has been criticised. The Law Reform Commission stated that, "with respect this is too extreme a statement at variance with human experience". Nevertheless, the case stands as strong authority for the proposition that, where a trial before a judge or judges only is anticipated, it is difficult to allege contempt in the form of prejudgment. This would exclude all civil actions, other than High Court actions for defamation, assault or false imprisonment, from the scope of this form of contempt.

---

[23]   [1994] I.L.R.M. 577.

After Trial: Sentence Pending

The case of *Kelly v O'Neill & Brady*[24] examined the issue of contempt in the context of an article having been written in the Irish Times after the trial had concluded but before sentence was passed. On May 15, 1993 Kelly had been convicted by a jury of two offences, that is, of having in his possession cocaine, and of having the same substance in his possession for the purpose of supplying it to others. The trial judge postponed sentencing until May 27, 1993.

The *Irish Times* article entitled "Gardaí believe Kelly was involved in Other Major Crimes" was published on May 17, 1993. It reported what it regarded as other major crimes that it believed Kelly was involved in. Kelly sought attachment of the respondents for alleged contempt of court.

The applicant claimed that the article contained malicious and pernicious lies. The respondents considered themselves free to comment on what they believed to be a matter of public importance, namely, the fact of the jury's decision and the applicant's previous court appearances and actions once the proceedings had passed out of the hands of the jury. They contended they had not intended to interfere in any way with the determination by the trial of the appropriate sentence.

The trial judge, having heard their arguments, concluded that as a matter of fact and law he was incorruptible but that the article did constitute contempt of the Circuit Court and he imposed a fine. The decision was appealed to the High Court who stated a consultative case for the opinion of the Supreme Court and posed the two following questions:

(a) Can it be contempt of court to publish an article in the terms of that complained of after a criminal trial has passed from the station of the jury and where the remainder of the hearing will take place before a judge sitting alone?

(b) Given the constitutional right to freedom of expression of the press, could the publication of the article complained of ever constitute contempt of court when published after conviction and before sentencing?

The main category of criminal contempt which the Supreme Court had to consider was whether the article, given the nature of the two

---

[24]   Unreported, Supreme Court, December 2, 1999.

questions posed, consisted of "any act done or writing published calculated to obstruct or interfere with the due course of justice or the lawful process of the courts". In other words, was the *sub judice* rule of any relevance in a criminal trial before a judge or judges sitting alone? However, the Supreme Court was not persuaded that due process ceases once the jury have returned their verdict because of the assumed immunity of the judges from frailties to which juries are acknowledged to be subject and, consequently, they answered yes to the first question. In relation to the second question, Keane J. took the view that what the court was being asked to consider was whether the conclusion which had been reached on the first question should be modified in light of the constitutionally guaranteed right to freedom of expression of the press. He was satisfied it should not, and he expressed his views as follows:

"Freedom of expression is undoubtedly a value of critical importance in a democratic society, but like every other right guaranteed, either expressly or by implication, by the Constitution it is not an absolute right. The limitations on freedom of expression required by the machinery of contempt of court were found not to be of themselves a violation of the right of freedom of expression guaranteed by the European Convention on Human Rights in *Sunday Times v UK*.[25]

I appreciate that deferring publication of an article of this nature until after sentence has been imposed might be commercially unattractive to a newspaper concerned, but the restraint is in a different category from the absolute prohibition on publication required by *scandalising the courts* which suggests that an even greater caution should be exercised by the courts in that area.

A temporary restraint on a publication of this nature, lasting sometimes for no more than a day or two, and at most a few weeks, seems to me a not disproportionate restriction, when weighed in the balance against the damage which could be done to the administration of justice if the press, television, radio or anyone else were to have an unrestricted licence, subject only to the law of defamation, to comment freely and publish material, however untrue and damaging concerning a trial at a stage when it was still in progress and the accused, although found guilty, was

---

[25] *Sunday Times v UK* (1979) E.H.R.R. 245.

still entitled to the solemn constitutional guarantee of a trial in due course of law."

He also answered the second question in the affirmative.

Effect on a Litigant or Appellant

Apart from the risk that a publication prejudging the issues in proceedings may affect the tribunal trying those issues, there is also a risk that extensive publicity, particularly of the campaigning type, might have an effect by making a plaintiff, defendant or appellant feel that he had no chance of success in pursuing his case.

Photographs

It is important to note that the publication of a photograph of an accused person is capable of amounting to contempt in a case where visual identification is in question. It may prejudice the accused by fostering an inaccurate identification and may also prejudice the prosecution by lessening the value of an identification witness.[26]

CIVIL CONTEMPT

The main difference between civil contempt proceedings and criminal contempt proceedings is that the object in civil contempt proceedings is to get a person or body to comply with a court order. From a journalist's point of view, the main dangers occur where a journalist either ignores a court order, e.g. an injunction, or reports a matter in ignorance, for example, that the material being covered has been the subject of a court order.

A person failing to obey a court order can be attached and committed. This means they can be brought before the courts and imprisoned until they purge their contempt. Because a person's liberty is at stake there are strict rules governing the procedure. These are set out in the Rules of the Superior Courts.

Generally speaking, a person whose committal or attachment is being sought, is served with a notice of motion which contains a penal endorsement, effectively a warning that they could be sent to prison if

---

[26]   See *McArthur* [1983] I.R.L.M. 355.

found in contempt. Such a motion must be served on the offending person personally with a copy of the order allegedly being broken.

The court has complete discretion whether or not to order committal or attachment, even in cases where the contempt is clear-cut. Generally, if the court is satisfied that the contempt was a genuine error on the part of a journalist an apology may suffice. This is more likely to happen where the court is happy that it would have been difficult for the journalist to know of the existence of the order.

In *Watters v Daily Star*,[27] Judge Mathews had already determined that comments made in a newspaper article were defamatory and ordered an apology be printed on terms agreed with the plaintiff. Subsequent to that and before the apology was printed, the newspaper printed a further article which stated: "We may have to apologise to this revolting pervert ... but will we mean it? HELL NO", and also reported: "Larry Murphy the Beast of Baltinglass had been rumoured to have become close to Watters 'another twisted pervert' in Dublin's Arbour Hill Prison."

The court found that these statements constituted not only a further defamatory statement, but also a contempt of court, as an earlier order had been made under s.33 of the Defamation Act 2009 which prohibited the defendant from publishing or further publishing the false and defamatory statements. He considered that the report was a calculated breach of his earlier order and he directed the publication of a suitable summary of the earlier judgment.

Judge Mathews considered that the report was not a report after conclusion of the proceedings, as the apology had not yet been printed. He stated:

> "I am unable to avoid the conclusion that in publishing as it did in the format complained of the newspaper breached the order prohibiting the Defendant from publishing or further publishing false and defamatory statements in respect of which the application was originally brought. Further the newspaper in declaring that it would, if obliged to publish an apology, publish it but would not mean such apology clearly in my judgment published matters directed at interfering with the due administration of justice in these proceedings *because* such matters were published before a form of correction and apology were to be published in accordance

---

[27] Unreported, Circuit Court, Judge Mathews, December 2010.

with the terms of the Defamation Act, 2009. To come to such a conclusion is not to unduly restrict the freedom of the press to comment on a matter of public interest rather it is to restrict the circumstances in which a libel complained of might be republished and a form of correction order and apology directed brought to nought the publication of such matters *before* the conclusion of the proceedings. The tendency to interfere with the due administration of justice in any particular set of proceedings has to be determined by reference to the nature of the publication and all relevant authorities agree that it is *not relevant* for this purpose to determine what the actual effect the publication upon the proceedings had been or what it will probably be. If the publication is of a character which might have an effect upon the proceedings it will be deemed to have the necessary tendency unless the possibility of interference is so removed or theoretical that the de minimis principle should be applied."[28]

Protection of Journalists' Sources

The principal worry most journalists have is the extent to which they will be able to protect their sources. Journalists like to be able to assure confidential contacts that there will be no question of them revealing their source. In England the need for the protection of journalists' sources was recognised with the passing of the Contempt of Court Act 1981. Under that Act, a journalist shall not be required to disclose his source unless it can be established to the satisfaction of the court that the disclosure is necessary in the interests of:

(a) national security,

(b) justice,

(c) the prevention of crime, or

(d) the prevention of disorder.

This section was tested all the way to the House of Lords, and from there, to the European Court of Human Rights in *X v Morgan Grampian (Publishers)*.[29] In this case, two associated privately owned companies prepared a business plan for the purposes of negotiating a

---

[28] Emphasis in original.
[29] [1991] 1 A.C. 1.

substantial loan to raise additional working capital. A copy of the plan was stolen and a trainee journalist was contacted by a confidential source and given information about the companies, including the projected loan. The trainee journalist decided to write an article on the companies and telephoned them and the bankers to check certain facts.

The companies immediately applied for an ex parte injunction prohibiting publication of anything contained in the draft plan. They also applied under s.10 of the Contempt of Court Act 1981 requiring the journalist to disclose the source of his information, claiming it was in the interests of justice that he do so. In finding for the companies, one of the judges stated:

> "Construing the phrase 'in the interests of Justice' in this sense immediately emphasises the importance of the balancing exercise. It will not be sufficient *per se*, for the party seeking disclosure of a source protected by s. 10 to show merely that he was unable without disclosure to exercise the legal right or avert the threatened legal wrong on which he bases his claim in order to establish the necessity of disclosure. The judge's task will always be to weigh in the scales the importance of enabling the ends of justice to be attained in the circumstances of the particular case on the one hand against the importance of protecting the source on the other hand. In this balancing exercise it is only if the judge is satisfied that disclosure in the interests of justice is of such preponderating importance as to overtake the statutory privilege against disclosure that the threshold of necessity will be reached."

The journalist lost the case but refused to identify his source or hand his notes into court and was fined £5,000. The matter went before the European Court of Human Rights[30] who found that the English court order breached art.10 of the European Convention on Human Rights.

The approach by the Irish courts since the enactment of the European Convention on Human Right Act 2003 does not favour an absolute privilege in favour of sources but will balance the public interest in the administration of justice in disclosure with the competing public interest of the protection of the rights of journalists in not disclosing their sources.

---

[30] *Goodwin v UK* (1996) 22 E.H.R.R. 123.

In *Mahon and others v Keena and Kennedy*,[31] a Divisional High Court (three members of that court) considered the jurisprudence of the ECtHR on the issue of the protection of a journalist's sources and commented:

"The foregoing, as is obviously so, is the briefest of summaries of the outcome of these cases. Throughout all of these cases however great emphasis is laid upon the importance of the right to freedom of expression in a democratic society. Going hand in hand with this, is the critical importance of a free press as an essential organ in a democratic society. An essential feature of the operation of a free press is the availability of sources of information. Without sources of information journalists will be unable to keep society informed on matters which are or should be of public interest. Thus there is a very great public interest in the cultivation of and protection of journalistic sources of information as an essential feature of a free and effective press. As between the parties in this case there was no dispute whatever concerning these fundamental aspects of the right to freedom of expression as set out in Article 10 of the Convention.

These cases also illustrate on the part of the European Court of Human Rights a stalwart defence of freedom of expression, and a trend of strictly construing potential interferences with that right that might claim justification under the variety of justifiable interferences set out in Article 10(2). This approach by the European Court of Human Rights is particularly evident in cases involving publications relating to political matters. There was no reported case opened to us in which the European Court of Human Rights has upheld an order of a domestic court ordering the disclosure of a journalistic source. In only one case, a decision of the United Kingdom Court of Appeal in the case of *Ashworth Hospital Authority v. MGN Limited* (2001) WLR 2003 is there a judgment of a court directing disclosure of a journalistic source, having considered the balancing under Article 10, of the right to non-disclosure against the competing interest in that case namely the protection of confidential information held by a hospital authority.

It is important to bear in mind that where a journalist asserts the right not to disclose or the privilege against non-disclosure,

---

[31]   [2007] IEHC 348.

invariably this is not the only right or interest in issue. As in this case the rights and interests of other persons or institutions have also to be considered.

That is an exercise that in a democratic society based on the rule of law is reserved to courts established by law for that purpose.

As the history of these cases show journalists should have little to fear and certainly no grounds for thinking that their right not to reveal sources does not or would not be given just consideration and vindicated where appropriate."

Nevertheless, if there is a greater public interest that justifies the release of the information then the protection will no longer apply. On appeal to the Supreme Court, Fennelly J. stated in the clearest terms, not only the importance of the privilege but also that ultimately the matter will be decided by the court:

"Who would decide whether the journalist's source had to be protected? There can be only one answer. In the event of conflict, whether in a civil or criminal context, the courts must adjudicate and decide, while allowing all due respect to the principle of journalistic privilege. No citizen has the right to claim immunity from the processes of the law."

CHAPTER ELEVEN

PRIVACY

Meaning of Privacy

The Law Reform Commission described privacy as a concept that:

> "… includes a wider range of personal interests or claims which place limits on the right of society and of its members to acquire knowledge of, and to take action regarding, another person. At its core lies the desire of the individual to maintain control over information, possessions and conduct of a personal kind, and … to deny or control access thereto by others."[1]

The challenge for the journalist in this area is in trying to identify:

- Is the information sought of such a nature that it is subject to a right of privacy?
- Do the means that the journalist uses in gathering the information amount to a breach of a right of privacy?

Constitutional and European Convention Protections

The Constitution of Ireland protects a right of privacy. While there is no specific provision in the Constitution expressing a right to privacy, it has long been accepted by the courts in Ireland that privacy is one of the unenumerated rights in the Constitution.[2]

In addition, the courts must also have regard to the European Convention on Human Rights (the "ECHR") and must also interpret legislation (in so far as is possible to do so) in a manner that is in accordance with the European Convention on Human Rights. Article 8 of that Convention explicitly guarantees a right to "private" life:

1. Everyone has the right to respect for his private and family life, his home and his correspondence.

---

[1] Law Reform Commission, *Report on Privacy* (1998), p.24 para.2.1.
[2] *Kennedy and Arnold v Attorney General* [1987] I.R. 587.

2. There shall be no interference by a public authority with the exercise of this right except such as is in accordance with the law and is necessary in a democratic society in the interests of national security, public safety or the economic well-being of the country, for the prevention of disorder or crime, for the protection of health or morals, or for the protection of the rights and freedoms of others.

If called upon, the courts will consider and, if necessary, uphold those rights if they are being unlawfully interfered with. The right to privacy is not absolute and is balanced against the rights of others, the exigencies of the common good, and certain other constitutional rights such as freedom of expression. For example, in *Haughey v Moriarty*,[3] the right of privacy in banking transactions was considered by the court in connection with the investigations of the Moriarty Tribunal. The court acknowledged in that case, that an encroachment on the right to privacy of the plaintiffs was permitted only to the extent that was necessary for the conduct of the work of the inquiry.

A journalist should be aware of the distinction between a media organisation serving the public interest and a tribunal carrying out its investigation in the public interest. A tribunal, on the one hand, is acting on authority lawfully bestowed upon it, either by statute or by a resolution of the Houses of the Oireachtas to investigate a matter of public importance in accordance with defined terms of reference. A newspaper, on the other hand, stands alone, without the benefit of a presumption that its actions are constitutional or without any form of formal lawful authority. Therefore, it does not have any immediate lawful authority to breach the privacy rights of the citizens of the State.

In *Kennedy and Arnold v Ireland*, both plaintiffs who were journalists, recovered damages against the State for what was a breach of their rights of privacy—by the unlawful tapping of their telephone conversations. It has subsequently been confirmed in *Herrity v Associated Newspapers (Ireland) Ltd*[4] that the right to sue for a breach of privacy rights is not limited to actions against the State and its institutions. An action in damages for breach of privacy rights may be brought against the person or body who interferes with those rights.

If the information that a journalist seeks to publish has been obtained in breach of a privacy right, it may be difficult to convince a

---

[3] [1999] 3 I.R. 1.
[4] [2008] IEHC 249.

court that there is an overwhelming public interest in the disclosure of the information to the public at large.

This very issue arose in the case of *Herrity v Associated Newspapers (Ireland) Ltd.*[5] The plaintiff was a married woman who brought proceedings against a newspaper seeking damages for breach of her privacy rights. A newspaper owned by the defendant published a number of articles regarding a relationship that she had with a priest following the breakdown of her marriage. The articles published contained transcript extracts of telephone conversations between the plaintiff and the priest, which had been secretly recorded at the instigation of the plaintiff's husband. The recordings were sent to the newspaper. Other conversations were also recorded and some extracts from those recordings were also transcribed and published in the newspaper. While the existence of the relationship with the priest was not disputed, the plaintiff claimed damages for breach of her right of privacy and breach of confidence and conspiracy.[6] After consideration of the case law in this area, Dunne J. considered that the following principles had been established in Irish law:

- There is a constitutional right of privacy.

- The right to privacy is not unqualified.

- The right to privacy may have to be balanced against other competing rights or interests.

- The right to privacy may be derived from the nature of information at issue, i.e. matters which are entirely private and in relation to which there can be no basis for disclosure to others.

- Competing interests may intervene that prevent the information from remaining private but there may still be a right to complain about the means by which the information was obtained.

- The right to sue for damages is not confined to actions against the State.

---

[5] [2008] IEHC 249.

[6] The issues of confidence and conspiracy were not addressed in the judgment as the High Court held in favour of the plaintiff, having found that the taping of her telephone conversations was a deliberate and conscious violation of her constitutional rights. She was awarded €90,000.00.

Understanding Privacy Rights

The extent of a right to privacy may well be different in each case. Clarke J. in *Cogley v RTÉ*[7] commented on the fact that the more intimate the aspect of private life being interfered with, the more serious must the reason be for interference with this right.

By acting in a particular way a person may also relinquish what would normally be protected by a right of privacy. For example, if one initiates a court action for defamation, the extent of that plaintiff's right to privacy will be limited as against the person or body against whom the action is brought. That body may need to penetrate what would in normal circumstances be regarded as the person's private life in order to successfully defend the claim. So by bringing an action in the courts, the plaintiff may have limited his own rights of privacy in relation to matters that are relevant to that litigation. Following that logic, in defending a personal injury claim, an insurer may well argue that by sending a private investigator to carry out surveillance on the plaintiff, no infringement of privacy rights has occurred because of the relevance of the surveillance to the action being brought by the plaintiff.

In *Trent v Garda Commissioner*,[8] O'Donovan J. considered that:

> "... it is perfectly reasonable that, when a citizen makes a complaint against a member of the Garda Siochana, the Garda authorities would try to ascertain what type of person the complainant was so that they might assess his/her reliability. Accordingly it seems to me that ... enquiries into Mr Trent's background and circumstance were perfectly legitimate and in no way offended his constitutional right to privacy."

In *Aherne and Aherne v RTÉ*,[9] a Prime Time program had been made concerning the Leas Cross Nursing Home. Anticipating the broadcast of the program, the owners of the home sought an injunction preventing the program from including "secretly" filmed footage from inside the home. The plaintiffs contended that the material was obtained in breach of their right to privacy and so should not be broadcast. Clarke J. considered that what may in normal circumstances be private material, having regard to competing factors such as the public interest, might not retain that status.

---

[7] [2005] IEHC 180.
[8] [1999] IEHC 84.
[9] [2005] IEHC 180.

A distinction is also made in that case between the manner in which a right of privacy has been infringed and the information that has been gathered in respect of that infringement. In the Leas Cross case, there seemed to be a broad acceptance that the secret filming was in itself a breach of a right to privacy, but that the information obtained from that breach was not protected as there was a greater interest in disclosure because of the very significant issues of public importance at stake. In the same judgment, Clarke J. was satisfied that the pixilation of the faces of the patients was a satisfactory way of protecting the privacy rights of the patients.

The defendants in *Herrity v Associated Newspapers (Ireland) Ltd* argued that there was public interest in the disclosure of the information, given the nature of the role of a catholic priest in Irish society and seeing as the story related to a relationship between the plaintiff and a priest. While Dunne J. accepted that there was a public interest arising in the story, she did not consider that the public interest was such as to set at nought the restrictions on disclosure of telephone conversations imposed by the Postal and Telecommunications Services Act 1983.

Photographs

In *Campbell v MGN*,[10] the plaintiff, a well-known fashion model sued following the publication in the *Mirror Newspaper* which carried a front page story entitled, "Naomi: I am a drug addict". The story then referred to the attendance of the plaintiff at a support group. The House of Lords unanimously concluded that, through the introduction of art.8 of the European Convention on Human Rights into English law, there was a right to control the dissemination of private information. That case was very significant in English law because it established a clear authority that a breach of one's private life was actionable in a claim for damages. That principle had already been established in Ireland since the *Arnold and Kennedy* case in which the plaintiffs recovered damages against the State arising from a wrongful interference with their right to privacy. The *Campbell* case was also significant, in that the House of Lords accepted that the publication of a photograph of someone which reveals the subject to be in a situation of humiliation or severe embarrassment, even if it takes place in a public place, may be an infringement of the privacy of his or her personal information. In

---

[10]   [2004] UKHL 22.

addition, the publication of a photograph, taken of someone in a private place may also be an infringement, even though there was nothing embarrassing about the picture itself.

In a decision of the ECtHR in *Von Hannover v Germany*,[11] the applicant was a member of the royal family of Monaco. Photographs of the applicant in restaurants, on horseback and canoeing with her children had been published in German magazines. The applicant claimed the photos interfered with her article 8 rights. The court upheld her complaint and held that:

> "[private life] in the Court's view, includes a person's physical and psychological integrity; the guarantee afforded by Article 8 of the Convention is primarily intended to ensure the development, without outside interference, of the personality of each individual in his relations with other human beings …".

The court went on to conclude that:

> "… there is no doubt that the publication by various German Magazines of photos of the applicant in her daily life either on her own or with other people falls within the scope of her private life."

Recently, in Ireland, the issue of photographs was dealt with in the High Court by *Ruth Hickey and Jesse Isaac Agnew (A minor suing by his mother and Next Friend Ruth Hickey) v Sunday Newspapers Ltd*.[12] This case concerned the photographs taken of a child in the arms of his father and were accompanied by the by-line, "exclusive/Twink's Ex Shows off Love Child". The child was photographed outside the registry of births, a public place. Kearns P. stated:

> "It is thus far from easy to determine where the parameters to the right of privacy may lie when placed in balance with the right of freedom of expression. One intuitively feels that a right of privacy is less easily established in public places where a person, in the words of T.S. Eliot, has had time "to prepare a face to meet the faces that you meet". That is particularly the case when one is performing a function of a public nature which I am satisfied the plaintiff and Mr Agnew were performing on this occasion.

---

[11] [2004] E.C.H.R. 294.
[12] [2010] IEHC 349.

> This was not a private celebration or event in the plaintiff's own home or at some other location to which a legitimate expectancy of privacy attached. That is not to say, however, that there will never be occasions where a person photographed in a public place can successfully invoke privacy rights."

The case is useful as it isolates certain facts, which the learned High Court President considered relevant in deciding that the publication of the photographs was not a breach of privacy:

(a) The photographs were taken when both the photographer and the plaintiffs were in a public place and performing a routine public function.

(b) The photographs did not disclose anything that could not have been seen by anyone else who turned up at the registry office at the relevant time.

(c) The existence of the child, his age and the identity of his parents were already matters of public record. The defendant could have gone into the registry office, found the information, and published it.

(d) Nothing in the publication exposed the plaintiffs or either of them to any risk of physical harm from any person with ill-intent.

(e) No evidence was adduced to establish the contention that a campaign of surveillance had been carried out on the first-named plaintiff, her partner or child.

(f) The features of the child were not recognisable from the photograph. Furthermore, the child himself could not have suffered any hurt or humiliation from any aspect of the two publications having regard to his age at the relevant time.

(g) The plaintiffs were at the relevant time performing, in the court's view, a public function which they were required to fulfil. No evidence was placed before the court to suggest that it was necessary to bring the child to the registry office on the occasion in question.

(h) The first-named plaintiff, and her partner, themselves elected to bring the child to the registry office. Furthermore, the first-named plaintiff had spoken to a journalist with the specific intention of publicity being accorded to the very matters in respect of which the court considered that she was in the action seeking to claim privacy of.

(i) A voicemail message reproduced in the defendant's newspaper was already posted on the internet and was in the public domain.

A significant factor in the court's decision was the fact that the court considered that the first plaintiff had actively sought publicity from the press and media concerning her partnership with Mr Agnew and the birth of their child, and had made public statements concerning her family life. Some further illumination on what the court might consider not to be an infringement of privacy rights was contained in the judgment:

> "Were I to hold otherwise, it would represent a radical ratcheting up of the right to privacy at the expense of the right of freedom of expression to a degree which, in my view, should more properly be the subject matter of legislation. A finding in favour of the plaintiffs would also give rise to a situation where a newspaper might feel itself inhibited from publishing a photograph of any public person attending, for example a funeral, or leaving or entering a court building or polling station. In any of these situations it is not difficult to imagine circumstances where a claimant could invoke some consideration of privacy."

Privacy of Sex Life

An important case on the law of privacy is the case of *Max Mosley v Newsgroup Newspapers*.[13] Judge Eady in a very convincing and clear judgment commented:

> "Nevertheless, the underlying sentiments are readily understood in everyday language; namely, that people's sex lives are to be regarded as essentially their own business – provided at least that the participants are genuinely consenting adults and there is no question of exploiting the young or vulnerable."

He concluded that the clandestine recording of sexual activity on private property must be taken to engage a person's article 8 rights.

---

[13] [2008] EWHC 1777 (Q.B.).

Freedom of Expression v Privacy

The courts, including the European Court of Human Rights, have recognised the need to balance the right to privacy with a right of freedom of expression. The assessment undertaken by the courts in this regard is more accurately described as balancing a person's rights of privacy with the public's need to be aware of certain information. Freedom of expression is a right that is guaranteed by art.10 of the ECHR.

In *Von Hannover v Germany,* the ECtHR stated that protection of private life guaranteed by art.8 has to be balanced against freedom of expression guaranteed by art.10. In its decision the court recognised that the freedom not only encompasses information or ideas that are favourably received, but also information that offended. The court stated:

> "In that connection the press plays an essential role in a democratic society. Although it must not overstep certain bounds, in particular in respect of the reputation and rights of others, its duty is nevertheless to impart—in a manner consistent with its obligations and responsibilities—information and ideas on all matters of public interest ... Journalistic freedom also covers possible recourse to a degree of exaggeration, or even provocation."[14]

In that case though, the court concluded that the decisive factor in balancing the protection of private life and the freedom of expression lies in the contribution that the published photos and articles make to public debate. The court held:

> "... it is clear in the instant case that they made no such contribution since the applicant exercises no official function and the photos and articles related exclusively to details of her private life."

The approach of the Irish courts has been broadly similar although perhaps more generous to the media.

In *National Irish Bank v RTÉ,*[15] RTÉ had come into possession of information that RTÉ alleged disclosed a scheme that the plaintiffs had used which would enable customers to evade tax. When the plaintiff sought to restrain the defendant from publishing information

---

[14]   [2004] E.C.H.R. 294 at para.58.
[15]   [1998] 2 I.R. 465.

which might identify their customers, the High Court refused the application. That refusal was upheld on appeal to the Supreme Court. Lynch J. held that there was a public interest in defeating wrong doing which may outweigh the public interest in maintaining confidentiality and that was such a case.

In *Aherne v RTÉ*, Clarke J. took a similar approach in refusing an application for an injunction to restrain the broadcast of a program about Leas Cross Nursing Home. He noted that:

> "... both the constitution itself and the law generally recognises the need for a vigorous and informed public debate on issues of importance. Any measures which would improve an excessive or unreasonable interference with the conditions necessary for such debate would require very substantial justification. Thus the reluctance of the courts in this jurisdiction (and also the European Court of Human Rights) to justify prior restraint save in unusual circumstances and after careful scrutiny."

Because the legitimate public interest issues raised were of a "very high weight" in the RTÉ programme, the court considered that those issues weighed against the granting of the injunction.

Dunne J. in *Herrity* stated:

> "The right of freedom of expression extends the same protection to worthless, prurient and meretricious publication as it does to serious worthy and socially valuable works. The undoubted fact that news media frequently and implausibly invoke the public interest to cloak worthless and even offensive material does not affect the principle."

Dunne J. considered that it does not follow that the right to freedom of expression is a more significant right than the right of privacy.

> "Accordingly, it seems to me that there is a balancing exercise engaged in circumstances where the right to freedom of expression conflicts with the right of privacy."

In that case she considered that:

> "I cannot see how anyone can assert a right to freedom of expression to publish transcripts of private telephone conversations

where the legislature has expressly prohibited the interception of telecommunications messages. This is precisely a situation in which the State has seen fit to lay down by Statute an exception to the right of freedom of expression. There is a hierarchy of constitutional rights and as a general proposition, I think, that cases in which the right to privacy will prevail over the right to freedom of expression may well be few and far between. However, this may not always be the case and there are circumstances where it seems to me the right to privacy could be such that it would prevail over the right to freedom of expression …

There may be other circumstances where the right to privacy prevails. For example, could a newspaper be entitled to publish details of a diagnosis of serious illness in respect of an individual bearing in mind the nature of the confidential doctor patient relationship? What if the individual was a well known public figure? Would it make a difference if the individual was a celebrity or, say, a senior politician? I would have thought that the circumstances which could justify a publication of such private information would seldom arise and only if there was some clear, demonstrable public interest."

Eady J. in *Mosley v Newsgroup Newspapers*[16] also considered whether there was a competing public interest in the publication of the images and information which he had already decided were subject to the plaintiff's article 8 rights. He quoted a passage from the ECtHR decision of *Leempoel v Belgium*[17]:

"In matters relating to striking a balance between protecting private life and the freedom of expression that the Court had had to rule upon, it has always emphasised … the requirement that the publication of information, documents or photographs in the press should serve the public interest and make a contribution to the debate of general interest … Whilst the right for the public to be informed, a fundamental right in a democratic society that under particular circumstances may even relate to aspects of the private life of public persons, particularly where political personalities are involved … publications whose sole aim is to satisfy the curiosity of a certain public as to the details of the private life of

---

[16]   [2008] EWHC 1777 (Q.B.).
[17]   App. No. 64772/01, November 9, 2006.

a person, whatever their fame, should not be regarded as contributing to any debate of general interest to society."

And he then concluded:

"In the light of the strict criteria I am required to apply, in the modern climate, I could not hold that any of the visual images, whether published in the newspaper or on the website, can be justified in the public interest. Nor can it be said in this case that even the information conveyed in the verbal descriptions would qualify."

Statutory Protections

There is no general statutory prohibition on interference with privacy rights. It is left to the courts to interpret what privacy rights are under the Constitution and the ECHR. There are, however, a number of statutory provisions that prohibit interference with certain aspects of a person's privacy. Those most relevant to the journalist include:

- The Data Protection Acts 1988–2003 which regulate the use of personal data.
- The restrictions under the Freedom of Information Acts 1997–2004 that arise where a disclosure would involve the disclosure of personal information.[18]
- The right to privacy in certain photographs and films under the Copyright and Related Rights Act 2000.[19]
- The Broadcasting Act 2009 provides in its broadcasting code "that in programmes broadcast by a broadcaster, and in the means employed to make such programmes, the privacy of the individual is not unreasonably encroached upon".[20]
- Section 98(1) of the Postal and Telecommunications Services Act 1983 provides for the criminalisation of interception or promotion of the interception by third parties, of telecommunications messages.

---

[18] Section 28 of the Freedom of Information Acts 1997–2004.
[19] Section 114 of the Copyright and Related Rights Act 2000.
[20] Section 42(2)(d) of the Broadcasting Act 2009.

Data Protection

The disclosure and processing of personal data is regulated by the Data Protection Acts 1988–2003.

The processing of personal data in particular ways is heavily regulated by those Acts. For example, within the legislation, there is a prohibition on processing "sensitive" personal data, an obligation to inform the data subject that you are processing personal data about him, and a right of access of the data subject to that data together with many more obligations.

However, if the data processing is undertaken solely with a view to the publication of any journalistic, literary or artistic material which the data controller (the person in charge of data protection in the organisation) believes, having regard to the special importance of the public interest in freedom of expression, would be in the public interest and that compliance with the Data Protection Acts would be incompatible with those journalistic purposes, the data processing is exempt from certain provisions of the Data Protection Acts. The sections of the Acts that this journalistic exemption applies to are:

- Section 2 which sets out the general data protection principles, other than the requirement that security measures be taken to protect the data;
- Section 2A which set the criteria for making data processing legitimate;
- Section 2B on the prohibition on processing sensitive personal data;
- Section 2D on the information to be given to the data subject;
- Section 4 on the right of access to the material;
- Section 5 on the right to have the data rectified;
- Section 6A on the right to object to the processing; and
- Section 6B on the right not to be subject to automated decision-making.

CHAPTER TWELVE

COPYRIGHT

Meaning of Copyright

The main piece of legislation governing copyright regulation in the State is the Copyright and Related Rights Act 2000 (the "2000 Act"). Although that Act modernised the law of copyright, the provisions of the earlier Copyright Act 1963 (the "1963 Act"), though now largely repealed are still relevant to works created before the 2000 Act came into force.

Copyright is a property right in a work, which permits the person who owns the copyright or persons authorised by him or her to undertake certain acts concerning the work which are restricted by the law of copyright. Copyright does not extend to the ideas and principles which underlie any element of a work.[1]

Copyright subsists in certain types of works[2]:

1. Original literary, dramatic, musical or artistic works;
2. Sound recordings, films, broadcasts or cable programmes;
3. The typographical arrangement of published editions; and
4. Original databases.

Duration of Copyright

The term of protection of literary, dramatic, musical and artistic works is the lifetime of the author and a period of 70 years after the author's death, irrespective of the date when the work is published or otherwise lawfully made available to the public.[3] Protection of cinematograph films is 70 years after the death of the last of the following persons to survive: the principal director, the author of the screenplay, the author of the dialogue and the composer of music specifically created for use in the cinematograph film.[4] Sound recordings are protected for 50 years

---

[1] Section 17(3) of the Copyright and Related Rights Act 2000.
[2] Section 17(1) of the Copyright and Related Rights Act 2000.
[3] Section 24 of the Copyright and Related Rights Act 2000.
[4] Section 24 of the Copyright and Related Rights Act 2000.

after the sound recording is made or, if published or lawfully communicated to the public during this 50 year period, then for 50 years from the
earliest date of publication or communication to the public.[5] Broadcasting
organisations have protection for a term of 50 years after the first
transmission of a broadcast.[6] The copyright in a cable programme expires
50 years after the cable programme was first lawfully included in a cable
programme service.[7] The copyright in a typographical arrangement of a
published edition expires 50 years after the date on which it is first
lawfully made available to the public.[8] For a computer generated work,
the term is 70 years after the date the work was first lawfully made
available to the public.[9] Since 1995, a 25 year term of economic rights was
granted to a person who publishes or communicates to the public for the
first time, a work on which copyright has expired.[10]

Protection of Rights

Many people think that the "C" surrounded by a circle (©) is essential
to establishing copyright but this is not the case. Nevertheless, it is
always advisable to use it if you are establishing a copyright. If someone
infringes the copyright in a work the owner has a right of action
against that person. He can protect the right by an action in the courts
for damages, by way of an injunction seeking to prevent the infringement or an action seeking to make the person infringing the right to
account to the owner for the profits of that infringement.[11]

Ownership Rights and Journalism

Ownership rests in the author or co-author. In the case of a sound
recording, the author is the producer.[12] In the case of a film, it is the
principal director and the producer.[13] In the case of a broadcast, it is the
person or organisation making the broadcast.[14] For a cable programme,

---

[5] Section 26 of the Copyright and Related Rights Act 2000.
[6] Section 27 of the Copyright and Related Rights Act 2000.
[7] Article 8 of the European Communities (Term of Copyright) Regulations 1995 which
    was subsequently substituted by s.34 of the Copyright and Related Rights Act 2000.
[8] Section 29 of the Copyright and Related Rights Act 2000.
[9] Section 30 of the Copyright and Related Rights Act 2000.
[10] Section 34 of the Copyright and Related Rights Act 2000.
[11] Section 127(1) of the Copyright and Related Rights Act 2000.
[12] Section 21(a) of the Copyright and Related Rights Act 2000.
[13] Section 21(b) of the Copyright and Related Rights Act 2000.
[14] Section 21(c) of the Copyright and Related Rights Act 2000.

it is the organisation providing the cable service.[15] For a typographical arrangement of a published edition, it is the publisher.[16] The person taking the photographs is the author of any photos taken.[17]

In *Donoghue v Allied Newspapers Ltd*,[18] a journalist wrote a series of racing stories for a newspaper using anecdotes provided by a jockey. The journalist put the stories into a literary form sometimes putting the stories into dialogues or conversations. As the journalist recreated the anecdotes giving the stories a certain style it was held by the court that the jockey was not the owner or part owner of the stories and could not therefore prevent the newspaper from using the stories again.

Employers and Freelancers

Normally, the author of the work is the first owner of copyright unless the work is employee created, in which case the owner is usually the employer.[19] If the author is a freelance journalist, for example, and there has been no agreement made to the contrary, as the author, the freelancer owns the copyright.

Whether or not someone is an employee is a matter that might not be clear all of the time. If a dispute arises an assessment will be carried out by the court as to the nature of the relationship between the parties. This necessarily involves an inquiry as to whether the person was employed under a contract for services or a contract of service. The determination of this question involves a comprehensive assessment of the nature of the relationship between the parties including the mutuality of obligations between the parties regarding both the provision of work and the execution of the work, the degree of control exerted by the newspaper over the journalist and whether the journalist is in business in his own account.[20]

Newspapers and Periodicals

There are some special rules that apply when the employee works for a newspaper or magazine. For works created during the existence of the 1963 Act and prior to January 1, 2001 a scheme of shared ownership of

---

15 Section 21(d) of the Copyright and Related Rights Act 2000.
16 Section 21(e) of the Copyright and Related Rights Act 2000.
17 Section 21(f) of the Copyright and Related Rights Act 2000.
18 [1937] 3 All E.R. 503.
19 Section 23 of the Copyright and Related Rights Act 2000
20 *Minister for Agriculture & Food v Barry* [2008] IEHC 216.

copyright exists so that in circumstances where the employer is the proprietor of a newspaper magazine or periodical, then although the employer has copyright in the work made for that purpose, the copyright is limited only to republication in similar other newspapers, magazines or periodicals. Otherwise, the journalist has copyright and may republish in a different source other than a newspaper, magazine or periodical.[21]

If a work (other than a computer program), is made after January 1, 2001 by an author in the course of employment by the proprietor of a newspaper or periodical, the copyright vests exclusively in the employer. However, the author may use the work for *any purpose*, other than for the purposes of making available that work to newspapers or periodicals, without infringing the copyright in the work.[22]

The distinction would at first sight appear to be of little consequence, but the vesting of ownership in works created after January 1, 2001 in the employer rather than the former joint ownership, permits the employer to enter into agreements with other media organisations to use scripts prepared by the journalist/employee for purposes beyond newspapers or periodicals.

Licences

If a journalist owns the copyright, the legal mechanism that permits a media organisation to publish the work is in effect the grant of a licence to that organisation. There is no absolute necessity to create a written document to this effect as the grant of a licence may be inferred by reason of the conduct of the parties or the custom that applies in the relevant industry. A freelance journalist submitting an article to a newspaper editor would probably be regarded as a licence permitting the editor to publish without further reference to the journalist.

The Importance of Private Contracts

If a work is employee created, generally ownership of the copyright is vested in the employer, unless the parties have an agreement to the contrary.[23] While it is possible that the copyright may vest jointly in a

---

[21] Section 10(2) of the Copyright Act 1963.
[22] Section 23(2) of the Copyright and Related Rights Act 2000.
[23] Section 23(1)(a) of the Copyright and Related Rights Act 2000.

number of authors, the presence of two authors would suggest that it would be prudent to enter into an agreement concerning copyright ownership. Likewise, where an editor is involved in the alteration of the work, written contracts should be entered into so as to specify ownership, let alone the rights to alter and further utilise the work. In the case of ghost writers, there is usually an obvious need for the ghost writer to enter into a contract to vest copyright ownership in someone else. It is also possible for the person who is the prospective owner of a copyright work not yet completed to vest in advance the ownership of copyright in someone else.[24]

The benefit of copyright may be transferred to someone else but this must be done in writing signed by the person assigning the right.[25]

Infringement

An infringement of copyright occurs under the 2000 Act by any person who undertakes or authorises another to undertake a restricted act without the permission of the owner that relates to a work created after January 1, 2001.[26] For works created prior to that date, the 1963 Act applies. Under the 1963 Act's provisions an infringement occurs if any of the following acts are carried out:

(a) reproducing the work in any material form;
(b) publishing the work;
(c) performing the work in public;
(d) broadcasting the work;
(e) causing the work to be transmitted to subscribers to a diffusion service;
(f) making any adaptation of the work;
(g) doing, in relation to an adaptation of the work, any of the acts mentioned in paragraphs (a) to (e) of this subsection.

The restricted acts under the 2000 Act are[27]:

(a) to copy the work;
(b) to make the work available to the public;

---

[24] Section 121 of the Copyright and Related Rights Act 2000.
[25] Section 47(3) of the Copyright Act 1963 and s.120 of the Copyright and Related Rights Act 2000.
[26] Section 37(3) of the Copyright and Related Rights Act 2000.
[27] Section 37(1) of the Copyright and Related Rights Act 2000.

(c) to make an adaptation of the work or undertake either of the above actions in relation to the adaptation of the work.

Copying

The infringement occurs by copying even if the copying is carried out electronically.[28] Extracting an image from a film or a broadcast and creating a photograph from the image would also be an infringement.[29] A small change was made to the legislation in 2004 which clarifies that temporary acts of reproduction will not be regarded as an infringement where the sole purpose behind the reproduction is either for transmission within a network to third parties or is to be used for a lawful purpose which has no independent economic significance.[30]

Make Available to the Public

An amendment to the 2000 Act clarifies that it shall not be an infringement to put on display a copy of a literary or artistic work in a place to which the public have access.[31]

Adaptation

Translations, arrangements and adaptation from one type of work to another are infringements.[32]

Some Exceptions

Express or Implied Permission

If the owner authorises the particular use complained of, it follows that there can be no infringement. As a defence, this is likely to arise in circumstances where the person who is alleged to have infringed another's copyright asserts that he or she has either an express or an implied authority to do so from the owner.

---

[28] Section 39(1)(a) of the Copyright and Related Rights Act 2000.
[29] Section 39(1)(c) of the Copyright and Related Rights Act 2000.
[30] Article 4 of the European Communities (Copyright and Related Rights) Regulations 2004.
[31] Section 40 of the Copyright and Related Rights Act 2000 was amended to reflect this exception.
[32] Section 43 of the Copyright and Related Rights Act 2000.

Educational Use

Educational establishments are authorised to copy a broadcast or cable programme provided it is for educational purposes.[33]

Fair Dealing

The defence of "fair dealing" has been described as simply reasonable use. This will involve an analysis to determine the original purpose behind the work, the purpose of the person who allegedly infringed the copyright, and the size of the extracts used. Since the 2000 Act, it is statutorily confirmed that "fair dealing" can only be available where the work has lawfully been made available to the public in the first place and the purpose to which the use is made of the work will not unreasonably prejudice the interests of the owner of the copyright.[34]

Prior to 2000, the defence of "fair dealing" applied only to literary, dramatic, musical and artistic works. After the 2000 Act, the defence was extended to cover films, sound recordings, broadcasts, cable programmes, non-electronic original databases and the typographical arrangements of published editions.[35] Fair dealing with a work (other than a photograph) for the purpose of reporting current events does not infringe copyright where the report is accompanied by a sufficient acknowledgement.[36]

Government and Court Operations

If any act is authorised by a statute, the actions taken pursuant to a statute cannot be regarded as a breach of copyright.[37] Similarly, no breach of copyright will arise from any matter arising in the conduct of court proceedings or on the reporting of those proceedings.[38] However, this exception does not extend to the copying of another's court report.[39] Work carried out in parliamentary proceedings bears a similar exemption.[40]

---

[33] Section 56(1) of the Copyright and Related Rights Act 2000.
[34] Section 51(4) of the Copyright and Related Rights Act 2000.
[35] Section 50(2) of the Copyright and Related Rights Act 2000.
[36] Section 51 of the Copyright and Related Rights Act 2000.
[37] Section 76 of the Copyright and Related Rights Act 2000.
[38] Section 71(1) of the Copyright and Related Rights Act 2000.
[39] Section 71(2) of the Copyright and Related Rights Act 2000.
[40] Section 71(1) of the Copyright and Related Rights Act 2000.

Chapter Thirteen

FREEDOM OF INFORMATION

Freedom of Information Act 1997

The Freedom of Information Act 1997, together with subsequent amendments and regulations require Government Departments, certain Government bodies, local authorities, the HSE, universities, technical and colleges of education, RTÉ, TG4 and certain other bodies to provide information on request to members of the public. It also provides the practical framework to allow for the provision of this information, along with a review and an appeal process. A list of bodies that are subject to the terms of the freedom of information legislation (FOI) can best be found at the website of the Office of the Information Commissioner.[1]

Underlying Principles

The underlying principles of the Act include the need to ensure that decisions taken by public bodies are open to public scrutiny; that citizens who are affected by decisions know how they were arrived at; and to know what information is held about them by State bodies.

The Act is broad in its application. So broad in fact, that a decision to refuse to provide information under the Act is presumed not to have been justified unless the body responsible for the decision shows to the satisfaction of the Information Commissioner that the decision was in fact justified.[2]

In *Deely v The Information Commissioner*,[3] McKechnie J. referred to the long title of the FOI Act and commented:

"As can thus be seen the clear intention is that, subject to certain specific and defined exceptions, the rights so conferred on members of the public and their exercise should be as extensive as possible, this viewed, in the context of and in a way to

---

[1] *http://www.oic.gov.ie.*
[2] Section 34(12)(b) of the FOI Act 1997.
[3] [2001] 3 I.R. 439.

positively further the aims, principles and policies underpinning the statute, subject only to necessary restrictions.

It is in my view a piece of legislation independent in existence, forceful in its aim and liberal in outlook and philosophy."

In *Sheedy v Information Commissioner*,[4] Fennelly J. (in a dissenting judgment in the Supreme Court) illustrated his clear view that the passing of the Freedom of Information Act was a significant legislative step:

"The passing of the Freedom of Information Act constituted a legislative development of major importance. By it, the Oireachtas took a considered and deliberate step which dramatically alters the administrative assumptions and culture of centuries. It replaces the presumption of secrecy with one of openness. It is designed to open the workings of government and administration to scrutiny. It is not designed simply to satisfy the appetite of the media for stories. It is for the benefit of every citizen. It lets light in to the offices and filing cabinets of our rulers."

Records

A record is defined as including any papers, memorandum, photographs, film or recording, or any form in which data is held whether manual, mechanical or electronic. The type of record that may be obtained includes any records necessary to understand a current record. If records are already publicly available or are available under any other enactment (for example the Data Protection legislation), then they may not be obtained under FOI.

Records generated by the public bodies in question after the commencement date of the 1997 Act can be sought under the freedom of information legislation. The commencement dates for most bodies was April 21, 1998 and with respect to the former health boards (now the HSE), October 20, 1998. A person who makes a request is entitled to any personal information held about him as a distinct category of record irrespective of the time the records were created.

---

[4] [2005] 2 I.R. 272.

The Head

Each public body must appoint a Chief Information Officer termed "the head" who is ultimately responsible for decisions taken under FOI within that body.

General Information Manuals

Before embarking on a freedom of information request, it is sometimes wise to first request from the public body concerned, a copy of the reference book or manuals that each organisation is obliged to have available for inspection by the public under ss.15 and 16 of the 1997 Act.[5] The first manual includes such information as the structure of the body, its functions, powers and duties, the services it provides to the public, the classes of records held, the details of the staff responsible for the provision of information, and the rights of review and appeal against the decisions of the body. This manual will no doubt assist a journalist in assessing the information held by each organisation and how to access it. The second manual[6] contains the internal rules and guidelines and an index only of precedents,[7] which are used by that body in decision-making processes that it engages in with respect to any schemes delivered by that body. The manual should contain provisions that clarify the rights of citizens in the first instance and also any obligations, penalties or sanctions that apply to the citizens if they fail to comply with their obligations. If the information is of such a nature that it is exempted elsewhere under the Act, then it follows that this information need not be published in the manuals. There is an express requirement on the public body to review the second manual every three years.

Making a Request

Alternatively, if the journalist is satisfied that the body will have the information that he is seeking, a simple request can be made for the information. A request should contain a number of essential pieces of information:

---

[5] Section 15 of the FOI Act 1997.
[6] Section 16 of the FOI Act 1997.
[7] Section 16(6) requires that a copy of any precedent shall be made available upon request.

- that the request is made pursuant to the FOI Acts;
- sufficient information to identify the record;
- the preferred medium for delivery of the information; and
- the fees payable.

Fees Payable

The charging regime is set out in s.47 of the 1997 Act. There are no charges payable with respect to personal information relating to the applicant (or other approved persons under the Act), a request for an amendment to the records, or a statement of reasons delivered to a person affected by a decision of the body.[8]

An upfront fee must accompany any application other than those outlined above which is, for the most part, the case in an application by a journalist. Currently the upfront fee normally payable by a person, such as a journalist, is €15. Reduced rates apply for medical cardholders and certain other types of application. With respect to an application that will involve the search and retrieval or copying of records there is a fee payable of €20.95 per hour and a copy charge of €0.04 cent per page copied. There is a charge for copying the information onto a computer disc of €10.16 in addition to the hourly charge.

Response Time

The body concerned must then respond within 10 working days with an acknowledgment of the request and decide within 20 working days whether or not to refuse or grant the request.[9] If the request is granted, the body must at this stage determine the means of access to the material sought and give written notification to the requester. This time limit may be extended by the head by up to a further period of 20 days if the request contains such a large number of records that the 20 day period cannot be met. If another public body holds the material sought, the recipient of the request will probably suggest that the application be withdrawn and resubmitted to the appropriate body concerned. Alternatively, the body must forward the request on to the appropriate public body within 10 days of initial receipt. If the records

---

[8] Section 18 of the FOI Act 1997.
[9] Sections 7(2) and 8(1) of the FOI Act 1997 respectively.

are partly held in a number of public bodies, then the first body must notify the requester of this fact and deliver the documents within its own organisation in accordance with the time limits above.

If no copying or search fees are payable, then access to the record must be made available immediately. Otherwise, the records are made available within five days of the provision of the fees. Access is usually given in the form requested (usually copying or computer disc). Sometimes, it involves an opportunity to inspect the actual record. Access to actual records can be restricted for various reasons, principally though, such a request is refused if the granting of the record in an alternative form would be significantly more efficient.

Deferral of Access

Access to records may be deferred for particular reasons[10]:

- If the record was prepared exclusively for the information of either or both of the Houses of the Oireachtas, or a committee of either of those Houses and will within a reasonable time be provided for that purpose.
- If it is in the public interest for the relevant Minister to make the contents of the record known first to the Houses of the Oireachtas or in some other public way. If so, the Minister must do so within 25 working days of receiving the request.
- If disclosure of certain material would not be in the public interest on or before a certain day. The relevant material with respect to which disclosure is deferred under this heading is factual information and analyses thereof; reports into an investigation of public bodies or a particular function of such bodies; and expert studies of a scientific or technical nature which are not created for the purposes of a decision of a public body.

Contents of a Decision

The following details should be included in the notification of a decision on an FOI request:

- The decision.
- The date of the decision.

---

[10]   Section 11 of the FOI Act 1997.

- The name and designation of the officer dealing with the request. This may be omitted if the disclosure of his details might prejudice his safety.

- A list of records covered by the request.

- If the application is granted, then the arrangements for access and the period during which the record will remain available together with the amount of any fees for search, retrieval and copying.

- If access to the record is deferred, then the reasons for the deferral and the period of its deferral must be stated.

- Particulars of rights of review and appeal, including procedures, fees and time limits involved.

- If refused, the reasons for the refusal must be stated.

Refusals

The public body may refuse the request for a number of stated reasons set out in the legislation. If a refusal occurs, then it must be accompanied by the reasons for the refusal and particulars of any matter relating to the public interest that were taken into consideration.[11] A simple reference to the section of the Act under which the refusal is permitted is not sufficient. The content of the refusal must be detailed enough to allow the requester to make an informed decision on whether or not to appeal.

A refusal is permissible for any of the following reasons:

- That the record is exempted under Pt III of the 1997 Act.

- That the record is excluded under s.46 of the 1997 Act.

- That the request ought to be refused for administrative reasons[12] such as an incomplete request, likely publication of the information within 60 days, frivolous or vexatious requests, non-payment of fees, and voluminous requests that would constitute an unreasonable interference with the work of the body concerned.[13]

Exemptions

The statutory scheme in place provides for the protection of some information relating to key areas of activity and information that is

---

[11]   Section 8(2)(d).
[12]   Section 10 of the FOI Act 1997, as amended by the 2003 Act.
[13]   Section 10 of the FOI Act 1997, as amended by the 2003 Act.

confidential. The measures considered by the legislature necessary to protect this information are contained in Pt III of the 1997 Act as amended. The measures are designed to protect key areas of government activity, court matters, parliamentary matters and third party information of a confidential nature. The legislation permits exemption from disclosure for different reasons. The various protection measures are examined below.

In some cases, a consultation process is required before a head releases certain types of material, such as confidential, commercially sensitive or personal information. This process involves the notification of the body or person to whom the information relates. Normally the process will be initiated within 10 working days of the request (extendable by 10 working days). The person to whom the information relates is then given a period of 15 working days to make submissions. Thereafter, the head must make a final decision within 10 working days of the receipt of the submission or the expiry of the period for submissions, whichever comes sooner.[14]

Deliberations of Government

Most records that relate to cabinet meetings, discussions between Government Ministers, Ministers of State, the Attorney General or a committee of officials certified by a secretary general as having been established in direct support of government deliberations will fall within a class of documents that is expressly excluded.[15] A head of department has no discretion to release those documents. This is not so if more than 10 years have elapsed since the government decision was taken or where the record contains merely factual information where the decision to which it relates has been published.

Deliberations of Public Bodies

If the record relates to the deliberative processes of a public body, a head may refuse to release the record unless the public interest is better served by its release.[16] As with the government exemption, documents that are of a factual or technical nature are not protected by this section. It offers no shelter either for reports that relate to the

---

14   Section 29 of the FOI Act 1997.
15   Section 19(1) of the FOI Act 1997.
16   Section 20 of the FOI Act 1997.

performance or effectiveness of public bodies. If a secretary general has certified that the record relates to a deliberative process in a Department of State, it must also be refused. Those certificates must be revoked once the decision has been taken and replaced with a new certificate to that effect.[17]

Operation of Public Bodies

If the disclosure could harm certain operations of the public body, such as its investigative functions, its effectiveness or the negotiating positions of those bodies, then those records may be protected unless, in the opinion of the head, the public interest is better served by disclosure.[18]

Legal and Legislative Protections

Documents which contain legal advice have always been regarded by the courts as privileged in favour of the person or body that sought the advice. This protection is maintained under the FOI Acts and the test is whether the record would be exempt from production in court or its disclosure would be regarded as a contempt of court.[19]

The private papers of elected representatives of the European Parliament,[20] local authorities or the HSE are also exempt, as are records relating to the appointment or business of tribunals and inquiries.[21]

Public Safety and Law Enforcement

Any information which could reasonably be expected to endanger life or the safety of any person may be protected. A similar discretion exists if the disclosure could prejudice or impair law enforcement or public safety. Documents that relate to policy are excluded from the operation of this exclusion if the head considers that the public interest would, on balance, be better served by their release.[22]

---

[17] Section 20(1A) of the FOI Act 1997.
[18] Section 21 of the FOI Act 1997.
[19] Section 22 of the FOI Act 1997.
[20] The private papers of Oireachtas members are excluded under s.46 of the FOI Act 1997.
[21] Section 22 of the FOI Act 1997.
[22] Section 23 of the FOI Act 1997.

Foreign Affairs, Northern Ireland and Defence

A head may refuse documents that, if disclosed, could adversely affect international relations, defence, security, and matters concerning Northern Ireland or the operation of the Independent Commission for the Location of Victims' Remains.[23] If the information relates to confidential diplomatic communications, a record of an EU or international body containing information, the release of which is prohibited by that body, intelligence or subversive activity or the tactics or operations of the defence forces, then the head has no discretion and must refuse to disclose the information.[24] A Minister may also sign a certificate that documents falling within either of the classifications just mentioned are exempt if the Minister is satisfied that the information sought is of exceptional sensitivity or seriousness. Review of these certificates is undertaken by other members of the Government rather than by the Information Commissioner.

Information Obtained in Confidence

If the information that was obtained in confidence is both important and such that releasing it would jeopardise the future delivery of similar information, the head shall protect the information unless it is on balance not in the public interest to do so. Even then, there is a consultation process that he must undertake prior to making a decision to release. If the disclosure would constitute a breach of a duty of confidence whether arising under an agreement, by statute or at common law, there is no discretion to release the material.[25]

Personal Information

In most cases access to private information is denied unless the public interest outweighs the right to privacy of the individual concerned or if the release of the information would benefit the individual. If a head is considering the release of the material then he must engage in a consultation process.[26]

---

[23]   Section 24 of the FOI Act 1997, as amended.
[24]   Section 24(2) of the FOI Act 1997, as amended.
[25]   Section 26 of the FOI Act 1997.
[26]   Section 28 of the FOI Act 1997.

Research and Natural Resources

If bodies are engaged in research and the premature disclosure of information is likely to expose that body or person to serious disadvantage then the information may be withheld. Similarly, information which could be reasonably expected to prejudice the well-being of a cultural heritage or natural resource or the habitat or species of flora or fauna may be withheld. Disclosure may be made in either case where the public interest would on balance be better served by granting the request rather than refusing it.[27]

Economic Interests of the State and Other Public Bodies

If the information sought could reasonably be expected to have serious adverse effects for the financial interests of the State or the ability of the Government to manage the economy, or disclosure could unduly disturb the ordinary business of the community or result in undue benefit or loss to any person, then the information may be protected. The head is permitted to release the information if on balance the public interest would be better served by granting the request.[28]

Other Statutory Protections

The head does not have discretion to release information which is expressly prohibited to be disclosed by other legislative measures.[29] Furthermore, the Act requires a review from time to time of any provisions that expressly prohibit disclosure.

Some of the types of information that may be withheld include:

- Memoranda for government.
- Records of government decisions other than those published to the general public.
- Documents containing advice for members of the Government, Ministers of State, the Attorney General, and the Secretary to the Government relating to matters of government.

---

[27] Section 30 of the FOI Act 1997.
[28] Section 30 of the FOI Act 1997.
[29] Section 32 of the FOI Act 1997.

- Minutes of government meetings that refer to statements made at those meetings.

- Information that records the deliberations of public bodies and the disclosure of which would be contrary to the public interest.

- Information that would prejudice the effectiveness of tests, exams, investigations or audits.

- Information that would attract legal professional privilege or in respect of which the disclosure would be a contempt of court.

- Opinions, advice and recommendations considered by either House of the Oireachtas or by a member of either House for the purposes of the proceedings of those Houses.

- Information that would impair the detection or investigation of offences or law enforcement, the fairness of criminal proceedings, the security of prisons and certain places of detention.

- Information concerning the security of buildings, ships or aircraft.

- Information concerning Garda or Defence force's communications systems.

- Information that would reveal the identity of certain informants.

- Information that would facilitate the commission of an offence.

- Information that could adversely affect defence security, international relations, matters relating to Northern Ireland or matters relating to the functions of the Independent Commission for the Location of Victims' Remains.

- Information that a Minister certifies as of exceptional sensitivity and seriousness.

- Commercially sensitive information.

- Information that may damage research or natural resources.

- Information that if disclosed might have serious adverse effects for the financial interests of the State.

- Secrecy provisions in other legislation.

Restrictions of FOI

Unlike some of the exemptions under the FOI legislation referred to above, the Act also excludes certain records from the application of the Act in any respect. These restrictions are permitted by s.46 of the 1997 Act and are not subject to any of the public interest related tests outlined above. Any decision to refuse to disclose information grounded on this section is still subject to review internally and by the Information Commissioner. Some of the types of records that are excluded under s.46 include:

- Court and tribunal records.
- Records of the Attorney General.
- Records of the Information Commissioner arising from a review or investigation.
- Records relating to audits by the Comptroller and Auditor General.
- Records relating to investigations by the Ombudsman.
- Records relating to the President.
- Records given to a Minister or Minister of State for use by him in the Oireachtas.
- Private papers of a TD or Senator that are submitted in accordance with the standing orders of either House of the Oireachtas.
- Information provided in confidence to a public body that relates to the enforcement of criminal law.
- Records already publicly available.

Review Procedures

There is an initial review of a refusal of appeal to a higher authority within the organisation and a subsequent right of appeal to the Information Commissioner. The internal review must always be taken before an appeal is taken to the Information Commissioner. This review, when requested, must be completed within three weeks.[30] The application fee for an internal review is €75 and €150 for review by the Information Commissioner. The following decisions are matters that the requester can apply to review:

- Refusal of all or part of a request.
- Deferral of access to records prepared solely for the Oireachtas.
- A decision to grant access in a form other than that requested.
- The deletion of certain exempt material from a record.

---

[30] Section 14(4) of the FOI Act 1997.

- Refusal to correct personal information that the requester believes is incomplete, incorrect or misleading.
- A decision relating to the rights of a person to obtain reasons for decisions on acts of the public body affecting that person.
- A decision relating to the charging of a fee or deposit.

Some matters automatically bypass the review procedure and are dealt with directly by the Information Commissioner, for example:

- If the Act requires consultation with third parties.
- Any initial decision which was taken by a head of a public body.
- Deferrals of access on the grounds of imminent public release of the information.
- Deferral of access on the grounds that it is not in the public interest for the requester to become aware of a significant decision which the body proposes to make.
- Extension of time for deciding on a request.

If a head is considering a refusal to disclose information because the disclosure of information could affect trade secrets of third parties, the consent of the Information Commissioner is required before refusal in the first instance.[31]

The Information Commissioner

The Office of the Information Commissioner[32] is an independent appointment by the President on the advice of the Government following a resolution by both the Dáil and the Seanad recommending the appointment.[33] The primary function of this office is the independent review of the refusals of disclosure by public bodies.

His or her powers include the power to affirm, vary or annul the decision and make further decisions relating to the request as are appropriate.[34] The starting point of the review by the Information Commissioner is an assumption that the decision to refuse was

---

[31]   Sections 27 and 29 of the FOI Act 1997.
[32]   The Information Commissioner's office is located at 18 Lower Leeson Street, Dublin 2.
[33]   Section 33 of the FOI Act 1997.
[34]   Section 34 of the FOI Act 1997.

unjustified. This places the onus on the body making the refusal to fully explain the decision to refuse by reference to specific provisions in the Acts.

In most cases, the application to the Information Commissioner for an appeal or review against a refusal ought to be made within two weeks of the decision to refuse.[35] The decision itself then binds both parties subject only to an appeal to the High Court on a point of law.[36]

In exercising this function, the Information Commissioner can also request the body concerned to furnish further documentation, require the attendance of witnesses or even enter any premises occupied by a public body for the purposes of the investigation. The Information Commissioner can review the following decisions:

- Most decisions made after internal review.
- Initial decisions on requests made personally by a head of a public body.
- Decisions on charges.
- Decisions to extend the time for consideration of requests.
- Decisions to defer the provision of access to a record or a matter of such public interest that the Minister first wishes to inform the Houses of the Oireachtas.
- Decisions to which the consultation procedures with third parties apply.
- Decisions to refuse a request for a record on the grounds that restrictions under s.46 apply (see above).

The following matters are not reviewable by the Information Commissioner:

- A delegated decision taken before an internal review is conducted.
- A refusal based on a secretary general's certificate.
- A refusal based on a ministerial certificate. The Taoiseach and other Ministers undertake this review.
- FOI decisions that concern the Office of the Information Commissioner and if the incumbent Commissioner is the

---

[35] Section 34(4) of the FOI Act 1997.
[36] Section 42 of the FOI Act 1997.

Ombudsman, the Office of the Ombudsman. Appeals from decisions in this regard are direct to the High Court.[37]

Appeal to the High Court

The appeal to the High Court of a decision of the Information Commissioner is restricted to appeals on a point of law[38]. The appeal must be filed within eight weeks after notice of the decision was given.[39] The distinction between what is a point of law and a point of fact is to a layperson sometimes difficult to understand. In the main, points of law involve the legal interpretation of the provisions of the Act and their application to the facts of the case. A simple determination of fact by the Information Commissioner is not a matter that is open to appeal to the High Court. An example of the application of the distinction between the two types of determination, fact and law, in the context of freedom of information can be seen in *Sheedy v Information Commissioner*.[40] The *Irish Times* applied to the Department of Education for disclosure of the school reports of a number of schools. The Department refused to disclose the reports on three grounds. First, on the ground that s.53 of the Education Act 1998 prohibited the disclosure of material that would lead to the compilation of information that could lead to the comparative performance of schools. Second, that the disclosure could lead to deterioration in the school reporting procedure as it would have a chilling effect on the interaction between teachers and school inspectors. Third, that the reports contained information that was imparted in circumstances imposing an obligation of confidence.

The Information Commissioner overturned the decision of the Department on all grounds. The school principal of one of the schools appealed to the High Court. In the High Court, Gilligan J. found in favour of the Information Commissioner. The school principal appealed the matter to the Supreme Court. The Supreme Court found for the school principal on the first ground but upheld the decision of the Information Commissioner on the other grounds. Kearns J. in discussing the second ground stated:

---

[37]   Section 42 of the FOI Act 1997.
[38]   Section 43 of the FOI Act 1997.
[39]   Section 42 of the FOI Act 1997.
[40]   [2005] 2 I.R. 272.

"In my view the onus of evidence of prejudice fell on the Department and, in the absence of same the Commissioner was entitled, under section 34 of the Act of 1997, to hold against the Department. A mere assertion of an expectation of non co-operation from teaching staff could never constitute sufficient evidence in this regard, particularly in the circumstances shown to apply, namely, that as a consequence of both circular 12/83 and section 13 of the 1998 Act, there was no choice left to schools or their staff as to whether or not to co-operate with the Department's inspectors in terms of furnishing the information sought. Nor do I believe that any exhaustive analysis conducted by reference to detailed evidence was necessary before the Commissioner could decide to apply the public interest provision of section 21(2) to direct release of the reports. *Once there was some evidence before him as to the circumstances in which these reports are compiled, as undoubtedly was the case here, the well established principles of O'Keefe v An Bord Pleanála make it clear that his decision is not to be interfered with.*[41] This assessment, which involved a balancing exercise between the various competing interests, was one uniquely within his particular remit."[42]

The passage above demonstrates that the court will not interfere with a decision if there is *some* evidence (or fact) upon which the decision could be arrived at provided the decision is based on a correct application of the law to those facts.

A further appeal from the High Court also lies to the Supreme Court.[43]

---

[41] Emphasis added.

[42] [2005] 2 I.R. 272 at 299.

[43] Section 42(8) of the FOI Act 1997 that purported to restrict an appeal was removed in the 2003 Act.

APPENDICES

INDEX TO BOOK OF PLEADINGS

THE HIGH COURT

BETWEEN:

X

Plaintiff

-and-

Y NEWSPAPERS LTD

Defendant

SAMPLE BOOK OF PLEADINGS

Index

Plenary Summons
Memorandum of Appearance
Statement of Claim
Affidavit of Verification
Defendant's Notice for Particulars
Plaintiff's Replies to Particulars
Defence
Affidavit of Verification
Reply to Defence
Plaintiff's Notice for Particulars
Defendant's Replies to Particulars
Defendant's Notice for Further Particulars
Plaintiff's Replies to Further Particulars
Amended Defence
Notice for Particulars of Amended Defence
Notice to Admit Facts

THE HIGH COURT

Record No. 4321P/2011

Between:

JOHN SMITH

Plaintiff

and

MICHAEL MILITANT
AND
DAILY SCREAM LIMITED

Defendants

GENERAL ENDORSEMENT OF CLAIM

The Plaintiff's claim is for:

(a)   Damages for defamation.

(b)   An injunction restraining the defendants and each of them, their servants or agents, and any person having notice of the making of an Order of this Honourable Court from publishing of and concerning the plaintiff the words set out in the Schedule to the Statement of Claim in this action or any words to the same effect.

(c)   *An Order pursuant to s.33 of the Defamation Act 2009 prohibiting the publication or further publication by the defendants and each of them, their servants or agents, and any person having notice of the making of an Order of this Honourable Court, from publishing of and concerning the plaintiff the words set out in the Schedule to the Statement of Claim in this action or any words to the same effect.*[1]

(d)   Further or other relief.

(e)   Costs.

E. Morse S.C.
E. Holmes B.L.

---

[1] Italicised portion represents a suggested pleading for a defamation occurring after January 1, 2010.

THE HIGH COURT

BETWEEN

JOHN SMITH

Plaintiff

and

MICHAEL MILITANT
AND
DAILY SCREAM LTD

Defendants

STATEMENT OF CLAIM

Delivered this 1st day of April 1997 by Patrick Murphy solicitor for the plaintiff.

1. The plaintiff is a schoolteacher and resides at 25, Happy Valley, Dublin 31

[indication of status of each defendant and at their addresses].

2. The first named defendant is a freelance journalist and resides 34 Grubb St., Dublin. The second named defendant is a Limited Liability Company incorporated in the United Kingdom of Great Britain and Northern Ireland and carries on business at 17 Yellow Press Road, London WC 1.

[allegation of publication in Ireland]

3. The second named defendant is a newspaper publisher and publishes amongst other titles the Daily Scream, which is a tabloid newspaper of wide circulation. The said newspaper is printed in the United Kingdom and distributed, inter alia, within the jurisdiction of this Honourable Court.

[allegation of reference to the plaintiff and of falsity and malice]

4. On or about the 20th day of March 1997, the first named defendant wrote, for the publication by the second named defendant, the words set out in the First Schedule hereto. The second named defendant published the said words and distributed them, inter alia, within the jurisdiction of this Honourable Court.

5. The said words were so written and published by the defendants falsely and maliciously of and concerning the plaintiff.

[allegation of defamatory nature of the words and indication that innuendo is relied on]

6. The said words in their ordinary and natural meaning, further or in the alternative by innuendo, are grossly defamatory of the plaintiff and have damaged him in his character and reputation and exposed him to odium, ridicule and contempt.

7. The said words in their ordinary and natural meaning, further or in the alternative by innuendo, meant and were understood to mean:

[meanings alleged, by innuendo or otherwise]

(a) that the plaintiff is a drug dealer, that is one who deals in prohibited drugs for a reward;

(b) further or in the alternative that the plaintiff is with reasonable cause suspected of being a drug dealer;

(c) that the plaintiff has committed and continues to commit serious criminal offences;

(d) that the plaintiff is unfit to be retained in his employment as a schoolteacher and is unfit to hold his elected office as a County Councillor;

(e) that the plaintiff has betrayed the trust reposed in him in both of the aforesaid capacities;

(f) that the plaintiff is a hypocrite;

(g) that the plaintiff is unfit for the company of law-abiding people.

8. PARTICULARS OF FACTS, EXTRINSIC TO THE WORDS COMPLAINED OF, RELIED UPON TO GROUND THE INNUENDO MEANINGS

[particulars of express malice]

The plaintiff is a registered teacher at St. Elsewhere's school. He has pastoral responsibility for a class of pupils there. In that capacity he has been an active vocal campaigner against drug use and in particular the supply of drugs to young people.

9. The words complained of were published with express malice towards the plaintiff on the part of the defendants and each of them.

10. PARTICULARS OF MALICE

The defendants published the words in question knowing them to have been false or alternatively reckless as to whether they were true or false. They made no attempt to contact the plaintiff prior to publishing them or to afford him any opportunity to rebut or comment on them. In so doing they were motivated by a desire to increase the circulation of the Daily Scream by publishing a sensational story and by a desire to destroy the plaintiff's political career.

AND the plaintiff claims:

(a) Damages for defamation.

(b) An injunction restraining the defendants and each of them, their servants or agents, and any person having notice of the making of an Order of this Honourable Court from publishing of and concerning the plaintiff the words set out in the Schedule to the Statement of Claim in this action or any words to the same effect.

(c) *An Order pursuant to s.33 of the Defamation Act 2009 prohibiting the publication or further publication by the defendants and each of them, their servants or agents, and any person having notice of the making of an Order of this Honourable Court, from publishing of and concerning the plaintiff the words set out in the Schedule to the Statement of Claim in this action or any words to the same effect.*[1]

(d)   Further or other relief.

(e)   Costs.

E. Morse S.C.
S. Holmes B.L.

SCHEDULE

NET CLOSES ON DRUGS' MR BIG

The Daily Scream has learnt that an arrest is imminent in the hunt for Dublin's drug czar. While no name is mentioned officially, well-placed sources are increasingly interested in John Smith, the outspoken anti-drugs campaigner who, they suggest, has been leading a double life. An official spokesman refused to confirm or deny that Smith (53) is the prime target.

(The said words were accompanied by a photograph of the plaintiff with a caption "Smith, double life?")

---

[1] Italicised portion represents a suggested pleading for a defamation occurring after January 1, 2010.

THE HIGH COURT

Record No. 4321P/2011

Between

JOHN SMITH

Plaintiff

and

MICHAEL MILITANT
AND
DAILY SCREAM LIMITED

Defendants

AFFIDAVIT OF VERIFICATION

I, John Smith, 25 Happy Valley Dublin 31, Schoolteacher, the plaintiff in the above entitled proceedings aged 18 years and upwards **MAKE OATH AND SAY** as follows:

1. I beg to refer to the contents of the Statement of Claim, delivered herein on behalf of the Plaintiff on the 20th day of December 2010 and upon a true copy of which marked "A", I have signed my name to the swearing hereof.

2. The assertions, allegations and information contained in the said Statement of Claim which are within my own knowledge are true.

3. I honestly believe that the assertions, allegations and information contained in the said Statement of Claim which are not within my knowledge are true.

4. I am aware that it is an offence to make a statement in this Affidavit that is false or misleading in any material respect and that I know to be false or misleading.

SWORN the 21st day of December 2010.

By the said **John Smith** who is personally known to me, at Sunshine Street, in the City of Dublin, before me a commissioner for Oaths/Practising Solicitor, and I know the deponent.

Commissioner for Oaths/Practising Solicitor.

Filed on behalf of the Plaintiff by Patrick Murphy, Solicitor for the Plaintiff.

THE HIGH COURT

Record No. 4321P/2011

Between:

JOHN SMITH

Plaintiff

and

MICHAEL MILITANT
AND
DAILY SCREAM LIMITED

Defendants

DEFENCE

Delivered this 2nd day of January 2011 by Black and Grey Solicitors for the Defendants

1. Paragraphs 1 and 2 of the Statement of Claim herein are admitted.

2. The words complained of in their ordinary and natural meaning or by innuendo, do not bear the meanings set out in the Statement of Claim and are not defamatory,

3. The said words in their true meaning, and without the special meanings pleaded, are true in substance and in fact.

4. *The said words in their true meaning, and without the special meanings pleaded, are true in all material respects.*

5. Insofar as the said words consist of statements of fact, they are true and accurate; insofar as they consist of comment they are fair comment made without malice on a matter of public interest, to wit the progress of official enquiries into serious crime.

6. *Insofar as the said words consist of statements of fact, they are true and accurate; insofar as they consist of opinions, those opinions were honestly held by the Defendants on matters of public interest, to wit the progress of official enquiries into serious crime.* *

7. *The words complained of were published in good faith and in the course of the discussion of a subject of public interest, which was for the public benefit, to wit the progress of official enquiries into serious crime and, in respect of which it was fair and reasonable to publish the words complained of.* *

8. The Plaintiff has not been damaged in his character or reputation or exposed to odium ridicule or contempt as alleged or at all.

9. The Plaintiff is not entitled to the relief claimed or to any relief.

H Poirot S.C.
J Marples B.L.

---

* Suggested defences under the Defamation Act 2009.

Number 40 of 1961.

DEFAMATION ACT, 1961

ARRANGEMENT OF SECTIONS

PART I
Preliminary and General

PART II
Criminal Proceedings for Libel

PART III
Civil Proceedings for Defamation

FIRST SCHEDULE.
ENACTMENTS REPEALED

SECOND SCHEDULE.
STATEMENTS HAVING QUALIFIED PRIVILEGE

ACTS REFERRED TO

Local Government Act, 1941	1941, No. 23
Wireless Telegraphy Act, 1926	1926, No. 45
Broadcasting Authority Act, 1960	1960, No. 10
Telegraph Act, 1863	1863, c. 112
Libel Amendment Act, 1888	1888, c. 64

Number 40 *of* 1961.

DEFAMATION ACT, 1961

AN ACT TO CONSOLIDATE WITH AMENDMENTS CERTAIN
ENACTMENTS RELATING TO THE LAW OF DEFAMATION.
[17*th August*, 1961.]
BE IT ENACTED BY THE OIREACHTAS AS FOLLOWS :—

PART I

PRELIMINARY AND GENERAL

1.—This Act may be cited as the Defamation Act, 1961.

Short title.

2.—In this Act—

Interpretation generally.

"*local authority*" has the same meaning as in the *Local Government Act, 1941*;

"*newspaper*" except in section 27, means any paper containing public news or observations thereon, or consisting wholly or mainly of advertisements, which is printed for sale and is published in the State or in Northern Ireland either periodically or in parts or numbers at intervals not exceeding thirty-six days;

"*proprietor*" means, as well as the sole proprietor of any newspaper, in the case of a divided proprietorship, the persons who, as partners or otherwise, represent or are responsible for any share or interest in the newspaper as between themselves and the persons in like manner representing or responsible for the other shares or interests therein, and no other person.

3.—(1) This Act shall come into operation on the 1st day of January, 1962.

Commencement and proceedings affected.

(2) *Part III* of this Act shall apply for the purposes of any proceedings begun after the commencement of this Act, whenever the cause of action arose, but shall not affect any proceedings commenced before the commencement of this Act.

4.—The enactments specified in the *First Schedule* to this Act are hereby repealed.

Repeals.

PART II

Criminal Proceedings for Libel

Competence
of jury to give
general verdict
on trial of
indictment
for libel.

5.—(1) On every trial of an indictment for making or publishing any libel to which a plea of not guilty is entered, the jury may give a general verdict of guilty or not guilty upon the whole matter put in issue on the indictment, and the jury shall not be required or directed by the court to find the person charged guilty merely on the proof of the publication by him of the paper charged to be a libel and of the sense ascribed to such paper in the indictment.

(2) On every such trial the court shall, according to its discretion, give its opinion and directions to the jury on the matter in issue in like manner as in other criminal cases.

(3) Subsections (1) and (2) of this section shall not operate to prevent the jury from finding a special verdict, in their discretion, as in other criminal cases.

Plea of truth of
matters charged
on trial for
defamatory libel
and that
publication was
for public
benefit.

6.—On the trial of any indictment for a defamatory libel, the person charged having pleaded such plea as hereinafter mentioned, the truth of the matters charged may be inquired into but shall not amount to a defence, unless it was for the public benefit that the said matters charged should be published; and, to entitle the defendant to give evidence of the truth of such matters charged as a defence to such indictment, it shall be necessary for the person charged, in pleading to the said indictment, to allege the truth of the said matters charged, in the manner required in pleading a justification to an action for defamation, and further to allege that it was for the public benefit that the said matters charged should be published, and the particular fact or facts by reason of which it was for the public benefit that the said matters charged should be published, to which plea the prosecutor shall be at liberty to reply generally, denying the whole thereof; and if, after such plea, the person charged is convicted on such indictment, the court may, in pronouncing sentence, consider whether his guilt is aggravated or mitigated by the said plea and by the evidence given to prove or to disprove the same: provided that—

> (*a*) the truth of the matters charged in the alleged libel complained of by such indictment shall in no case be inquired into without such plea of justification;
>
> (*b*) in addition to such plea of justification, the person charged may enter a plea of not guilty;
>
> (*c*) nothing in this section shall take away or prejudice any defence under the plea of not guilty which it is competent to the person charged to make under such plea to any indictment for defamatory libel.

Evidence by
person charged
to rebut *prima
facie* case of
publication by
his agent.

7.—Whenever, upon the trial of an indictment for the publication of a libel, a plea of not guilty having been entered, evidence is given establishing a presumption of publication against the person charged by the act of any other person by his authority, it shall be competent for the person charged to prove that the publication was made without his authority, consent or knowledge and that the publication did not arise from want of due care or caution on his part.

8.—No criminal prosecution shall be commenced against any proprietor, publisher, editor or any person responsible for the publication of a newspaper for any libel published therein without the order of a Judge of the High Court sitting *in camera* being first had and obtained, and every application for such order shall be made on notice to the person accused, who shall have an opportunity of being heard against the application.

Order of Judge required for prosecution of newspaper proprietor, etc.

9.—A Justice of the District Court, upon the hearing of a charge against a proprietor, publisher or editor or any person responsible for the publication of a newspaper for a libel published therein, may receive evidence as to the publication being for the public benefit, as to the matters charged in the libel being true, as to the report being fair and accurate and published without malice and as to any matter which, under this or any other Act or otherwise, might be given in evidence by way of defence by the person charged on his trial on indictment, and the Justice, if of opinion after hearing such evidence that there is a strong or probable presumption that the jury on the trial would acquit the person charged, may dismiss the case.

Inquiry as to libel being for public benefit or being true.

10.—If a Justice of the District Court, upon the hearing of a charge against a proprietor, publisher, editor or any person responsible for the publication of a newspaper for a libel published therein, is of opinion that, though the person charged is shown to have been guilty, the libel was of a trivial character and that the offence may be adequately punished by virtue of the powers conferred by this section, the Justice shall cause the charge to be reduced into writing and read to the person charged and shall then ask him if he desires to be tried by a jury or consents to the case being dealt with summarily, and, if such person consents to the case being dealt with summarily, may summarily convict him, and impose on him a fine not exceeding fifty pounds, and the Summary Jurisdiction Acts shall apply accordingly.

Provisions as to summary conviction for libel.

11.—Every person who maliciously publishes any defamatory libel shall, on conviction thereof on indictment, be liable to a fine not exceeding two hundred pounds or to imprisonment for a term not exceeding one year or to both such fine and imprisonment.

Penalty for maliciously publishing defamatory libel.

12.—Every person who maliciously publishes any defamatory libel, knowing the same to be false, shall, on conviction thereof on indictment, be liable to a fine not exceeding five hundred pounds or to imprisonment for a term not exceeding two years or to both such fine and imprisonment.

Penalty for maliciously publishing libel known to be false.

13.—(1) Every person who composes, prints or publishes any blasphemous or obscene libel shall, on conviction thereof on indictment, be liable to a fine

Penalty for printing or publishing blasphemous or obscene libel.

not exceeding five hundred pounds or to imprisonment for a term not exceeding two years or to both such fine and imprisonment or to penal servitude for a term not exceeding seven years.

    (2)(*a*) In every case in which a person is convicted of composing, printing or publishing a blasphemous libel, the court may make an order for the seizure and carrying away and detaining in safe custody, in such manner as shall be directed in the order, of all copies of the libel in the possession of such person or of any other person named in the order for his use, evidence upon oath having been previously given to the satisfaction of the court that copies of the said libel are in the possession of such other person for the use of the person convicted.

    (*b*) Upon the making of an order under paragraph (*a*) of this subsection, any member of the Garda Síochána acting under such order may enter, if necessary by the use of force, and search for any copies of the said libel any building, house or other place belonging to the person convicted or to such other person named in the order and may seize and carry away and detain in the manner directed in such order all copies of the libel found therein.

    (*c*) If, in any such case, the conviction is quashed on appeal, any copies of the libel seized under an order under paragraph (*a*) of this subsection shall be returned free of charge to the person or persons from whom they were seized.

    (*d*) Where, in any such case, an appeal is not lodged or the conviction is confirmed on appeal, any copies of the libel seized under an order under paragraph (*a*) of this subsection shall, on the application of a member of the Garda Síochána to the court which made such order, be disposed of in such manner as such court may direct.

PART III

CIVIL PROCEEDINGS FOR DEFAMATION

Interpretation.
(Part III).

14.—(1) In this Part—

"*broadcast*" has the same meaning as in the *Wireless Telegraphy Act, 1926* (in this section referred to as the Act of 1926) and "*broadcasting*" shall be construed accordingly;

"*broadcasting station*" has the same meaning as in the Act of 1926, as amended by the *Broadcasting Authority Act, 1960*;

"*wireless telegraphy*" has the same meaning as in the Act of 1926.

(2) Any reference in this Part to words shall be construed as including a reference to visual images, gestures and other methods of signifying meaning.

(3) Where words broadcast by means of wireless telegraphy are simultaneously transmitted by telegraph as defined by the Telegraph Act, 1863, in accordance with a licence granted by the Minister for Posts and Telegraphs, the provisions of this Part shall apply as if the transmission were broadcasting by means of wireless telegraphy.

15.—For the purposes of the law of libel and slander the broadcasting of words by means of wireless telegraphy shall be treated as publication in permanent form.

Broadcast statements.

16.—Words spoken and published which impute unchastity or adultery to any woman or girl shall not require special damage to render them actionable.

Words imputing unchastity or adultery actionable without special damage.

17.—In any action for defamation, it shall be lawful for the defendant (after notice in writing of his intention so to do, duly given to the plaintiff at the time of filing or delivering the plea in the action) to give in evidence, in mitigation of damage, that he made or offered an apology to the plaintiff for such defamation before the commencement of the action, or as soon afterwards as he had an opportunity of doing so, in case the action shall have been commenced before there was an opportunity of making or offering such apology.

Offer of an apology admissible in evidence in mitigation of damages in action for defamation.

18.—(1) A fair and accurate report published in any newspaper or broadcast by means of wireless telegraphy as part of any programme or service provided by means of a broadcasting station within the State or in Northern Ireland of proceedings publicly heard before any court established by law and exercising judicial authority within the State or in Northern Ireland shall, if published or broadcast contemporaneously with such proceedings, be privileged.

(2) Nothing in subsection (1) of this section shall authorise the publication or broadcasting of any blasphemous or obscene matter.

Newspaper and broadcast reports of proceedings in court privileged.

19.—In an action for slander in respect of words calculated to disparage the plaintiff in any office, profession, calling, trade or business held or carried on by him at the time of the publication, it shall not be necessary to allege or prove special damage, whether or not the words are spoken of the plaintiff in the way of his office, profession, calling, trade or business.

Slander affecting official, professional or business reputation.

20.—(1) In an action for slander of title, slander of goods or other malicious falsehood, it shall not be necessary to allege or prove special damage—
   (*a*) if the words upon which the action is founded are calculated to cause pecuniary damage to the plaintiff and are published in writing or other permanent form; or
   (*b*) if the said words are calculated to cause pecuniary damage to the plaintiff in respect of any office, profession, calling, trade or business held or carried on by him at the time of the publication.

Slander of title, etc.

(2) *Section 15* of this Act shall apply for the purposes of subsection (1) of this section as it applies for the purposes of the law of libel and slander.

21.—(1) A person who has published words alleged to be defamatory of another person may, if he claims that the words were published by him innocently in relation to that other person, make an offer of amends under this section, and in any such case—

(*a*) if the offer is accepted by the party aggrieved and is duly performed, no proceedings for libel or slander shall be taken or continued by that party against the person making the offer in respect of the publication in question (but without prejudice to any cause of action against any other person jointly responsible for that publication);

(*b*) if the offer is not accepted by the party aggrieved, then, except as otherwise provided by this section, it shall be a defence, in any proceedings by him for libel or slander against the person making the offer in respect of the publication in question, to prove that the words complained of were published by the defendant innocently in relation to the plaintiff and that the offer was made as soon as practicable after the defendant received notice that they were or might be defamatory of the plaintiff, and has not been withdrawn.

(2) An offer of amends under this section must be expressed to be made for the purposes of this section, and must be accompanied by an affidavit specifying the facts relied upon by the person making it to show that the words in question were published by him innocently in relation to the party aggrieved; and for the purposes of a defence under paragraph (*b*) of subsection (1) of this section no evidence, other than evidence of facts specified in the affidavit, shall be admissible on behalf of that person to prove that the words were so published.

(3) An offer of amends under this section shall be understood to mean an offer—

(*a*) in any case, to publish or join in the publication of a suitable correction of the words complained of, and a sufficient apology to the party aggrieved in respect of those words;

(*b*) where copies of a document or record containing the said words have been distributed by or with the knowledge of the person making the offer, to take such steps as are reasonably practicable on his part for notifying persons to whom copies have been so distributed that the words are alleged to be defamatory of the party aggrieved.

(4) Where an offer of amends under this section is accepted by the party aggrieved—

(*a*) any question as to the steps to be taken in fulfilment of the offer as so accepted shall, in default of agreement between the parties, be referred to and determined by the High Court or, if proceedings in respect of the publication in question have been taken in the Circuit Court, by the Circuit Court, and the decision of such Court thereon shall be final;

(*b*) the power of the court to make orders as to costs in proceedings by the party aggrieved against the person making the offer in respect of the publication in question, or in proceedings in respect of the offer under paragraph (*a*) of this subsection, shall include power to order the payment by the person making the offer to the party aggrieved of costs on an indemnity basis and any expenses reasonably incurred or to be incurred by that party in consequence of the publication in question;

and if no such proceedings as aforesaid are taken, the High Court may, upon application made by the party aggrieved, make any such order for the payment of such costs and expenses as aforesaid as could be made in such proceedings.

(5) For the purposes of this section words shall be treated as published by one person (in this subsection referred to as the publisher) innocently in relation to another person if, and only if, the following conditions are satisfied, that is to say—

(*a*) that the publisher did not intend to publish them of and concerning that other person, and did not know of circumstances by virtue of which they might be understood to refer to him; or

(*b*) that the words were not defamatory on the face of them, and the publisher did not know of circumstances by virtue of which they might be understood to be defamatory of that other person,

and in either case that the publisher exercised all reasonable care in relation to the publication; and any reference in this subsection to the publisher shall be construed as including a reference to any servant or agent of the publisher who was concerned with the contents of the publication.

(6) Paragraph (*b*) of subsection (1) of this section shall not apply where the party aggrieved proves that he has suffered special damage.

(7) Paragraph (*b*) of subsection (1) of this section shall not apply in relation to the publication by any person of words of which he is not the author unless he proves that the words were written by the author without malice.

22.—In an action for libel or slander in respect of words containing two or more distinct charges against the plaintiff, a defence of justification shall not fail by reason only that the truth of every charge is not proved, if the words not proved to be true do not materially injure the plaintiff's reputation having regard to the truth of the remaining charges.

Justification.

23.—In an action for libel or slander in respect of words consisting partly of allegations of fact and partly of expression of opinion, a defence of fair comment shall not fail by reason only that the truth of every allegation of fact is not proved, if the expression of opinion is fair comment having regard to such of the facts alleged or referred to in the words complained of as are proved.

Fair comment.

24.—(1) Subject to the provisions of this section, the publication in a newspaper or the broadcasting by means of wireless telegraphy as part of any programme or service provided by means of a broadcasting station within

Qualified privilege of certain newspaper and broadcasting reports.

the State or in Northern Ireland of any such report or other matter as is mentioned in the *Second Schedule* to this Act shall be privileged unless the publication or broadcasting is proved to be made with malice.

(2) In an action for libel in respect of the publication or broadcasting of any such report or matter as is mentioned in Part II of the *Second Schedule* to this Act, the provisions of this section shall not be a defence if it is proved that the defendant has been requested by the plaintiff to publish in the newspaper in which the original publication was made or to broadcast from the broadcasting station from which the original broadcast was made, whichever is the case, a reasonable statement by way of explanation or contradiction, and has refused or neglected to do so, or has done so in a manner not adequate or not reasonable having regard to all the circumstances.

(3) Nothing in this section shall be construed as protecting the publication or broadcasting of any matter the publication or broadcasting of which is prohibited by law, or of any matter which is not of public concern and the publication or broadcasting of which is not for the public benefit.

(4) Nothing in this section shall be construed as limiting or abridging any privilege subsisting (otherwise than by virtue of section 4 of the Law of Libel Amendment Act, 1888) immediately before the commencement of this Act.

Agreements for indemnity.

25.—An agreement for indemnifying any person against civil liability for libel in respect of the publication of any matter shall not be unlawful unless at the time of the publication that person knows that the matter is defamatory, and does not reasonably believe there is a good defence to any action brought upon it.

Evidence of other damages recovered by plaintiff.

26.—In any action for libel or slander the defendant may give evidence in mitigation of damages that the plaintiff has recovered damages, or has brought actions for damages, for libel or slander in respect of the publication of words to the same effect as the words on which the action is founded, or has received or agreed to receive compensation in respect of any such publication.

Obligation on certain newspaper proprietors to be registered under the Registration of Business Names Act, 1916.

27.—(1) The proprietor of every newspaper having a place of business in the State shall, where such proprietor is not a company registered under the Companies Acts, 1908 to 1959, and is not required under the provisions of the Registration of Business Names Act, 1916, to be registered under that Act in respect of the business of carrying on such newspaper, be registered in the manner directed by that Act, and that Act shall apply to such proprietor in like manner as it applies to a firm or individual referred to in section 1 thereof.

(2) Every reference in the Registration of Business Names Act, 1916, to that Act shall be construed as a reference to that Act as extended by subsection (1) of this section.

(3) In this section "*newspaper*" means any paper containing public news or observations thereon, or consisting wholly or mainly of advertisements,

which is printed for sale and is published in the State either periodically or in parts
or numbers at intervals not exceeding twenty-six days.

28.—Nothing in this Part shall affect the law relating to criminal libel.   Saving.

FIRST SCHEDULE

ENACTMENTS REPEALED

Section 4.

PART I

ACTS OF THE PARLIAMENT OF IRELAND

Session and Chapter	Title
28 Hen. 8, c. 7 (Ir.).	An Act of Slaunder.
2 Geo. 1, c. 20 (Ir.).	An Act to limit the time for Criminal Prosecutions for words spoken.
33 Geo. 3, c. 43 (Ir.).	An Act to remove doubts respecting the functions of juries in cases of libel.

PART II

ACTS OF THE PARLIAMENT OF THE LATE UNITED KINGDOM OF GREAT BRITAIN AND IRELAND

Session and Chapter	Title
60 Geo. 3 & 1 Geo. 4, c. 8.	Criminal Libel Act, 1819.
3 & 4 Vic., c. 9.	Parliamentary Papers Act, 1840.
6 & 7 Vic., c. 96.	Libel Act, 1843.
8 & 9 Vic., c. 75.	Libel Act, 1845.
32 & 33 Vic., c. 24.	Newspapers Printers and Reading Rooms Repeal Act, 1869.
44 & 45 Vic., c. 60.	Newspaper Libel and Registration Act, 1881.
51 & 52 Vic., c. 64.	Law of Libel Amendment Act, 1888.
54 & 55 Vic., c. 51.	Slander of Women Act, 1891.

SECOND SCHEDULE
STATEMENTS HAVING QUALIFIED PRIVILEGE

Section 24.

PART I

STATEMENTS PRIVILEGED WITHOUT EXPLANATION OR CONTRADICTION

1. A fair and accurate report of any proceedings in public of a house of any legislature (including subordinate or federal legislatures) of any foreign sovereign State or any body which is part of such legislature or any body duly appointed by or under the legislature or executive of such State to hold a public inquiry on a matter of public importance.
2. A fair and accurate report of any proceedings in public of an international organization of which the State or the Government is a member or of any international conference to which the Government sends a representative.
3. A fair and accurate report of any proceedings in public of the International Court of Justice and any other judicial or arbitral tribunal deciding matters in dispute between States.
4. A fair and accurate report of any proceedings before a court (including a court martial) exercising jurisdiction under the law of any legislature (including subordinate or federal legislatures) of any foreign sovereign State.
5. A fair and accurate copy of or extract from any register kept in pursuance of any law which is open to inspection by the public or of any other document which is required by law to be open to inspection by the public.
6. Any notice or advertisement published by or on the authority of any court in the State or in Northern Ireland or any Judge or officer of such a court.

PART II

STATEMENTS PRIVILEGED SUBJECT TO EXPLANATION OR CONTRADICTION

1. A fair and accurate report of the findings or decision of any of the following associations, whether formed in the State or Northern Ireland, or of any committee or governing body thereof, that is to say:
    (*a*) an association for the purpose of promoting or encouraging the exercise of or interest in any art, science, religion or learning, and empowered by its constitution to exercise control over or adjudicate upon matters of interest or concern to the association or the actions or conduct of any persons subject to such control or adjudication;
    (*b*) an association for the purpose of promoting or safeguarding the interests of any trade, business, industry or profession or of the persons carrying on or engaged in any trade, business, industry or profession and empowered by its constitution to exercise control over or adjudicate

upon matters connected with the trade, business, industry or profession or the actions or conduct of those persons;

(*c*) an association for the purpose of promoting or safeguarding the interests of any game, sport or pastime, to the playing or exercise of which members of the public are invited or admitted, and empowered by its constitution to exercise control over or adjudicate upon persons connected with or taking part in the game, sport or pastime;

being a finding or decision relating to a person who is a member of or is subject by virtue of any contract to the control of the association.

2. A fair and accurate report of the proceedings at any public meeting held in the State or Northern Ireland, being a meeting *bona fide* and lawfully held for a lawful purpose and for the furtherance or discussion of any matter of public concern whether the admission to the meeting is general or restricted.

3. A fair and accurate report of the proceedings at any meeting or sitting of—

(*a*) any local authority, or committee of a local authority or local authorities, and any corresponding authority, or committee thereof, in Northern Ireland;

(*b*) any Judge or Justice acting otherwise than as a court exercising judicial authority and any corresponding person so acting in Northern Ireland;

(*c*) any commission, tribunal, committee or person appointed, whether in the State or Northern Ireland, for the purposes of any inquiry under statutory authority;

(*d*) any person appointed by a local authority to hold a local inquiry in pursuance of an Act of the Oireachtas and any person appointed by a corresponding authority in Northern Ireland to hold a local inquiry in pursuance of statutory authority;

(*e*) any other tribunal, board, committee or body constituted by or under, and exercising functions under, statutory authority, whether in the State or Northern Ireland;

not being a meeting or sitting admission to which is not allowed to representatives of the press and other members of the public.

4. A fair and accurate report of the proceedings at a general meeting, whether in the State or Northern Ireland, of any company or association constituted, registered or certified by or under statutory authority or incorporated by charter, not being, in the case of a company in the State, a private company within the meaning of the Companies Acts, 1908 to 1959, or, in the case of a company in Northern Ireland, a private company within the meaning of the statutes relating to companies for the time being in force therein.

5. A copy or fair and accurate report or summary of any notice or other matter issued for the information of the public by or on behalf of any Government department, local authority or the Commissioner of the Garda Síochána or by or on behalf of a corresponding department, authority or officer in Northern Ireland.

DEFAMATION ACT 2009

ARRANGEMENT OF SECTIONS

PART 1
PRELIMINARY AND GENERAL

PART 2
DEFAMATION

PART 3
DEFENCES

PART 4
REMEDIES

28. Declaratory order.
29. Lodgment of money in settlement of action.
30. Correction order.
31. Damages.
32. Aggravated and punitive damages.
33. Order prohibiting the publication of a defamatory statement.
34. Summary disposal of action.

PART 5
CRIMINAL LIABILITY

35. Abolition of certain common law offences.
36. Publication or utterance of blasphemous matter.
37. Seizure of copies of blasphemous statements.

PART 6
MISCELLANEOUS

38. Limitation of actions.
39. Survival of cause of action on death.
40. Agreements for indemnity.
41. Jurisdiction of courts.
42. Malicious falsehood.
43. Evidence of acquittal or conviction.
44. Press Council.

SCHEDULE 1
STATEMENTS HAVING QUALIFIED PRIVILEGE

PART 1
STATEMENTS PRIVILEGED WITHOUT EXPLANATION OR CONTRADICTION

PART 2
STATEMENTS PRIVILEGED SUBJECT TO EXPLANATION OR CONTRADICTION

SCHEDULE 2
MINIMUM REQUIREMENTS IN RELATION TO PRESS COUNCIL

ACTS REFERRED TO

Number 31 *of* 2009

DEFAMATION ACT 2009

AN ACT TO REVISE IN PART THE LAW OF DEFAMATION; TO
REPEAL THE DEFAMATION ACT 1961; AND TO PROVIDE
FOR MATTERS CONNECTED THEREWITH.

[*23rd July*, 2009]

BE IT ENACTED BY THE OIREACHTAS AS FOLLOWS:

PART 1

PRELIMINARY AND GENERAL

1.—(1) This Act may be cited as the Defamation Act 2009.

(2) This Act shall come into operation on such day or days as the
Minister may appoint, by order or orders, either generally or with reference
to any particular purpose or provision, and different days may be so
appointed for different purposes and different provisions.

*Short title and
commencement.*

2.—In this Act—

Definitions.

"Act of 1957" means the Statute of Limitations 1957;

"Act of 1961" means the Defamation Act 1961;

"cause of action" means a cause of action for defamation;

"correction order" has the meaning assigned to it by *section 30*;

"declaratory order" has the meaning assigned to it by *section 28*;

"defamation" shall be construed in accordance with *section 6(2)*;

"defamation action" means—

    (*a*) an action for damages for defamation, or

    (*b*) an application for a declaratory order,

whether or not a claim for other relief under this Act is made;

"defamatory statement" means a statement that tends to injure a person's
reputation in the eyes of reasonable members of society, and "defamatory"
shall be construed accordingly;

"defence of absolute privilege" has the meaning assigned to it by *section 17*;

"defence of qualified privilege" has the meaning assigned to it by *section 18*;

"defence of truth" has the meaning assigned to it by *section 16*;

"electronic communication" includes a communication of information in the
form of data, text, images or sound (or any combination of these) by means
of guided or unguided electromagnetic energy, or both;

"Minister" means the Minister for Justice, Equality and Law Reform;

"periodical" means any newspaper, magazine, journal or other publication that is printed, published or issued, or that circulates, in the State at regular or substantially regular intervals and includes any version thereof published on the internet or by other electronic means;

"plaintiff" includes a defendant counterclaiming in respect of a statement that is alleged to be defamatory;

"Press Council" has the meaning assigned to it by *section 44*;

"Press Ombudsman" has the meaning assigned to it by *paragraph 8* of *Schedule 2*;

"qualified offer" has the meaning assigned to it by *section 22*;

"special damages" has the meaning assigned to it by *section 31(7)*;

"statement" includes—

> (*a*) a statement made orally or in writing,
>
> (*b*) visual images, sounds, gestures and any other method of signifying meaning,
>
> (*c*) a statement—
>
>> (i) broadcast on the radio or television, or
>>
>> (ii) published on the internet, and
>
> (*d*) an electronic communication;

"summary relief" means, in relation to a defamation action—

> (*a*) a correction order, or
>
> (*b*) an order prohibiting further publication of the statement to which the action relates.

Saver.

3.—(1) A provision of this Act shall not affect causes of action accruing before its commencement.

(2) This Act shall not affect the operation of the general law in relation to defamation except to the extent that it provides otherwise (either expressly or by necessary implication).

Repeal.

4.—The Act of 1961 is repealed.

Review of operation of Act.

5.—(1) The Minister shall, not later than 5 years after the passing of this Act, commence a review of its operation.

(2) A review under *subsection (1)* shall be completed not later than one year after its commencement.

PART 2
DEFAMATION

Defamation.

6.—(1) The tort of libel and the tort of slander—

> (*a*) shall cease to be so described, and

(*b*) shall, instead, be collectively described, and are referred to in this Act, as the "tort of defamation".

(2) The tort of defamation consists of the publication, by any means, of a defamatory statement concerning a person to one or more than one person (other than the first-mentioned person), and "defamation" shall be construed accordingly.

(3) A defamatory statement concerns a person if it could reasonably be understood as referring to him or her.

(4) There shall be no publication for the purposes of the tort of defamation if the defamatory statement concerned is published to the person to whom it relates and to a person other than the person to whom it relates in circumstances where—

    (*a*) it was not intended that the statement would be published to the second-mentioned person, and

    (*b*) it was not reasonably foreseeable that publication of the statement to the first-mentioned person would result in its being published to the second-mentioned person.

(5) The tort of defamation is actionable without proof of special damage.

7.—(1) Section 77 of the Courts of Justice Act 1924 is amended, in paragraph (i) (inserted by section 4(*a*) of the Courts Act 1991), by the substitution of "the tort of defamation" for the words "slander, libel". *Amendment of certain enactments.*

(2) The Civil Liability Act 1961 is amended—

    (*a*) in section 11, by—

        (i) the substitution, in subsection (5), of "defamatory statement" for the words "libel or slander", and

        (ii) the insertion of the following subsection:

            "(7) In this section 'defamatory statement' has the same meaning as it has in the *Defamation Act 2009*.",

    and

    (*b*) in section 14(6), by the substitution of "a defamation action under the *Defamation Act 2009*" for the words "an action for libel or slander".

8.—(1) Where the plaintiff in a defamation action serves on the defendant any pleading containing assertions or allegations of fact, the plaintiff (or in the case of a defamation action brought on behalf of an infant or person of unsound mind by a next friend or a committee of the infant or person, the next friend or committee) shall swear an affidavit verifying those assertions or allegations. *Verifying affidavit.*

(2) Where the defendant in a defamation action serves on the plaintiff any pleading containing assertions or allegations of fact, the defendant shall swear an affidavit verifying those assertions or allegations.

(3) Where a defamation action is brought on behalf of an infant or a person of unsound mind by a next friend or a committee of the infant or person, an affidavit to which *subsection (1)* applies sworn by the next friend or committee concerned shall, in respect of assertions or allegations, of

which he or she does not have personal knowledge, state that he or she honestly believes the assertions or allegations, to be true.

(4) Where the plaintiff or defendant in a defamation action is a body corporate, the person swearing the affidavit on behalf of the body corporate under *subsection (1)* or *(2)*, as the case may be, shall, in respect of assertions or allegations, of which he or she does not have personal knowledge, state that he or she honestly believes the assertions or allegations to be true.

(5) An affidavit under this section shall be sworn and filed in court not later than 2 months after the service of the pleading concerned or such longer period as the court may direct or the parties may agree.

(6) If a person makes a statement in an affidavit under this section—

    (*a*) that is false or misleading in any material respect, and

    (*b*) that he or she knows to be false or misleading,

he or she shall be guilty of an offence.

(7) A person guilty of an offence under this section shall be liable—

    (*a*) on summary conviction, to a fine not exceeding €3,000, or imprisonment for a term not exceeding 6 months or to both, or

    (*b*) on conviction on indictment, to a fine not exceeding €50,000, or imprisonment for a term not exceeding 5 years, or to both.

(8) An affidavit sworn under this section shall include a statement by the deponent that he or she is aware that the making of a statement by him or her in the affidavit that is false or misleading in any material respect and that he or she knows to be false or misleading is an offence.

(9) In a defamation action—

    (*a*) the defendant shall, unless the court otherwise directs, be entitled to cross examine the plaintiff in relation to any statement made by the plaintiff in the affidavit sworn by him or her under this section, and

    (*b*) the plaintiff shall, unless the court otherwise directs, be entitled to cross examine the defendant in relation to any statement made by the defendant in the affidavit sworn by him or her under this section.

(10) Where a plaintiff or a defendant fails to comply with this section, the court may make such order as it considers just and equitable, including—

    (*a*) in the case of such a failure on the part of the plaintiff, an order dismissing the defamation action, and

    (*b*) in the case of such a failure by the defendant, judgment in favour of the plaintiff,

and may give such directions in relation to an order so made as the court considers necessary or expedient.

(11) The reference to court in subsection (5) shall—

    (*a*) in the case of a defamation action brought in the High Court, include a reference to the Master of the High Court, and

    (*b*) in the case of a defamation action brought in the Circuit Court, include a reference to the county registrar for the county in which the proceedings concerned were issued.

(12) (*a*) References in this section to plaintiff shall, in the case of a plaintiff who is deceased, be construed as references to his or her personal representative.

(*b*) References in this section to defendant shall, in the case of a defendant who is deceased, be construed as references to his or her personal representative.

(13) This section does not apply to an application for a declaratory order.

9.—A person has one cause of action only in respect of the publication of a defamatory statement concerning the person even if more than one defamatory imputation in respect of that person is borne by that statement.

Imputation.

10.—Where a person publishes a defamatory statement concerning a class of persons, a member of that class shall have a cause of action under this Act against that person if—

(*a*) by reason of the number of persons who are members of that class, or

(*b*) by virtue of the circumstances in which the statement is published,

the statement could reasonably be understood to refer, in particular, to the member concerned.

Defamation of class of persons.

11.—(1) Subject to *subsection (2)*, a person has one cause of action only in respect of a multiple publication.

(2) A court may grant leave to a person to bring more than one defamation action in respect of a multiple publication where it considers that the interests of justice so require.

(3) In this section "multiple publication" means publication by a person of the same defamatory statement to 2 or more persons (other than the person in respect of whom the statement is made) whether contemporaneously or not.

Multiple publication.

12.—The provisions of this Act apply to a body corporate as they apply to a natural person, and a body corporate may bring a defamation action under this Act in respect of a statement concerning it that it claims is defamatory whether or not it has incurred or is likely to incur financial loss as a result of the publication of that statement.

Defamation of a body corporate.

13.—(1) Upon the hearing of an appeal from a decision of the High Court in a defamation action, the Supreme Court may, in addition to any other order that it deems appropriate to make, substitute for any amount of damages awarded to the plaintiff by the High Court such amount as it considers appropriate.

(2) In this section "decision" includes a judgment entered pursuant to the verdict of a jury.

Appeals in defamation actions.

14.—(1) The court, in a defamation action, may give a ruling—

Meaning.

(*a*) as to whether the statement in respect of which the action was brought is reasonably capable of bearing the imputation pleaded by the plaintiff, and

(*b*) (where the court rules that that statement is reasonably capable of bearing that imputation) as to whether that imputation is reasonably capable of bearing a defamtory meaning,

upon an application being made to it in that behalf.

(2) Where a court rules under *subsection (1)* that—

(*a*) the statement in respect of which the action was brought is not reasonably capable of bearing the imputation pleaded by the plaintiff, or

(*b*) that any imputation so pleaded is not reasonably capable of bearing a defamatory meaning,

it shall dismiss the action in so far only as it relates to the imputation concerned.

(3) An application under this section shall be brought by notice of motion and shall be determined, in the case of a defamation action brought in the High Court, in the absence of the jury.

(4) An application under this section may be brought at any time after the bringing of the defamation action concerned including during the course of the trial of the action.

PART 3
DEFENCES

Abolition of certain defences.

15.—(1) Subject to *sections 17(1)* and *18(1)*, any defence that, immediately before the commencement of this Part, could have been pleaded as a defence in an action for libel or slander is abolished.

(2) In this section—

"defence" shall not include a defence under—

(*a*) statute,

(*b*) an act of the institutions of the European Communities, or

(*c*) regulations made for the purpose of giving effect to an act of the institutions of the European Communities;

"European Communities" has the same meaning as it has in the European Communities Act 1972;

"statute" means—

(*a*) an Act of the Oireachtas, or

(*b*) a statute that was in force in Saorstát Éireann immediately before the date of the coming into operation of the Constitution and that continues to be of full force and effect by virtue of Article 50 of the Constitution.

Truth.

16.—(1) It shall be a defence (to be known and in this Act referred to as the "defence of truth") to a defamation action for the defendant to prove that the statement in respect of which the action was brought is true in all material respects.

(2) In a defamation action in respect of a statement containing 2 or more distinct allegations against the plaintiff, the defence of truth shall not fail by reason only of the truth of every allegation not being proved, if the words not proved to be true do not materially injure the plaintiff's reputation having regard to the truth of the remaining allegations.

17.—(1) It shall be a defence to a defamation action for the defendant to prove that the statement in respect of which the action was brought would, if it had been made immediately before the commencement of this section, have been considered under the law in force immediately before such commencement as having been made on an occasion of absolute privilege.

Absolute privilege.

(2) Subject to section 11(2) of the Committees of the Houses of the Oireachtas (Compellability, Privileges and Immunities of Witnesses) Act 1997, and without prejudice to the generality of *subsection (1)*, it shall be a defence to a defamation action for the defendant to prove that the statement in respect of which the action was brought was—

(*a*) made in either House of the Oireachtas by a member of either House of the Oireachtas,

(*b*) contained in a report of a statement, to which *paragraph (a)* applies, produced by or on the authority of either such House,

(*c*) made in the European Parliament by a member of that Parliament,

(*d*) contained in a report of a statement, to which *paragraph (c)* applies, produced by or on the authority of the European Parliament,

(*e*) contained in a judgment of a court established by law in the State,

(*f*) made by a judge, or other person, performing a judicial function,

(*g*) made by a party, witness, legal representative or juror in the course of proceedings presided over by a judge, or other person, performing a judicial function,

(*h*) made in the course of proceedings involving the exercise of limited functions and powers of a judicial nature in accordance with Article 37 of the Constitution, where the statement is connected with those proceedings,

(*i*) a fair and accurate report of proceedings publicly heard before, or decision made public by, any court—

(i) established by law in the State, or

(ii) established under the law of Northern Ireland,

(*j*) a fair and accurate report of proceedings to which a relevant enactment referred to in section 40 of the Civil Liability and Courts Act 2004 applies,

(*k*) a fair and accurate report of proceedings publicly heard before, or decision made public by, any court or arbitral tribunal established by an international agreement to which the State is a party including the Court of Justice of the European Communities, the Court of First Instance of the European Communities, the European Court of Human Rights and the International Court of Justice, (*l*) made in proceedings before a committee appointed by either House of the Oireachtas or jointly by both Houses of the Oireachtas,

(*m*) made in proceedings before a committee of the European Parliament,

(*n*) made in the course of proceedings before a tribunal established under the Tribunals of Inquiry (Evidence) Acts 1921 to 2004, where the statement is connected with those proceedings,

(*o*) contained in a report of any such tribunal,

(*p*) made in the course of proceedings before a commission of investigation established under the Commissions of Investigation Act 2004, where the statement is connected with those proceedings,

(*q*) contained in a report of any such commission,

(*r*) made in the course of an inquest by a coroner or contained in a decision made or verdict given at or during such inquest,

(*s*) made in the course of an inquiry conducted on the authority of a Minister of the Government, the Government, the Oireachtas, either House of the Oireachtas or a court established by law in the State,

(*t*) made in the course of an inquiry conducted in Northern Ireland on the authority of a person or body corresponding to a person or body referred to in *paragraph (s)*,

(*u*) contained in a report of an inquiry referred to in *paragraph (s) or (t)*,

(*v*) made in the course of proceedings before an arbitral tribunal where the statement is connected with those proceedings,

(*w*) made pursuant to and in accordance with an order of a court established by law in the State.

(3) Section 2 of the Committees of the Houses of the Oireachtas (Privilege and Procedure) Act 1976 is amended by the insertion of the following subsection:

"(3) In this section 'utterance' includes a statement within the meaning of the *Defamation Act 2009;*".

(4) A defence under this section shall be known as, and is referred to in this Act, as the "defence of absolute privilege".

Qualified privilege.

18.—(1) Subject to *section 17*, it shall be a defence to a defamation action for the defendant to prove that the statement in respect of which the action was brought would, if it had been made immediately before the commencement of this section, have been considered under the law (other than the Act of 1961) in force immediately before such commencement as having been made on an occasion of qualified privilege.

(2) Without prejudice to the generality of *subsection (1)*, it shall, subject to *section 19*, be a defence to a defamation action for the defendant to prove that—

(*a*) the statement was published to a person or persons who—

(i) had a duty to receive, or interest in receiving, the information contained in the statement, or

(ii) the defendant believed upon reasonable grounds that the said person or persons had such a duty or interest, and

(*b*) the defendant had a corresponding duty to communicate, or interest in communicating, the information to such person or persons.

(3) Without prejudice to the generality of *subsection (1)*, it shall be a defence to a defamation action for the defendant to prove that the statement to which the action relates is—

(*a*) a statement to which *Part 1* of *Schedule 1* applies,

(*b*) contained in a report, copy, extract or summary referred to in that Part, or

(*c*) contained in a determination referred to in that Part.

(4) Without prejudice to the generality of *subsection (1)*, it shall be a defence to a defamation action for the defendant to prove that the statement to which the action relates is contained in a report, copy or summary referred to in *Part 2* of *Schedule 1*, unless it is proved that the defendant was requested by the plaintiff to publish in the same medium of communication in which he or she published the statement concerned, a reasonable statement by way of explanation or a contradiction, and has refused or failed to do so or has done so in a manner that is not adequate or reasonable having regard to all of the circumstances.

(5) Nothing in *subsection (3)* shall be construed as—

(*a*) protecting the publication of any statement the publication of which is prohibited by law, or of any statement that is not of public concern and the publication of which is not for the public benefit, or

(*b*) limiting or abridging any privilege subsisting apart from *subsection (3)*.

(6) A defence under this section shall be known, and is referred to in this Act, as the "defence of qualified privilege".

(7) In this section—

"duty" means a legal, moral or social duty;

"interest" means a legal, moral or social interest.

19.—(1) In a defamation action, the defence of qualified privilege shall fail if, in relation to the publication of the statement in respect of which the action was brought, the plaintiff proves that the defendant acted with malice.

Loss of defence of qualified privilege.

(2) The defence of qualified privilege shall not fail by reason only of the publication of the statement concerned to a person other than an interested person if it is proved that the statement was published to the person because the publisher mistook him or her for an interested person.

(3) Where a defamation action is brought against more than one defendant, the failure of the defence of qualified privilege in relation to one of the defendants by virtue of the application of *subsection (1)* shall not cause the failure of the defence in relation to another of the defendants unless that other defendant was vicariously liable for such acts or omissions of the first-mentioned defendant as gave rise to the cause of action concerned.

(4) Section 11(4) of the Civil Liability Act 1961 is repealed.

(5) In this section "interested person" means, in relation to a statement, a person who, under *section 18(2)(a)*, had a duty or interest in receiving the information contained in the statement.

Honest
opinion.

20.—(1) It shall be a defence (to be known, and in this section referred to, as the "defence of honest opinion") to a defamation action for the defendant to prove that, in the case of a statement consisting of an opinion, the opinion was honestly held.

(2) Subject to *subsection (3)*, an opinion is honestly held, for the purposes of this section, if—

    (*a*) at the time of the publication of the statement, the defendant believed in the truth of the opinion or, where the defendant is not the author of the opinion, believed that the author believed it to be true,

    (*b*) (i) the opinion was based on allegations of fact—

        (I)   specified in the statement containing the opinion, or

        (II) referred to in that statement, that were known, or might reasonably be expected to have been known, by the persons to whom the statement was published,

      or

    (ii) the opinion was based on allegations of fact to which—

        (I)   the defence of absolute privilege, or

        (II) the defence of qualified privilege,

      would apply if a defamation action were brought in respect of such allegations,

      and

    (*c*) the opinion related to a matter of public interest.

(3) (*a*) The defence of honest opinion shall fail, if the opinion concerned is based on allegations of fact to which *subsection (2)(b)(i)* applies, unless—

    (i) the defendant proves the truth of those allegations, or

    (ii) where the defendant does not prove the truth of all of those allegations, the opinion is honestly held having regard to the allegations of fact the truth of which are proved.

  (*b*) The defence of honest opinion shall fail, if the opinion concerned is based on allegations of fact to which *subsection (2)(b)(ii)* applies, unless—

    (i) the defendant proves the truth of those allegations, or

    (ii) where the defendant does not prove the truth of those allegations—

        (I) the opinion could not reasonably be understood as implying that those allegations were true, and

        (II) at the time of the publication of the opinion, the defendant did not know or could not reasonably have been expected to know that those allegations were untrue.

(4) Where a defamatory statement consisting of an opinion is published jointly by a person ("first-mentioned person") and another person ("joint

publisher"), the first-mentioned person shall not fail in pleading the defence of honest opinion in a subsequent defamation action brought in respect of that statement by reason only of that opinion not being honestly held by the joint publisher, unless the first-mentioned person was at the time of publication vicariously liable for the acts or omissions, from which the cause of action in respect of that statement accrued, of the joint publisher.

21.—The matters to which the court in a defamation action shall have regard, for the purposes of distinguishing between a statement consisting of allegations of fact and a statement consisting of opinion, shall include the following:

> (*a*) the extent to which the statement is capable of being proved;
> (*b*) the extent to which the statement was made in circumstances in which it was likely to have been reasonably understood as a statement of opinion rather than a statement consisting of an allegation of fact; and
> (*c*) the words used in the statement and the extent to which the statement was subject to a qualification or a disclaimer or was accompanied by cautionary words.

Distinguishing between allegations of fact and opinion.

22.—(1) A person who has published a statement that is alleged to be defamatory of another person may make an offer to make amends.

(2) An offer to make amends shall—

> (*a*) be in writing,
> (*b*) state that it is an offer to make amends for the purposes of this section, and
> (*c*) state whether the offer is in respect of the entire of the statement or an offer (in this Act referred to as a "qualified offer") in respect of—
>> (i) part only of the statement, or
>> (ii) a particular defamatory meaning only.

(3) An offer to make amends shall not be made after the delivery of the defence in the defamation action concerned.

(4) An offer to make amends may be withdrawn before it is accepted and where such an offer is withdrawn a new offer to make amends may be made.

(5) In this section "an offer to make amends" means an offer—

> (*a*) to make a suitable correction of the statement concerned and a sufficient apology to the person to whom the statement refers or is alleged to refer,
> (*b*) to publish that correction and apology in such manner as is reasonable and practicable in the circumstances, and
> (*c*) to pay to the person such sum in compensation or damages (if any), and such costs, as may be agreed by them or as may be determined to be payable,

whether or not it is accompanied by any other offer to perform an act other than an act referred to in *paragraph (a), (b)* or *(c)*.

Offer to make amends.

23.—(1) If an offer to make amends under *section 22* is accepted the following provisions shall apply:

  (*a*) if the parties agree as to the measures that should be taken by the person who made the offer to ensure compliance by him or her with the terms of the offer, the High Court or, where a defamation action has already been brought, the court in which it was brought may, upon the application of the person to whom the offer was made, direct the party who made the offer to take those measures;

  (*b*) if the parties do not so agree, the person who made the offer may, with the leave of the High Court or, where a defamation action has already been brought, the court in which it was brought, make a correction and apology by means of a statement before the court in such terms as may be approved by the court and give an undertaking as to the manner of their publication;

  (*c*) if the parties do not agree as to the damages or costs that should be paid by the person who made the offer, those matters shall be determined by the High Court or, where a defamation action has already been brought, the court in which it was brought, and the court shall for those purposes have all such powers as it would have if it were determining damages or costs in a defamation action, and in making a determination under this paragraph it shall take into account the adequacy of any measures already taken to ensure compliance with the terms of the offer by the person who made the offer;

  (*d*) no defamation action shall be brought or, if already brought, proceeded with against another person in respect of the statement to which the offer to make amends applies unless the court considers that in all the circumstances of the case it is just and proper to so do.

(2) Subject to *subsection (3)*, it shall be a defence to a defamation action for a person to prove that he or she made an offer to make amends under *section 22* and that it was not accepted, unless the plaintiff proves that the defendant knew or ought reasonably to have known at the time of the publication of the statement to which the offer relates that—

  (*a*) it referred to the plaintiff or was likely to be understood as referring to the plaintiff, and

  (*b*) it was false and defamatory of the plaintiff.

(3) Where the defendant in a defamation action made a qualified offer only, *subsection (2)* shall apply in relation to that part only of the action that relates to the part of the statement or the meaning, as the case may be, to which the qualified offer relates.

(4) A person who makes an offer to make amends is not required to plead it as a defence in a defamation action.

(5) If a defendant in a defamation action pleads the defence under this section, he or she shall not be entitled to plead any other defence in the action, and if the defence is pleaded in respect of a qualified offer only he or

she shall not be entitled to plead any other defence in respect of that part of the action that relates to the part of the statement or the meaning, as the case may be, to which the qualified offer relates.

24.—(1) In a defamation action the defendant may give evidence in mitigation of damage that he or she—

Apology.

    (*a*) made or offered an apology to the plaintiff in respect of the statement to which the action relates, and

    (*b*) published the apology in such manner as ensured that the apology was given the same or similar prominence as was given to that statement, or offered to publish an apology in such a manner,

as soon as practicable after the plaintiff makes complaint to the defendant concerning the utterance to which the apology relates, or after the bringing of the action, whichever is earlier.

(2) In a defamation action, a defendant who intends to give evidence to which *subsection (1)* applies shall, at the time of the filing or delivery of the defence to the action, notify the plaintiff in writing of his or her intention to give such evidence.

(3) In a defamation action, an apology made by or on behalf of a defendant in respect of a statement to which the action relates—

    (*a*) does not constitute an express or implied admission of liability by that defendant, and

    (*b*) is not relevant to the determination of liability in the action.

(4) Evidence of an apology made by or on behalf of a person in respect of a statement to which the action relates is not admissible in any civil proceedings as evidence of liability of the defendant.

25.—In a defamation action it shall be a defence, to be known as the "defence of consent", for a person to prove that the plaintiff consented to the publication of the statement in respect of which the action was brought.

Consent to publish.

26.—(1) It shall be a defence (to be known, and in this section referred to, as the "defence of fair and reasonable publication") to a defamation action for the defendant to prove that—

Fair and reasonable publication on a matter of public interest.

    (*a*) the statement in respect of which the action was brought was published—

        (i) in good faith, and

        (ii) in the course of, or for the purpose of, the discussion of a subject of public interest, the discussion of which was for the public benefit,

    (*b*) in all of the circumstances of the case, the manner and extent of publication of the statement did not exceed that which was reasonably sufficient, and

    (*c*) in all of the circumstances of the case, it was fair and reasonable to publish the statement.

(2) For the purposes of this section, the court shall, in determining whether it was fair and reasonable to publish the statement concerned, take into account such matters as the court considers relevant including any or all of the following:

(*a*) the extent to which the statement concerned refers to the performance by the person of his or her public functions;

(*b*) the seriousness of any allegations made in the statement;

(*c*) the context and content (including the language used) of the statement;

(*d*) the extent to which the statement drew a distinction between suspicions, allegations and facts;

(*e*) the extent to which there were exceptional circumstances that necessitated the publication of the statement on the date of publication;

(*f*) in the case of a statement published in a periodical by a person who, at the time of publication, was a member of the Press Council, the extent to which the person adhered to the code of standards of the Press Council and abided by determinations of the Press Ombudsman and determinations of the Press Council;

(*g*) in the case of a statement published in a periodical by a person who, at the time of publication, was not a member of the Press Council, the extent to which the publisher of the periodical adhered to standards equivalent to the standards specified in *paragraph (f)*;

(*h*) the extent to which the plaintiff's version of events was represented in the publication concerned and given the same or similar prominence as was given to the statement concerned;

(*i*) if the plaintiff's version of events was not so represented, the extent to which a reasonable attempt was made by the publisher to obtain and publish a response from that person; and

(*j*) the attempts made, and the means used, by the defendant to verify the assertions and allegations concerning the plaintiff in the statement.

(3) The failure or refusal of a plaintiff to respond to attempts by or on behalf of the defendant, to elicit the plaintiff's version of events, shall not—

(*a*) constitute or imply consent to the publication of the statement, or

(*b*) entitle the court to draw any inference therefrom.

(4) In this section—

"court" means, in relation to a defamation action brought in the High Court, the jury, if the High Court is sitting with a jury;

"defamation action" does not include an application for a declaratory order.

Innocent
publication.

27.—(1) It shall be a defence (to be known as the "defence of innocent publication") to a defamation action for the defendant to prove that—

(*a*) he or she was not the author, editor or publisher of the statement to which the action relates,

(*b*) he or she took reasonable care in relation to its publication, and (*c*) he or she did not know, and had no reason to believe, that what he or she did caused or contributed to the publication of a statement that would give rise to a cause of action in defamation.

(2) A person shall not, for the purposes of this section, be considered to be the author, editor or publisher of a statement if—

(*a*) in relation to printed material containing the statement, he or she was responsible for the printing, production, distribution or selling only of the printed material,

(*b*) in relation to a film or sound recording containing the statement, he or she was responsible for the processing, copying, distribution, exhibition or selling only of the film or sound recording,

(*c*) in relation to any electronic medium on which the statement is recorded or stored, he or she was responsible for the processing, copying, distribution or selling only of the electronic medium or was responsible for the operation or provision only of any equipment, system or service by means of which the statement would be capable of being retrieved, copied, distributed or made available.

(3) The court shall, for the purposes of determining whether a person took reasonable care, or had reason to believe that what he or she did caused or contributed to the publication of a defamatory statement, have regard to—

(*a*) the extent of the person's responsibility for the content of the statement or the decision to publish it,

(*b*) the nature or circumstances of the publication, and

(*c*) the previous conduct or character of the person.

PART 4
REMEDIES

28.—(1) A person who claims to be the subject of a statement that he or she alleges is defamatory may apply to the Circuit Court for an order (in this Act referred to as a "declaratory order") that the statement is false and defamatory of him or her.

Declaratory order.

(2) Upon an application under this section, the court shall make a declaratory order if it is satisfied that—

(*a*) the statement is defamatory of the applicant and the respondent has no defence to the application,

(*b*) the applicant requested the respondent to make and publish an apology, correction or retraction in relation to that statement, and

(*c*) the respondent failed or refused to accede to that request or, where he or she acceded to that request, failed or refused to give the apology, correction or retraction the same or similar prominence as was given by the respondent to the statement concerned.

(3) For the avoidance of doubt, an applicant for a declaratory order shall not be required to prove that the statement to which the application concerned relates is false.

(4) Where an application is made under this section, the applicant shall not be entitled to bring any other proceedings in respect of any cause of action arising out of the statement to which the application relates.

(5) An application under this section shall be brought by motion on notice to the respondent grounded on affidavit.

(6) Where a court makes a declaratory order, it may, in addition, make an order under *section 30* or *33*, upon an application by the applicant in that behalf.

(7) The court may, for the purposes of making a determination in relation to an application under this section in an expeditious manner, give directions in relation to the delivery of pleadings and the time and manner of trial of any issues raised in the course of such an application.

(8) No order in relation to damages shall be made upon an application under this section.

(9) An application under this section shall be made to the Circuit Court sitting in the circuit where—

(*a*) the statement to which the application relates was published, or

(*b*) the defendant or one of the defendants, as the case may be, resides.

Lodgment of money in settlement of action.

29.—(1) In an action for damages for defamation the defendant may, upon giving notice in writing to the plaintiff, pay a sum of money into court in satisfaction of the action when filing his or her defence to the action.

(2) A payment to which this section applies shall be deemed to be a payment under such rule of court for the time being in force as provides for the payment into court of a sum of money in satisfaction of an action for damages for defamation.

(3) Where a payment to which this section applies is made, the plaintiff in the action concerned may accept the payment—

(*a*) in accordance with the rule referred to in *subsection (2)*, or

(*b*) inform the court in which the action was brought, on notice to the defendant, of his or her acceptance of the payment in full settlement of the action.

(4) The defendant shall not be required to admit liability in an action for damages for defamation when making a payment to which this section applies.

Correction order.

30.—(1) Where, in a defamation action, there is a finding that the statement in respect of which the action was brought was defamatory and the defendant has no defence to the action, the court may, upon the application of the plaintiff, make an order (in this Act referred to as a "correction order") directing the defendant to publish a correction of the defamatory statement.

(2) Without prejudice to the generality of *subsection (1)*, a correction order shall—

(*a*) specify—

(i) the date and time upon which, or

(ii) the period not later than the expiration of which,
the correction order shall be published, and
(*b*) specify the form, content, extent and manner of publication of the
correction,
and shall, unless the plaintiff otherwise requests, require the correction to be
published in such manner as will ensure that it is communicated to all or
substantially all of those persons to whom the defamatory statement was
published.

(3) Where a plaintiff intends to make an application under this section,
he or she shall so inform—
(*a*) the defendant by notice in writing, not later than 7 days before the
trial of the action, and
(*b*) the court at the trial of the action.

(4) An application under this section may be made at such time during
the trial of a defamation action as the court or, where the action is tried in
the High Court sitting with a jury, the trial judge directs.

31.—(1) The parties in a defamation action may make submissions to the
court in relation to the matter of damages.

Damages.

(2) In a defamation action brought in the High Court, the judge shall
give directions to the jury in relation to the matter of damages.

(3) In making an award of general damages in a defamation action,
regard shall be had to all of the circumstances of the case.

(4) Without prejudice to the generality of *subsection (3)*, the court in a
defamation action shall, in making an award of general damages, have regard
to—
(*a*) the nature and gravity of any allegation in the defamatory statement
concerned,
(*b*) the means of publication of the defamatory statement including the
enduring nature of those means,
(*c*) the extent to which the defamatory statement was circulated,
(*d*) the offering or making of any apology, correction or retraction by the
defendant to the plaintiff in respect of the defamatory statement,
(*e*) the making of any offer to make amends under *section 22* by the
defendant, whether or not the making of that offer was pleaded as
a defence,
(*f*) the importance to the plaintiff of his or her reputation in the eyes of
particular or all recipients of the defamatory statement,
(*g*) the extent (if at all) to which the plaintiff caused or contributed to,
or acquiesced in, the publication of the defamatory statement,
(*h*) evidence given concerning the reputation of the plaintiff,
(*i*) if the defence of truth is pleaded and the defendant proves the truth
of part but not the whole of the defamatory statement, the extent
to which that defence is successfully pleaded in relation to the
statement,

(*j*) if the defence of qualified privilege is pleaded, the extent to which the defendant has acceded to the request of the plaintiff to publish a reasonable statement by way of explanation or contradiction, and

(*k*) any order made under *section 33*, or any order under that section or correction order that the court proposes to make or, where the action is tried by the High Court sitting with a jury, would propose to make in the event of there being a finding of defamation.

(5) For the purposes of *subsection (4)(c)*, a defamatory statement consisting of words that are innocent on their face, but that are defamatory by reason of facts known to some recipients only of the publication containing the defamatory statement, shall be treated as having been published to those recipients only.

(6) The defendant in a defamation action may, for the purposes of mitigating damages, give evidence—

(*a*) with the leave of the court, of any matter that would have a bearing upon the reputation of the plaintiff, provided that it relates to matters connected with the defamatory statement,

(*b*) that the plaintiff has already in another defamation action been awarded damages in respect of a defamatory statement that contained substantially the same allegations as are contained in the defamatory statement to which the first-mentioned defamation action relates.

(7) The court in a defamation action may make an award of damages (in this section referred to as "special damages") to the plaintiff in respect of financial loss suffered by him or her as a result of the injury to his or her reputation caused by the publication of the defamatory statement in respect of which the action was brought.

(8) In this section "court" means, in relation to a defamation action brought in the High Court, the jury, if the High Court is sitting with a jury.

Aggravated
and punitive
damages.

32.—(1) Where, in a defamation action—

(*a*) the court finds the defendant liable to pay damages to the plaintiff in respect of a defamatory statement, and

(*b*) the defendant conducted his or her defence in a manner that aggravated the injury caused to the plaintiff's reputation by the defamatory statement,

the court may, in addition to any general, special or punitive damages payable by the defendant to the plaintiff, order the defendant to pay to the plaintiff damages (in this section referred to as "aggravated damages") of such amount as it considers appropriate to compensate the plaintiff for the aggravation of the said injury.

(2) Where, in a defamation action, the court finds the defendant liable to pay damages to the plaintiff in respect of a defamatory statement and it is proved that the defendant—

(*a*) intended to publish the defamatory statement concerned to a person other than the plaintiff, (*b*) knew that the defamatory statement would be understood by the said person to refer to the plaintiff, and

(*c*) knew that the statement was untrue or in publishing it was reckless as to whether it was true or untrue,

the court may, in addition to any general, special or aggravated damages payable by the defendant to the plaintiff, order the defendant to pay to the plaintiff damages (in this section referred to as "punitive damages") of such amount as it considers appropriate.

(3) In this section "court" means, in relation to a defamation action brought in the High Court, the jury, if the High Court is sitting with a jury.

33.—(1) The High Court, or where a defamation action has been brought, the court in which it was brought, may, upon the application of the plaintiff, make an order prohibiting the publication or further publication of the statement in respect of which the application was made if in its opinion—

Order prohibiting the publication of a defamatory statement.

(*a*) the statement is defamatory, and

(*b*) the defendant has no defence to the action that is reasonably likely to succeed.

(2) Where an order is made under this section it shall not operate to prohibit the reporting of the making of that order provided that such reporting does not include the publication of the statement to which the order relates.

(3) In this section "order" means—

(*a*) an interim order,

(*b*) an interlocutory order, or

(*c*) a permanent order.

34.—(1) The court in a defamation action may, upon the application of the plaintiff, grant summary relief to the plaintiff if it is satisfied that—

Summary disposal of action.

(*a*) the statement in respect of which the action was brought is defamatory, and

(*b*) the defendant has no defence to the action that is reasonably likely to succeed.

(2) The court in a defamation action may, upon the application of the defendant, dismiss the action if it is satisfied that the statement in respect of which the action was brought is not reasonably capable of being found to have a defamatory meaning.

(3) An application under this section shall be brought by motion on notice to the other party to the action and shall be grounded on an affidavit.

(4) An application under this section shall not be heard or determined in the presence of a jury.

PART 5
Criminal Liability

Abolition of certain common law offences.

35.—The common law offences of defamatory libel, seditious libel and obscene libel are abolished.

Publication or utterance of blasphemous matter.

36.—(1) A person who publishes or utters blasphemous matter shall be guilty of an offence and shall be liable upon conviction on indictment to a fine not exceeding €25,000.

(2) For the purposes of this section, a person publishes or utters blasphemous matter if—

    (*a*) he or she publishes or utters matter that is grossly abusive or insulting in relation to matters held sacred by any religion, thereby causing outrage among a substantial number of the adherents of that religion, and

    (*b*) he or she intends, by the publication or utterance of the matter concerned, to cause such outrage.

(3) It shall be a defence to proceedings for an offence under this section for the defendant to prove that a reasonable person would find genuine literary, artistic, political, scientific, or academic value in the matter to which the offence relates.

(4) In this section "religion" does not include an organisation or cult—

    (*a*) the principal object of which is the making of profit, or

    (*b*) that employs oppressive psychological manipulation—

        (i) of its followers, or

        (ii) for the purpose of gaining new followers.

Seizure of copies of blasphemous statements.

37.—(1) Where a person is convicted of an offence under *section 36*, the court may issue a warrant—

    (*a*) authorising any member of the Garda Síochána to enter (if necessary by the use of reasonable force) at all reasonable times any premises (including a dwelling) at which he or she has reasonable grounds for believing that copies of the statement to which the offence related are to be found, and to search those premises and seize and remove all copies of the statement found therein,

    (*b*) directing the seizure and removal by any member of the Garda Síochána of all copies of the statement to which the offence related that are in the possession of any person,

    (*c*) specifying the manner in which copies so seized and removed shall be detained and stored by the Garda Síochána.

(2) A member of the Garda Síochána may—

    (*a*) enter and search any premises,

    (*b*) seize, remove and detain any copy of a statement to which an offence under *section 36* relates found therein or in the possession of any person,

in accordance with a warrant under *subsection (1)*.

(3) Upon final judgment being given in proceedings for an offence under *section 36*, anything seized and removed under *subsection (2)* shall be disposed of in accordance with such directions as the court may give upon an application by a member of the Garda Síochána in that behalf.

PART 6
MISCELLANEOUS

38.—(1) Section 11 of the Act of 1957 is amended—

Limitation of actions.

    (*a*) in subsection (2), by the substitution of the following paragraph for paragraph (*c*):

        "(*c*) A defamation action within the meaning of the *Defamation Act 2009* shall not be brought after the expiration of—

            (i) one year, or

            (ii) such longer period as the court may direct not exceeding 2 years,

            from the date on which the cause of action accrued.",

and

    (*b*) the insertion of the following subsections:

        "(3A) The court shall not give a direction under subsection (2)(*c*)(ii) (inserted by *section 38(1)(a)* of the *Defamation Act 2009*) unless it is satisfied that—

          (*a*) the interests of justice require the giving of the direction,

          (*b*) the prejudice that the plaintiff would suffer if the direction were not given would significantly outweigh the prejudice that the defendant would suffer if the direction were given,

and the court shall, in deciding whether to give such a direction, have regard to the reason for the failure to bring the action within the period specified in subparagraph (i) of the said subsection (2)(*c*) and the extent to which any evidence relevant to the matter is by virtue of the delay no longer capable of being adduced.

        (3B) For the purposes of bringing a defamation action within the meaning of the *Defamation Act 2009*, the date of accrual of the cause of action shall be the date upon which the defamatory statement is first published and, where the statement is published through the medium of the internet, the date on which it is first capable of being viewed or listened to through that medium.".

(2) Section 49 of the Act of 1957 is amended by the substitution of the following subsection for subsection (3):

        "(3) In the case of defamation actions within the meaning of the *Defamation Act 2009*, subsection (1) of this section shall have effect as if for the words 'six years' there were substituted the words 'one year or such longer period as the court may direct not exceeding two years'.".

39.—(1) Section 6 of the Civil Liability Act 1961 is amended by the insertion of the following definitions:

" 'Act of 2009' means the *Defamation Act 2009*;

'aggravated damages' has the same meaning as it has in the Act of 2009;

'punitive damages' has the same meaning as it has in the Act of 2009.".

(2) Section 7 of the Civil Liability Act 1961 is amended by—

(*a*) the insertion of the following subsection:

"(1A) On the death of a person on or after the commencement of *section 39(2)(a)* of the *Act of 2009*, a cause of action for defamation vested in him immediately before his death shall survive for the benefit of his estate.",

and

(*b*) the insertion of the following subsection:

"(2A) Where by virtue of subsection (1A) of this section, a cause of action for defamation survives for the benefit of the estate of a deceased person, the damages recoverable for the benefit of the estate of that person shall not include general damages, punitive damages or aggravated damages.".

(3) Section 8 of the Civil Liability Act 1961 is amended by—

(*a*) the insertion of the following subsection:

"(1A) On the death of a person on or after the commencement of *section 39(3)(a)* of the *Act of 2009* a cause of action subsisting against him shall survive against his estate.",

(*b*) by the insertion of the following subsection:

"(2A) Where by virtue of subsection (1A) of this section, a cause of action for defamation survives against the estate of a deceased person, the damages recoverable against the estate of that person shall not include general damages, punitive damages or aggravated damages.".

40.—An agreement to indemnify any person against civil liability for defamation in respect of the publication of any statement shall be lawful unless at the time of the publication that person knows that the statement is defamatory, and does not reasonably believe that there is a defence to any action brought upon it that would succeed.

41.—The Third Schedule to the Courts (Supplemental Provisions) Act 1961 is amended by—

(*a*) the insertion, in column (2) at reference number 6, of "a defamation action within the meaning of the Defamation Act 2009," between "other than" and "an action", and

(*b*) the insertion of the following:

"

7A	A defamation action under of the *Defamation Act 2009*.	Where the amount the claim does not exceed €50,000.	At the election of the plaintiff— (a) the judge of the circuit where the tort is alleged to have been committed, or (b) the judge of the circuit where the defendant or one of the defendants resides or carries on business.

".

42.—(1) In an action for slander of title, slander of goods or other malicious falsehood, the plaintiff shall be required to prove that the statement upon which the action is founded— *Malicious falsehood.*

    (*a*) was untrue,

    (*b*) was published maliciously, and

    (*c*) referred to the plaintiff, his or her property or his or her office, profession, calling, trade or business.

(2) In an action for slander of title, slander of goods or other malicious falsehood, the plaintiff shall be required to prove—

    (*a*) special damage, or

    (*b*) that the publication of the statement was calculated to cause and was likely to cause financial loss to the plaintiff in respect of his or her property or his or her office, profession, calling, trade or business.

43.—(1) Where a person has been acquitted of an offence in the State, the fact of his or her acquittal, and any findings of fact made during the course of proceedings for the offence concerned, shall be admissible in evidence in a defamation action. *Evidence of acquittal or conviction.*

(2) Where a person has been convicted of an offence in the State, the fact of his or her conviction, and any findings of fact made during the course of proceedings for the offence concerned, shall be admissible in evidence in a defamation action.

44.—(1) The Minister may by order declare that such body as is specified in the order shall be recognised for the purposes of this Act, and a body standing so recognised, for the time being, shall be known, and in this Act is referred to, as the "Press Council". *Press Council.*

(2) Not more than one body shall stand recognised under this section for the time being.

(3) No body (other than a body that stands recognised under this section for the time being) shall be known as, or describe itself as, the Press Council.

(4) The Minister shall not make an order under *subsection (1)* unless he or she is satisfied that the body in respect of which he or she proposes to make the order complies with the minimum requirements specified in *Schedule 2.*

(5) If the Minister is of the opinion that a body for the time being standing recognised by order under this section no longer complies with the provisions of *Schedule 2*, he or she may revoke that order.

(6) The Minister shall, before making an order under *subsection (5)*, allow the body for the time being standing recognised under this section to make representations to him or her.

(7) Whenever an order is proposed to be made under this section a draft of the order shall be laid before each House of the Oireachtas and the order shall not be made unless a resolution approving of the draft has been passed by each such House.

Section 18.

SCHEDULE 1

STATEMENTS HAVING QUALIFIED PRIVILEGE

PART 1
STATEMENTS PRIVILEGED WITHOUT EXPLANATION OR CONTRADICTION

1. A fair and accurate report of any matter to which the defence of absolute privilege would apply (other than a fair and accurate report referred to in *section 17(2)(i)* or *(k)*).
2. A fair and accurate report of any proceedings publicly heard before, or decision made public by a court (including a court-martial) established under the law of any state or place (other than the State or Northern Ireland).
3. A fair and accurate report of the proceedings (other than court proceedings) presided over by a judge of a court established under the law of Northern Ireland.
4. A fair and accurate report of any proceedings in public of a house of any legislature (including a subordinate or federal legislature) of any state other than the State.
5. A fair and accurate report of proceedings in public of any body duly appointed, in the State, on the authority of a Minister of the Government, the Government, the Oireachtas, either House of the Oireachtas or a court established by law in the State to conduct a public inquiry on a matter of public importance.
6. A fair and accurate report of proceedings in public of any body duly appointed, in Northern Ireland, on the authority of a person or body corresponding to a person or body referred to in *paragraph 5* to conduct a public inquiry on a matter of public importance.
7. A fair and accurate report of any proceedings in public of any body—
    (*a*) that is part of any legislature (including a subordinate or federal legislature) of any state (other than the State), or
    (*b*) duly appointed in a state other than the State, on the authority of a person or body corresponding to a person or body referred to in *paragraph 5*,
to conduct a public inquiry on a matter of public importance.

8. A fair and accurate report of any proceedings in public of an international organisation of which the State or Government is a member or the proceedings of which are of interest to the State.

9. A fair and accurate report of any proceedings in public of any international conference to which the Government sends a representative or observer or at which governments of states (other than the State) are represented.

10. A fair and accurate copy or extract from any register kept in pursuance of any law which is open to inspection by the public or of any other document which is required by law to be open to inspection by the public.

11. A fair and accurate report, copy or summary of any notice or advertisement published by or on the authority of any court established by law in the State or under the law of a Member State of the European Union, or any judge or officer of such a court.

12. A fair and accurate report or copy or summary of any notice or other document issued for the information of the public by or on behalf of any Department of State for which a Minister of the Government is responsible, local authority or the Commissioner of the Garda Síochána, or by or on behalf of a corresponding department, authority or officer in a Member State of the European Union.

13. A fair and accurate report or copy or summary of any notice or document issued by or on the authority of a committee appointed by either House of the Oireachtas or jointly by both Houses of the Oireachtas.

14. A determination of the Press Ombudsman referred to in *paragraph 9(2)* of *Schedule 2*.

15. A determination of the Press Council referred to in *paragraph 9(4)* of *Schedule 2* or a report of the Press Council relating to the past performance of its functions.

16. Any statement published pursuant to, and in accordance with, a determination of the Press Ombudsman or the Press Council.

17. Any statement made during the investigation or hearing of a complaint by the Press Ombudsman in accordance with *Schedule 2*.

18. Any statement made during the hearing of an appeal from a determination of the Press Ombudsman in accordance with *Schedule 2*.

19. Any statement published by a person in accordance with a requirement under an Act of the Oireachtas whether or not that person is the author of the statement.

PART 2

Statements Privileged Subject to Explanation or Contradiction

1. A fair and accurate report of the proceedings, findings or decisions of an association, or a committee or governing body of an association, whether incorporated or not in the State or in a Member State of the European Union, relating to a member of the association or to a person subject, by contract or otherwise, to control by the association.

2. A fair and accurate report of the proceedings at any public meeting, held in the State or in a Member State of the European Union, being a meeting held for a

lawful purpose and for the discussion of any matter of public concern whether the admission to the meeting is general or restricted.

3. A fair and accurate report of the proceedings at a general meeting, whether in the State or in a Member State of the European Union, of any company or association established by or under statute or incorporated by charter.

4. A fair and accurate report of the proceedings at any meeting or sitting of any local authority or the Health Service Executive, and any corresponding body in a Member State of the European Union.

5. A fair and accurate report of a press conference convened by or on behalf of a body to which this Part applies or the organisers of a public meeting within the meaning of *paragraph 2* to give an account to the public of the proceedings or meeting.

6. A fair and accurate report of a report to which the defence of qualified privilege would apply.

7. A copy or fair and accurate report or summary of any ruling, direction, report, investigation, statement (including any advice, admonition or censure given or administered by the Irish Takeover Panel under section 20 of the Irish Takeover Panel Act 1997) or notice made, given, prepared, published or served by the Irish Takeover Panel.

Section 44.

SCHEDULE 2

Minimum Requirements in Relation to Press Council

1. The Press Council shall be a company limited by guarantee.

2. The principal objects of the Press Council shall be to—
   (*a*) ensure the protection of freedom of expression of the press,
   (*b*) protect the public interest by ensuring ethical, accurate and truthful reporting by the press,
   (*c*) maintain certain minimum ethical and professional standards among the press,
   (*d*) ensure that the privacy and dignity of the individual is protected.

3. The Press Council shall be independent in the performance of its functions.

4. The owner of any periodical in circulation in the State or part of the State shall be entitled to be a member of the Press Council.

5. (1) The number of directors of the Press Council shall be 13, of whom—
   (*a*) 7 shall be directors (in this Schedule referred to as "independent public interest directors") who represent the public interest,
   (*b*) 5 shall be directors who represent the interests of owners and publishers of periodicals,
   (*c*) one shall be a director who represents the interests of journalists.
   (2) One of the independent public interest directors of the Press Council shall be appointed as chairperson of the Press Council.

6. (1) The independent public interest directors shall—
   (*a*) be persons who are of standing in the community,

(*b*) be persons who are independent of—

> (i) the interests of owners and publishers of periodicals, and
>
> (ii) the interests of journalists, and

(*c*) be selected for appointment as independent public interest directors—

> (i) by a panel of persons who are, in the opinion of the Minister, independent of the interests referred to in *paragraph 5(1)(b) and (c)*,
>
> (ii) in accordance with a selection process that is advertised to members of the public in a manner that the Minister considers to be sufficient.

(2) The criteria for selecting persons for appointment as independent public interest directors shall be published in such manner as will enable them to be inspected by members of the public.

7. (1) The Press Council shall be funded from subscriptions paid by members of the Press Council calculated in accordance with such rules as the Press Council shall make for that purpose.

(2) The Press Council shall not accept gifts or funding from any person other than subscriptions referred to in *subparagraph (1)*.

8. (1) The Press Council shall have authority to receive, hear and determine complaints concerning the conduct of its members.

(2) The Press Council shall appoint a person (in this Act referred to as the "Press Ombudsman") to investigate, hear and determine complaints made to the Press Council concerning the conduct of its members.

9. (1) The procedures for investigating, hearing and determining a complaint to the Press Ombudsman shall—

(*a*) where appropriate, provide for the expeditious and informal resolution of the matter between the complainant and the member of the Press Council in respect of whom the complaint was made,

(*b*) provide for the determination of the matter by the Press Ombudsman, where all reasonable efforts made in accordance with *clause (a)* in relation to the matter have failed,

(*c*) provide for the taking of remedial action by the member of the Press Council in respect of whom the complaint was made consisting of any or all of the following:

> (i) the publication of the decision of the Press Ombudsman by such members of the Press Council as he or she directs and in such form and manner as he or she directs;
>
> (ii) the publication of a correction of inaccurate facts or information relating to the complainant in a manner that gives due prominence to the correction in the publication concerned;
>
> (iii) the publication of a retraction in respect of the material complained of; or
>
> (iv) such other action as the Ombudsman may, in the circumstances, deem appropriate.

(2) A determination of the Press Ombudsman in relation to a complaint may be appealed to the Press Council.

(3) Where an appeal is brought against the determination of the Press Ombudsman it shall be determined by the directors of the Press Council.

(4) A determination of the Press Council, upon an appeal from a determination of the Press Ombudsman, shall be published by such members of the Press Council as the directors of the Press Council direct and in such form and manner as they direct.

10. The Press Council shall adopt a code of standards which shall specify the standards to be adhered to, and the rules and practices to be complied with by the members of the Press Council including—

   (*a*) ethical standards and practices,

   (*b*) rules and standards intended to ensure the accuracy of reporting where a person's reputation is likely to be affected, and

   (*c*) rules and standards intended to ensure that intimidation and harassment of persons does not occur and that the privacy, integrity and dignity of the person is respected.

PRESS COUNCIL CODE OF PRACTICE*

PREAMBLE

The freedom to publish is vital to the right of the people to be informed. This freedom includes the right of a newspaper to publish what it considers to be news, without fear or favour, and the right to comment upon it.

Freedom of the press carries responsibilities. Members of the press have a duty to maintain the highest professional and ethical standards.

This Code sets the benchmark for those standards. It is the duty of the Press Ombudsman and Press Council of Ireland to ensure that it is honoured in the spirit as well as in the letter, and it is the duty of publications to assist them in that task.

In dealing with complaints, the Ombudsman and Press Council will give consideration to what they perceive to be the public interest. It is for them to define the public interest in each case, but the general principle is that the public interest is invoked in relation to a matter capable of affecting the people at large so that they may legitimately be interested in receiving and the press legitimately interested in providing information about it.

PRINCIPLE 1 – TRUTH AND ACCURACY

1.1 In reporting news and information, newspapers and periodicals shall strive at all times for truth and accuracy.

1.2 When a significant inaccuracy, misleading statement or distorted report or picture has been published, it shall be corrected promptly and with due prominence.

1.3 When appropriate, a retraction, apology, clarification, explanation or response shall be published promptly and with *due prominence*.

PRINCIPLE 2 – DISTINGUISHING FACT AND COMMENT

2.1 Newspapers and periodicals are entitled to advocate strongly their own views on topics.

---

* Code of Practice of the Press Council of Ireland.

2.2 Comment, conjecture, rumour and unconfirmed reports shall not be reported as if they were fact.

2.3 Readers are entitled to expect that the content of a publication reflects the best judgment of editors and writers and has not been inappropriately influenced by undisclosed interests. Wherever relevant, any significant financial interest of an organisation should be disclosed. Writers should disclose significant potential conflicts of interest to their editors.

PRINCIPLE 3 – FAIRNESS AND HONESTY

3.1 Newspapers and periodicals shall strive at all times for fairness and honesty in the procuring and publishing of news and information.

3.2 Publications shall not obtain information, photographs or other material through misrepresentation or subterfuge, unless justified by the public interest.

3.3 Journalists and photographers must not obtain, or seek to obtain, information and photographs through harassment, unless their actions are justified in the public interest.

PRINCIPLE 4 – RESPECT FOR RIGHTS

Everyone has constitutional protection for his or her good name. Newspapers and periodicals shall not knowingly publish matter based on malicious misrepresentation or unfounded accusations, and must take reasonable care in checking facts before publication.

PRINCIPLE 5 – PRIVACY

5.1 Privacy is a human right, protected as a personal right in the Irish Constitution and the European Convention on Human Rights, which is incorporated into Irish law. The private and family life, home and correspondence of everyone must be respected.

5.2 Readers are entitled to have news and comment presented with respect for the privacy and sensibilities of individuals. However, the right to privacy should not prevent publication of matters of public record or in the public interest.

5.3 Sympathy and discretion must be shown at all times in seeking information in situations of personal grief or shock. In publishing such information, the feelings of grieving families should be taken into account. This should not be interpreted as restricting the right to report judicial proceedings.

5.4 Public persons are entitled to privacy. However, where a person holds public office, deals with public affairs, follows a public career, or has sought or obtained publicity for his activities, publication of relevant details of his private life and circumstances may be justifiable where the information revealed relates to the validity of the persons conduct, the credibility of his public statements, the value of his publicly expressed views or is otherwise in the public interest.

5.5 Taking photographs of individuals in private places without their consent is not acceptable, unless justified by the public interest.

PRINCIPLE 6 – PROTECTION OF SOURCES

Journalists shall protect confidential sources of information.

PRINCIPLE 7 – COURT REPORTING

Newspapers and periodicals shall strive to ensure that court reports (including the use of photographs) are fair and accurate, are not prejudicial to the right to a fair trial and that the presumption of innocence is respected.

PRINCIPLE 8 – PREJUDICE

Newspapers and periodicals shall not publish material intended or likely to cause grave offence or stir up hatred against an individual or group on the basis of their race, religion, nationality, colour, ethnic origin, membership of the travelling community, gender, sexual orientation, marital status, disability, illness or age.

PRINCIPLE 9 – CHILDREN

9.1 Newspapers and periodicals shall take particular care in seeking and presenting information or comment about a child under the age of 16.

9.2 Journalists and editors should have regard for the vulnerability of children, and in all dealings with children should bear in mind the age of the child, whether parental or other adult consent has been obtained for such dealings, the sensitivity of the subject-matter, and what circumstances if any make the story one of public interest. Young people should be free to complete their time at school without unnecessary intrusion. The fame, notoriety or position of a parent or guardian must not be used as sole justification for publishing details of a childs private life.

PRINCIPLE 10 – PUBLICATION OF THE DECISION OF THE PRESS OMBUDSMAN / PRESS COUNCIL

10.1   When requested or required by the Press Ombudsman and/or the Press Council to do so, newspapers and periodicals shall publish the decision in relation to a complaint with due prominence.

10.2   The content of this Code will be reviewed at regular intervals.

NATIONAL UNION OF JOURNALISTS CODE OF CONDUCT

The NUJ's Code of Conduct has set out the main principles of British and Irish journalism since 1936. The code is part of the rules and all journalists joining the union must sign that they will strive to adhere to it.

Members of the National Union of Journalists are expected to abide by the following professional principles:

A journalist:

1. At all times upholds and defends the principle of media freedom, the right of freedom of expression and the right of the public to be informed

2. Strives to ensure that information disseminated is honestly conveyed, accurate and fair

3. Does her/his utmost to correct harmful inaccuracies

4. Differentiates between fact and opinion

5. Obtains material by honest, straightforward and open means, with the exception of investigations that are both overwhelmingly in the public interest and which involve evidence that cannot be obtained by straightforward means

6. Does nothing to intrude into anybody's private life, grief or distress unless justified by overriding consideration of the public interest

7. Protects the identity of sources who supply information in confidence and material gathered in the course of her/his work

8. Resists threats or any other inducements to influence, distort or suppress information

9. Takes no unfair personal advantage of information gained in the course of her/his duties before the information is public knowledge

10. Produces no material likely to lead to hatred or discrimination on the grounds of a person's age, gender, race, colour, creed, legal status, disability, marital status, or sexual orientation

11. Does not by way of statement, voice or appearance endorse by advertisement any commercial product or service save for the promotion of her/his own work or of the medium by which she/he is employed

12. Avoids plagiarism.

The NUJ believes a journalist has the right to refuse an assignment or be identified as the author of editorial that would break the letter or spirit of the code. The NUJ will fully support any journalist disciplined for asserting her/his right to act according to the code.

EUROPEAN CONVENTION FOR THE PROTECTION OF HUMAN RIGHTS, ARTICLES 2—18

Article 2 – Right to life

1 Everyone's right to life shall be protected by law. No one shall be deprived of his life intentionally save in the execution of a sentence of a court following his conviction of a crime for which this penalty is provided by law.

2 Deprivation of life shall not be regarded as inflicted in contravention of this article when it results from the use of force which is no more than absolutely necessary:

    a in defence of any person from unlawful violence;

    b in order to effect a lawful arrest or to prevent the escape of a person lawfully detained;

    c in action lawfully taken for the purpose of quelling a riot or insurrection.

Article 3 – Prohibition of torture

No one shall be subjected to torture or to inhuman or degrading treatment or punishment.

Article 4 – Prohibition of slavery and forced labour

1 No one shall be held in slavery or servitude.

2 No one shall be required to perform forced or compulsory labour.

3 For the purpose of this article the term "forced or compulsory labour" shall not include:

    a any work required to be done in the ordinary course of detention imposed according to the provisions of Article 5 of this Convention or during conditional release from such detention;

    b any service of a military character or, in case of conscientious objectors in countries where they are recognised, service exacted instead of compulsory military service;

    c any service exacted in case of an emergency or calamity threatening the life or well-being of the community;

    d any work or service which forms part of normal civic obligations.

Article 5 – Right to liberty and security

1 Everyone has the right to liberty and security of person. No one shall be deprived of his liberty save in the following cases and in accordance with a procedure prescribed by law:

    a the lawful detention of a person after conviction by a competent court;

b   the lawful arrest or detention of a person for non-compliance with the lawful order of a court or in order to secure the fulfilment of any obligation prescribed by law;

c   the lawful arrest or detention of a person effected for the purpose of bringing him before the competent legal authority on reasonable suspicion of having committed an offence or when it is reasonably considered necessary to prevent his committing an offence or fleeing after having done so;

d   the detention of a minor by lawful order for the purpose of educational supervision or his lawful detention for the purpose of bringing him before the competent legal authority;

e   the lawful detention of persons for the prevention of the spreading of infectious diseases, of persons of unsound mind, alcoholics or drug addicts or vagrants;

f   the lawful arrest or detention of a person to prevent his effecting an unauthorised entry into the country or of a person against whom action is being taken with a view to deportation or extradition.

2   Everyone who is arrested shall be informed promptly, in a language which he understands, of the reasons for his arrest and of any charge against him.

3   Everyone arrested or detained in accordance with the provisions of paragraph 1.c of this article shall be brought promptly before a judge or other officer authorised by law to exercise judicial power and shall be entitled to trial within a reasonable time or to release pending trial. Release may be conditioned by guarantees to appear for trial.

4   Everyone who is deprived of his liberty by arrest or detention shall be entitled to take proceedings by which the lawfulness of his detention shall be decided speedily by a court and his release ordered if the detention is not lawful.

5   Everyone who has been the victim of arrest or detention in contravention of the provisions of this article shall have an enforceable right to compensation.

Article 6 – Right to a fair trial

1   In the determination of his civil rights and obligations or of any criminal charge against him, everyone is entitled to a fair and public hearing within a reasonable time by an independent and impartial tribunal established by law. Judgment shall be pronounced publicly but the press and public may be excluded from all or part of the trial in the interests of morals, public order or national security in a democratic society, where the interests of juveniles or the protection of the private life of the parties so require, or to the extent strictly necessary in the opinion of the court in special circumstances where publicity would prejudice the interests of justice.

2   Everyone charged with a criminal offence shall be presumed innocent until proved guilty according to law.

3   Everyone charged with a criminal offence has the following minimum rights:

a   to be informed promptly, in a language which he understands and in detail, of the nature and cause of the accusation against him;

b   to have adequate time and facilities for the preparation of his defence;

c   to defend himself in person or through legal assistance of his own choosing or, if he has not sufficient means to pay for legal assistance, to be given it free when the interests of justice so require;

    d to examine or have examined witnesses against him and to obtain the attendance and examination of witnesses on his behalf under the same conditions as witnesses against him;

    e to have the free assistance of an interpreter if he cannot understand or speak the language used in court.

Article 7 – No punishment without law

1 No one shall be held guilty of any criminal offence on account of any act or omission which did not constitute a criminal offence under national or international law at the time when it was committed. Nor shall a heavier penalty be imposed than the one that was applicable at the time the criminal offence was committed.

2 This article shall not prejudice the trial and punishment of any person for any act or omission which, at the time when it was committed, was criminal according to the general principles of law recognised by civilised nations.

Article 8 – Right to respect for private and family life

1 Everyone has the right to respect for his private and family life, his home and his correspondence.

2 There shall be no interference by a public authority with the exercise of this right except such as is in accordance with the law and is necessary in a democratic society in the interests of national security, public safety or the economic well-being of the country, for the prevention of disorder or crime, for the protection of health or morals, or for the protection of the rights and freedoms of others.

Article 9 – Freedom of thought, conscience and religion

1 Everyone has the right to freedom of thought, conscience and religion; this right includes freedom to change his religion or belief and freedom, either alone or in community with others and in public or private, to manifest his religion or belief, in worship, teaching, practice and observance.

2 Freedom to manifest one's religion or beliefs shall be subject only to such limitations as are prescribed by law and are necessary in a democratic society in the interests of public safety, for the protection of public order, health or morals, or for the protection of the rights and freedoms of others.

Article 10 – Freedom of expression

1 Everyone has the right to freedom of expression. This right shall include freedom to hold opinions and to receive and impart information and ideas without interference by public authority and regardless of frontiers. This article shall not prevent States from requiring the licensing of broadcasting, television or cinema enterprises.

2 The exercise of these freedoms, since it carries with it duties and responsibilities, may be subject to such formalities, conditions, restrictions or penalties as are prescribed by law and are necessary in a democratic society, in the interests of national security, territorial integrity or public safety, for the prevention of

disorder or crime, for the protection of health or morals, for the protection of the reputation or rights of others, for preventing the disclosure of information received in confidence, or for maintaining the authority and impartiality of the judiciary.

Article 11 – Freedom of assembly and association

1   Everyone has the right to freedom of peaceful assembly and to freedom of association with others, including the right to form and to join trade unions for the protection of his interests.

2   No restrictions shall be placed on the exercise of these rights other than such as are prescribed by law and are necessary in a democratic society in the interests of national security or public safety, for the prevention of disorder or crime, for the protection of health or morals or for the protection of the rights and freedoms of others. This article shall not prevent the imposition of lawful restrictions on the exercise of these rights by members of the armed forces, of the police or of the administration of the State.

Article 12 – Right to marry

Men and women of marriageable age have the right to marry and to found a family, according to the national laws governing the exercise of this right.

Article 13 – Right to an effective remedy

Everyone whose rights and freedoms as set forth in this Convention are violated shall have an effective remedy before a national authority notwithstanding that the violation has been committed by persons acting in an official capacity.

Article 14 – Prohibition of discrimination

The enjoyment of the rights and freedoms set forth in this Convention shall be secured without discrimination on any ground such as sex, race, colour, language, religion, political or other opinion, national or social origin, association with a national minority, property, birth or other status.

Article 15 – Derogation in time of emergency

1   In time of war or other public emergency threatening the life of the nation any High Contracting Party may take measures derogating from its obligations under this Convention to the extent strictly required by the exigencies of the situation, provided that such measures are not inconsistent with its other obligations under international law.

2   No derogation from Article 2, except in respect of deaths resulting from lawful acts of war, or from Articles 3, 4 (paragraph 1) and 7 shall be made under this provision.

3   Any High Contracting Party availing itself of this right of derogation shall keep the Secretary General of the Council of Europe fully informed of the measures which it has taken and the reasons therefor. It shall also inform the Secretary General of the Council of Europe when such measures have ceased to operate and the provisions of the Convention are again being fully executed.

Article 16 – Restrictions on political activity of aliens
Nothing in Articles 10, 11 and 14 shall be regarded as preventing the High
Contracting Parties from imposing restrictions on the political activity of aliens.

Article 17 – Prohibition of abuse of rights
Nothing in this Convention may be interpreted as implying for any State, group
or person any right to engage in any activity or perform any act aimed at the
destruction of any of the rights and freedoms set forth herein or at their limitation
to a greater extent than is provided for in the Convention.

Article 18 – Limitation on use of restrictions on rights
The restrictions permitted under this Convention to the said rights and freedoms
shall not be applied for any purpose other than those for which they have been
prescribed.

EUROPEAN COMMUNITIES (DIRECTIVE 2000/31/EC) REGULATIONS 2003

(S.I. No. 68 of 2003) regs 16–18

16. (1) An intermediary service provider shall not be liable for information transmitted by him or her in a communication network if —

Liability of intermediary service providers - "mere conduit."

    (a) the information has been provided to him or her by a recipient of a relevant service provided by him or her (being a service consisting of the transmission in a communication network of that information), or

    (b) a relevant service provided by him or her consists of the provision of access to a communication network,

and, in either case, the following conditions are complied with —

        (i) the intermediary service provider did not initiate the transmission,

        (ii) the intermediary service provider did not select the receiver of the transmission, and

        (iii) the intermediary service provider did not select or modify the information contained in the transmission.

(2) References in paragraph (1) to an act of transmission and of provision of access include references to the automatic, intermediate and transient storage of the information transmitted in so far as this takes place for the sole purpose of carrying out the transmission in the communications network, and provided that the information is not stored for any period longer than is reasonably necessary for the transmission.

(3) This Regulation shall not affect the power of any court to make an order against an intermediary service provider requiring the provider not to infringe, or to cease to infringe, any legal rights.

17. (1) An intermediary service provider shall not be liable for the automatic, intermediate and temporary storage of information which is performed for the sole purpose of making more efficient that information's onward transmission to other users of the service upon their request, if —

Caching.

    (a) that storage is done in the context of the provision of a relevant service by the relevant service provider consisting of the transmission in a communication network of information provided by a recipient of that service, and

(b) the following conditions are complied with —

    (i) the intermediary service provider does not modify the information,

    (ii) the intermediary service provider complies with conditions relating to access to the information,

    (iii) the intermediary service provider complies with any rules regarding the updating of the information that have been specified in a manner widely recognised and used by industry,

    (iv) the intermediary service provider does not interfere with the lawful use of technology, widely recognised and used by industry to obtain data on the use of the information, and

    (v) the intermediary service provider acts expeditiously to remove or disable access to the information it has stored upon obtaining actual knowledge of the fact that the information at the initial source of the transmission has been removed from the network, or access to it has been disabled, or that a court or an administrative authority has ordered such removal or disablement.

(2) This Regulation shall not affect the power of any court to make an order against an intermediary service provider requiring the provider not to infringe, or to cease to infringe, any legal rights.

Hosting.   **18.** (1) An intermediary service provider who provides a relevant service consisting of the storage of information provided by a recipient of the service shall not be liable for the information stored at the request of that recipient if—

    (a) the intermediary service provider does not have actual knowledge of the unlawful activity concerned and, as regards claims for damages, is not aware of facts or circumstances from which that unlawful activity is apparent, or

    (b) the intermediary service provider, upon obtaining such knowledge or awareness, acts expeditiously to remove or to disable access to the information.

(2) Paragraph (1) shall not apply where the recipient of the service is acting under the authority or the control of the intermediary service provider referred to in that paragraph.

(3) This Regulation shall not affect the power of any court to make an order against an intermediary service provider requiring the provider not to infringe, or to cease to infringe, any legal rights.

GLOSSARY OF LEGAL TERMS

a fortiori: much more so and with greater force.

ab initio: from the outset.

abscond: to hide from or otherwise to evade the Jurisdiction of the court.

accessory, before the fact: one who, though absent at the time of commission of a felony, assists or commands another to commit the felony; **after the fact:** one who, though not present at the time of commission of the felony, actively assists a felon to avoid justice knowing that a felony has been committed.

accusatorial /adversarial system: a legal system where the responsibility to collect and present evidence lies with the party who seeks to introduce the evidence. In criminal matters the accused person is presumed to be innocent until proven guilty and the onus of proving guilt rests on the prosecution.

adverse possession: the acquiring by a squatter on property of rights of ownership to that property by flux of time.

affidavit: a written and sworn statement made by a person who is called a deponent.

affray: fighting by two or more persons in a public place which is of such a nature as would frighten reasonable people.

acquired bank asset: A bank asset such as a credit facility, security, asset that has been acquired by NAMA from a participating institution.

acquisition value: the value of a bank asset as determined by NAMA using the Valuation methodology set out in Part 5 of the NAMA Act 2009.

aid and abet: to intentionally assist a person committing a crime.

alibi: a defence to a criminal charge to the effect that the accused was elsewhere when the crime was committed.

Anton Piller order: *see* **injunction, quia timet.**

apology and offer to make amends: a factor which a court can take into account in assessing (and reducing) damages payable by a defendant in defamation proceedings.

appearance: *see* **pleadings.**

appellant: a person who appeals.

apportionment of fault: a judge hearing a case where there is more than one defendant can hold both defendants liable to varying degrees expressed as percentages of the overall award made to the plaintiff. Also, liability as between the plaintiff and defendants can be apportioned to reflect the plaintiff's own contributory negligence.

arraignment: the commencement of a criminal trial when the charges against the accused are read out in court and the accused is asked whether he/she pleads guilty or not guilty

articles of association: *see* **company.**

attachment and committal: the process whereby a person is brought before a court to explain their contempt of a court order (attachment) and their committal to prison for contempt upon failure or refusal to comply with the order of the court or to otherwise purge their contempt.

audi alteram partem: (hear the other side) a rule that requires a court or tribunal to hear both sides of a matter before it. *See* **fair procedures**.

auditor: an independent professional who undertakes to audit the books of account of a company and who must certify that the books are being properly kept.

bail: the process whereby a person accused of a criminal offence is set free until the date of the trial. An independent surety, who is a person who undertakes to have the accused person in attendance at the trial, is required. A bail bond is a sum of money usually provided by the surety which is lodged in court and is forfeited if the accused does not turn up for the trial.

bailiff: a person employed by the sheriff to serve and execute writs and orders (*see* **execution**).

balance of convenience: *see* **injunction**.

balance of probability: the burden of proof resting on the plaintiff in a civil action. Essentially, the plaintiff must prove that his version of events is more likely than not.

Bar Council: the governing body of the barrister's profession responsible for the internal regulation of the profession and external relations between the bar and other persons or groups.

barring order: an order preventing one spouse (or cohabiting partner) from entering the family home where the safety or welfare of the other spouse or of the children so requires.

battery: an unlawful touching of a person (a crime as well as a tort).

bench warrant: an order of a court for the immediate arrest of a person frequently issued where a person fails to appear at trial in a criminal case.

beyond reasonable doubt: the burden of proof in a criminal case. If there is any reasonable doubt regarding the evidence against an accused person, he/she is entitled to the benefit of the doubt and must be acquitted.

Bill: a piece of draft legislation.

binding to keep the peace: an order made by a criminal court whereby a person undertakes to keep the peace for a specified time and be of good behaviour.

bona fide: in good faith, honestly, innocently.

book of evidence: statements of evidence and a list of exhibits upon which the prosecution intends to rely in a trial by Jury. It must be served on the accused before his trial.

byelaw: a law passed by a local authority or other body to whom statutory authority is granted. A byelaw will be limited in its application either in terms of the area or the persons it affects.

canon law: the body of law by which the Catholic Church is governed.

capital murder: *see* **aggravated murder**.

care order: an order issued by the District Court on the application of a health board, committing a child to the care of the health board where there is physical or sexual abuse or neglect or where the child's health, development or welfare is or is likely to be adversely affected.

case stated: a procedure for submitting a question or questions of law to a higher court to be determined. The points raised are argued before the higher court which makes a determination and then remits the matter back to the original court for disposal. A case may be stated on the application of either party or by the court of its own motion.

causation: the necessary link between a person's actions and the eventual consequences of those actions. There must be a sufficient link between the actions and consequences for liability to attach to a person in crime or in tort.

cause of action: the facts which give rise to proceedings in a court.

certiorari: where an inferior court or tribunal or person exercising a legal power makes an error or fails to apply fair procedures before reaching its decision an aggrieved party can apply to the High Court by way of judicial review for an order of certiorari invalidating or quashing the decision (*see* **judicial review, natural justice, fair procedures**).

chancery: general description of cases involving the application of the law of equity to a particular dispute. Such cases are generally heard in the Chancery lists of the High Court and will typically involve injunctions and certain company law matters such as liquidations and receiverships.

charge: in the criminal law context an instruction to a jury issued by the trial judge which summarises the evidence and outlines the applicable law.

chattels: items of property which are not freehold real property. Generally, a chattel will be an item of personal property.

Chief Justice: the president of the Supreme Court and the most senior judge in Ireland.

Church penal process: this is the canon law judicial process to investigate an allegation of an offence and to determine whether or not to impose or declare a penalty for that offence.

circumstantial evidence: evidence which indirectly points to a particular conclusion on an issue in a case but which does not directly prove the issue.

civil bill: a document which initiates civil proceedings in the Circuit Court and which sets out the factual basis of the claim and the nature of the relief sought by the plaintiff.

civil law: depending on the context civil law is the body of law providing a citizen with a civil remedy (such as damages) and is contrasted with criminal law which involves the imposition of a penal sanction (such as imprisonment) on an offender. Civil law can also be contrasted with canon law (the law of the Roman Catholic Church). In addition a system of law which relies on a written code rather than a body of judge-made law is described as a civil law system. The Irish system is not based on such a code and thus in this context has what is called a common law system.

civil process: a document initiating a civil claim in the District Court setting out the facts and the nature of the relief sought by the plaintiff.

close of pleadings: the stage in civil litigation when all matters in issue between the parties have been set out in the pleadings (*see* **pleadings**).

codicil: an addition to or amendment of or explanation of a will but created after the execution of the original will.

commissioner for oaths: a person appointed to administer oaths to persons making sworn statements such as affidavits or statutory declarations.

common law: a system of laws not based on a written code but based on a body of laws derived from decisions of Judges in previous cases. However, written laws exist within a common law system and these laws are distinguished from common law by describing them as statute law.

company: a legal entity which has a legal personality separate and distinct from its members. It has separate rights and duties under the law and can sue and be sued in its own name. A limited company is one where the liability of the members to discharge the company's debts in the event of insolvency is limited to a certain amount. A limited company which does not offer its shares to the public is a private limited company whereas a company which offers shares to the public is called public limited company or plc. Every company must have a set of rules which are contained in its memorandum and articles of association. Every limited company must have directors, a secretary and auditors and must file annual returns (which are statements of the company's financial results) and other documents with the Companies Office.

competition law: an area of law principally administered by the competition authority which governs monopolies, mergers, restraint of trade and the fixing of pricing by commercial entities. The US equivalent is known as Anti-trust law.

complainant: a person who makes a complaint which gives rise to legal proceedings, e.g. the victim in a rape case.

concurrent sentences: separate sentences for separate offences which a judge orders to be served at the same time.

Congregation for the Doctrine of the Faith (CDF): This is one of the offices which assists the Pope in governing the universal Church. It was originally founded in 1542 as the Congregation of the Sacred Inquisition. Its main function now is to promote and safeguard the doctrine on faith and morals throughout the Catholic world: everything which in any way touches such matters falls within its remit. It deals with cases of child sexual abuse against clerics.

consecutive sentences: separate sentences for separate offences which a judge orders the accused to serve one after the other.

conspiracy: the crime of conspiracy is committed when two or more persons agree to effect an unlawful purpose. the tort of conspiracy is committed where two or more persons act with the intent to damage the business of another and whose actions cause such damage. A trade union organising a strike in relation to a trade dispute is immune from liability in conspiracy in circumstances set out in the Industrial Relations Act 1990.

constructive dismissal: the treatment of an employee by his employers such that the employee is entitled to deem himself to be dismissed by the employer.

consumer affairs, director of: an independent office holder, appointed by the Minister, with responsibility for dealing with complaints against businesses from members of the public and given certain powers to take action against businesses in breach of consumer protection legislation.

contempt of court: failure to comply with a court order or conduct which is likely to prejudice the fair trial of an accused person or other conduct which is disrespectful of the court. Contempt is punishable by imprisonment.

contributory: a person who is liable to contribute to the assets of a company in the event of its being wound up.

contributory negligence: a degree of fault on the part of the plaintiff in an action for damages which reduces his damages by an amount expressed as a percentage of the total award made by the trial judge.

conveyancing: the legal work involved in purchasing or selling real property.

counterclaim: a claim made by a defendant in an action which is pursued in the same action against the plaintiff.

court of first instance: the court where any matter is first heard and determined.

crime: an offence contrary to public law which gives rise to a penal sanction.

cross appeal: whereby both parties appeal the decision of a court.

curia: the Roman curia consists of the departments and ministries that assist the Pope in the government of the universal Church. A diocesan curia is composed of those people who assist a bishop to govern his diocese.

damages: a sum of money awarded to a person to compensate him for his loss. General damages are those damages which cannot be ascertained other than by a judicial assessment, e.g. damages for pain and suffering. Special damages are those amounts which are capable of precise calculation in advance of the hearing, e.g. medical expenses. Punitive or exemplary damages are awarded to a plaintiff in exceptional circumstances not to compensate the plaintiff but to punish the defendant. Nominal damages are awarded where the plaintiff has succeeded but has sustained no loss and contemptuous damages are awarded where it is thought necessary to express contempt for the plaintiff's conduct by a very small award.

data protection: statutory protection of information concerning individuals which is stored electronically. Persons storing such information are under obligations imposed by the Data Protection Act 1988 regarding their use of such information. Responsibility for supervising compliance with the Act rests with the Data Protection Commissioner.

de facto: a situation or state of affairs which exists in fact.

de jure: a situation or state of affairs which exists as a matter of law.

debenture: in company law, an instrument or deed whereby a company acknowledges its indebtedness to a particular person, which is issued as security for a loan advanced to the company.

declaration: an order of the High Court which declares the rights of a person in the particular circumstances before the court. Most commonly sought in Chancery and Judicial review proceedings.

decree: an order of a court. A decree nisi is a conditional order and a decree absolute is a final decree.

declarent: a person making a statutory declaration.

deed: a legal document which is formally sealed.

defence: a document which sets out the nature of a defendant's intended defence to a civil action

delegated legislation: written laws in the form of orders, byelaws or statutory instruments made by a person or body under authority provided by an Act of the Oireachtas.

deponent: a person making an affidavit.

direction order: an order made under the Credit Institutions (Stabilisation) Act 2010 which directs that a financial institution take or refrain from taking any action set out in the Act.

discovery: any party to a civil action has the right, before the trial of the action, to view and copy documents which are in the possession of or can be obtained by the other party, which are relevant to the proceedings between the parties. Discovery can be made on a voluntary basis or pursuant to an order of the court but in either case an affidavit is required by the party discovering the documents.

disqualification order: in company law, an order made by the High Court preventing a person from being an officer or servant or receiver or liquidator of any company.

embezzlement: a criminal offence committed by a person who fraudulently converts to his own use, property received by him on account of his employer.

Employment Appeals Tribunal (EAT): an industrial tribunal set up by the Redundancy Payment Act 1967 and modified by the Unfair Dismissal Act 1977, whose purpose is to adjudicate on disputes relating to the termination of employment. The tribunal can award damages of up to two years' remuneration or reinstatement (returning the employee to his former job with back pay and preserved benefits) re re-engagement (return to former job on terms fixed by the tribunal). There is a right of appeal to the Circuit Court from a decision of the tribunal and a further right of appeal to the High Court.

equality officer: a person appointed by the Labour Relations Commission whose function is to investigate complaints by employees in relation to the Employment Equality Act 1977 or the Anti-Discrimination (Pay) Act 1974. Following an investigation and oral hearing the Equality Officer makes a recommendation.

Equity: a body of law which developed in the old courts of chancery parallel to the common law and which originally addressed itself to the defects of the common law. Equity provided remedies such as injunctions and specific performance where the common law could only offer damages. Equity now co-exists with common law and equitable as well as common law remedies can now be sought in the same court.

Used in a broader context, equity can also mean simply the requirements of fairness and justice. In the context of company law, equity share capital denotes the type of share where the shareholder is not guaranteed a fixed dividend but will receive a dividend commensurate with the company's financial results.

estoppel: a principal of equity whereby a person's behaviour prevents him from relying on a particular argument which but for his behaviour would otherwise have been available to him.

ex parte: an application which is made in court without notice to the other party and where the other party has no right to address the court.

examinership: a statutory procedure whereby an examiner is appointed by the High Court for a short period to devise a scheme which either saves the company from liquidation or puts the company's affairs in order so as to facilitate a winding-up.

execution of judgment: the process of enforcing the judgment of a court as against the unsuccessful party.

extempore: a written judgment issued by a judge immediately after the evidence in a case has concluded.

fair procedures: the rules of procedure which must be applied by all courts, tribunals and persons exercising powers which affect another person's rights. The requirement is to give every party a proper hearing (*audi alteram partem*) and to be impartial and unbiased (*nemo judex in sua causa*).

felony: a crime which at one stage carried the death penalty. Contrasted with a misdemeanour which was a less serious offence and, generally carries a lighter penalty. The distinction no longer exists.

fiduciary: a special obligation or duty which falls on a person who is in control of the property of another. A fiduciary duty is strict and does not permit the person on whom the duty falls to be in a situation of conflict of interest or to profit secretly from his position. The directors of a company, for example, have a fiduciary duty to the company.

fraudulent trading: any officer or servant of a company who is a party to the carrying on of a company's business with intent to defraud creditors is guilty of the criminal offence of fraudulent trading and in addition may be made personally liable for the company's debts and may also be the subject of a disqualification order.

garnishee order: where A is indebted to B and B is indebted to C as a result of a judgment in C's favour, C can apply to the court for a garnishee order directing A to pay C out of the monies owed by A to B.

guardian ad litem: a person appointed to safeguard the interests of a minor involved in litigation.

habeas corpus: where it appears to the High Court that a person is being detained in custody in a manner which is unconstitutional a habeas corpus order is made directing that the person be brought before the court and reasons given as to the grounds of his detention. If after legal argument the person is found to have been unconstitutionally detained he must then be freed by the court.

hearsay: evidence given by a witness which evidence recites a statement made by another person. Hearsay evidence is generally inadmissible but there are a number of exceptions.

Holy See: the universal government of the Catholic Church of which the Pope is the ruler, The term Apostolic See is sometimes used.

in camera: hearing of a case in court where the public have been excluded in the interests of justice. Examples are cases involving infants, rape, matrimonial cases and applications for the appointment of an examiner.

indictable offence: an offence for which the accused has the right to be tried by a jury. However, the accused can and more often than not will exercise his right to be tried by a judge alone (known as summary trial) in the District Court where the maximum penalty is two years imprisonment.

indictment: a numbered list of charges against an accused person for which he is to be tried.

injunction: an order made by a court directing the taking of certain action by the defendant (a mandatory injunction) or the cessation of a certain action (a prohibitory injunction) with the penalty of committal to prison for contempt of court in the event of failure to comply. In urgent cases an interim injunction can be obtained *ex parte* which will last for a short time whereupon the defendant can then challenge the injunction before the court. An interlocutory injunction if granted will last as Iong as it takes for the case to reach a full hearing. A judge will only grant an interlocutory injunction if satisfied that damages will not be an adequate remedy and that the balance of convenience favours the granting of the injunction.

inquisitorial procedure: criminal procedure adopted in civil law jurisdictions where the judge initiates the investigation and examines witnesses. The presumption of innocence as it applies in common law countries such as Ireland does not apply in such legal systems.

insanity: a special verdict of not guilty by reason of insanity is delivered if the court or jury find that the accused was suffering from a mental disorder at the time of the commission of the offence and the disorder was such that the accused ought not be held responsible by reason of the fact that he or she did not know the nature and quality of the act, or did not know what he or she was doing was wrong or was unable to refrain from commiting the act..

insider dealing: a criminal offence (punishable by prohibition from dealing for 12 months) and a civil wrong (rendering the person liable to any person involved in the deal who was not in possession of the information and liable to the company) committed by any person connected to a company who deals in securities (shares, stocks, etc.) whilst in possession of information, which if known would materially affect the price of securities and which was not generally available to the public.

interlocutory: an application to the court by any party for relief before the close of pleadings and in advance of the trial date, e.g. an application for discovery or for an interlocutory injunction.

interrogatories: an interlocutory order (described above) which directs a party to answer a series of questions raised by the other party the purpose of which is to narrow down the scope of the case being made by the party upon whom the interrogatories are served.

intestacy: where a person dies without making a will. There are specific rules governing the distribution of the assets of a deceased person.

Iris Oifigiúil: a twice weekly government publication wherein official notice is given of various matters of interest to the business community, and the general public such as the appointment of receivers to companies or the striking-off of companies, etc

judge's rules: a set of guidelines for members of the Garda Siochána, regarding the interrogation of suspects in custody A statement obtained from a suspect in custody in breach of the rules is admissible if it is proven to have been made voluntarily.

judgment: a decree or order of a court stating that a specified sum of money is owing by one party (the judgment debtor) to another party (the judgment creditor). The term is also used to describe a decision of a court on a particular case. (Note that this is the usual spelling when referring to legal matters).

judgment mortgage: the process whereby a judgment creditor (a person to whom money is owed on foot of a judgment in his favour against the judgment debtor) can convert his judgment into a mortgage against the judgment debtor's property, The judgment debtor will then be unable to sell the mortgaged property until the debt is paid.

judicial review: a procedure provided for in the rules of court whereby an application to the High Court is made (by a party known as the applicant) to challenge the finding or determination of an inferior court (District or Circuit) or tribunal or other person exercising a quasi-judicial function (defined below). The grounds are that the respondent (the person who made the decision or determination) has acted beyond its jurisdiction (*i.e.* its lawful powers) or has failed to apply fair procedures. The applicant must apply *ex parte* in the judicial review list for leave to apply, and if successful the respondent must then choose whether or not to show cause (defend or oppose the order).

judicial separation: a formal decree of a court relieving the parties of their marital obligations though not dissolving the marriage. Provision may also be made by the judge with respect to maintenance of a spouse and children, custody of the children and the distribution or otherwise of the family home and other marital property.

Labour Court: a forum for the negotiation of industrial disputes set up by the Industrial Relations Act 1946. In addition to its role as a facilitator the Labour Court also adjudicates) on appeals from the recommendations of equality officers under the Employment Equality Act 1977 and the Anti-Discrimination (Pay) Act 1974. From the finding of the Labour Court there is an appeal to the High Court on a point of law only.

labour injunction: an injunction to restrain a strike.

Labour Relations Commission (LRC): a statutory body whose function is to promote and facilitate industrial relations. Most industrial disputes will be referred to the LRC before the Labour Court becomes involved.

land registry: a government office under the Department of Justice which houses registers noting the ownership of land.

larceny: the criminal offence of theft. Often mistaken for robbery, larceny does not involve violence or force but relates to an intentional taking without consent with the intention of permanently depriving the owner of his property.

legal cost accountant: a professional person engaged by solicitors to advise on appropriate fees on individual cases and who will represent the solicitor before the Taxing Master (*q.v.*) where there is a dispute over fees.

lien: the right to hold the property of another until such time as that other pays a debt or performs a legal obligation which was due to the person exercising the lien, e.g. a mechanic keeping a car until its owner pays a repair bill.

liquidated damages: where the damages payable or a formula by which it is possible to calculate the damages payable in the event of a breach of a contract by either party are agreed in advance and form part of the contract.

liquidator: company law, a person appointed by the High Court (called an official liquidator) or by a company's members or creditor whose function is to collect and realise a company's assets, to pay off its debts, distribute any remaining assets to the company's members and to dissolve the company. A provisional liquidator is one appointed by a court in advance of a formal winding-up application in circumstances where there is an urgency in relation to preserving the assets of the company.

locus standi: a plaintiff in an action must have a sufficient interest in the subject matter of the litigation in order to pursue the claim. If the plaintiff does not have sufficient interest he will not be entitled to proceed as he lacks locus standi.

lodgment: in a civil action a lodgment is a sum which a defendant pays into court and which he considers to be adequate to compensate the plaintiff, The lodgment can be made with or without an admission of liability. The fact of a lodgment or its amount is not disclosed to the trial judge and if an award of damages is made to the plaintiff at the hearing which does not exceed the amount of the lodgment the defendant is entitled to his costs from the date the lodgment is made. (Note that this is the usual spelling when referring to legal matters).

long term economic value: the long term value of an asset as assessed by NAMA which takes into account the market value and the long term economic value. It is possible that this value can exceed the market value by no more than such a fraction that the Minister prescribes by regulation.

man of straw: a person who has no financial resources, who will not be a mark for damages or the recovery of legal costs.

mandamus: a form of relief sought by way of judicial review which commands an inferior court or tribunal or person exercising quasi-judicial power to act in accordance with its/his legal duties.

manslaughter: the criminal offence of unlawful killing but without malice aforethought or intent. Voluntary manslaughter is an intentional killing where the killing is vitiated by the provocation of the accused. Involuntary manslaughter is committed where a person is killed by the accused's unlawful act or recklessness.

Mareva injunction: *see* **injunction, quia timet**.

Master of the High Court: a judicial officer of the High Court who sits in the Master's Court where various orders (e.g. Discovery) in relation to High Court civil litigation may be sought.

memorandum of association: *see* **company**.

memorial: a summary of a deed which is lodged in the Registry of Deeds when a deed is registered.

mens rea: the mental element of intention on the part of the accused which must generally be proven before the accused can be convicted.

minor offence: an offence which may be tried summarily, *i.e.* without a jury. Minor offences are tried in the District Court.

misdemeanour: *see* **felony**.

misdirection: an error on the part of a trial judge in instructing the jury on matters of law or evidence. In a civil case where a judge sits alone the judge must direct himself as to the law and thus can also misdirect himself. a misdirection is a ground for appeal.

motion: an application to a judge seeking some form of relief in advance of the date of trial. Unless the rules of court provide for an application *ex parte* a motion must be notified in advance to the other side by way of notice of motion.

Motor Insurers Bureau of Ireland (MIBI): a company formed pursuant to agreement with the Minister and funded by insurers who transact motor insurance business which deals with claims in respect of motor accidents caused by uninsured drivers, stolen vehicles and foreign registered vehicles.

murder: the unlawful killing of a person with malice aforethought which or conviction carries a mandatory life sentence.

NAMA: the National Asset Management Agency. This is a body corporate established with a separate legal entity to the State. The rules applicable to it's governance are derived from the National Asset Management Agency Act 2009. Its primary purpose is the acquisition of assets from Participating Institutions and dealing expeditiously with them.

NTMA: the National Treasury Management Agency. This body manages assets and liabilities on behalf of the Government was established in 1990. It is the agency that borrows on behalf of the State but has many other functions such as managing the pension reserve fund. It has a close association with NAMA in that it provides business and support services to that agency.

natural justice: the requirement that a court or tribunal or person exercising quasi-judicial power apply fair procedures to all parties to a dispute or matter (*see* **fair procedures**).

natural law: law which is thought to emanate from God as contrasted with man-made or positive law.

negligence: a common law tort; where a person owes another a duty to take care and breaches that duty causing damage to that other person which flows from the breach of duty, the person causing the damage is liable to the injured party in negligence.

nemo judex in sua causa: no man can be a judge in his own cause. A principle which requires a court, tribunal or administrative body or person to be impartial when deciding matters affecting the rights of persons (*see* **procedures**).

next friend: a person who pursues legal action on behalf of a minor. Usually a parent.

nolle prosequi: where the prosecution in a criminal case withdraws before the conclusion of the case. The proceedings are then stayed but can be reactivated by the State at a later date.

norms: rules or procedures

notary public: a person, usually a solicitor appointed by the Chief Justice, who is empowered to certify documents and deeds as authentic

novus actus interveniens: an act of negligence which is committed by a third party after the original act of negligence of a defendant in a civil case which absolves the defendant of liability

nuisance: a tort and in certain circumstances a crime which involves the unreasonable interference by a person with the rights of another. Public nuisance (which is a crime as well as a tort) is interference with the rights of the general public and only the Attorney General can sue unless a person can show particular damage over and above that sustained by the general public. Private nuisance is actionable by a private individual if he can show unreasonable interference with the enjoyment of his land.

nullity of marriage: a decree which declares that a valid marriage has never taken place or that if it has it has been rendered a nullity by reason of the occurrence of certain events such as the insanity of a spouse — often referred to as "an annulment".

obiter dictum: a statement of law made by a judge in the course of which does not go to the root of the decision but which nonetheless can be quoted in a subsequent case as a persuasive but not a binding authority.

occupier's liability: the liability in tort of a person occupying (not necessarily owning) land to persons who are injured whilst on the land. The tort is now governed by the Occupiers Liability Act 1995 which provides for the classification of persons entering the land of another (entrants) in three categories: visitors, recreational users and trespassers, with the strictest duty owed to the first category and lesser duties owed to the second and third.

participating institution: a credit institution such as a bank designated by the Minister for Finance under section 67 of the NAMA Act 2009.

partnership: the carrying on by two or more persons of a business in common with a view to making a profit

passing off: the tort committed by a person who passes off his goods as those of another.

patent: an industrial property right whereby an idea, plan, concept, process or product is protected and gives the patent holder the right to prevent all third parties from using the subject matter of the patent.

peace commissioner: a person appointed by order of the Minister for justice with responsibility for signing warrants and summonses and with the authority to administer oaths and declarations.

penal servitude: historically this sentence implied mandatory hard labour but nowadays there is no difference between such a sentence and one for imprisonment.

precept: an order from a bishop to a priest – usually restricting him in carrying out some or all of his priestly functions.

Personal Injuries Summons: a form of legal pleading that is used specifically for personal injuries litigation. It is a comprehensive form of summons which includes the details of the claim that are normally contained in a statement of claim (*see* **Statement of claim**).

pleadings: formal legal documents used in civil proceedings the purpose of which is to identify and clarify the matters in issue between the parties. (*See* **civil bill, civil process, defence, plenary summons, personal injuries summons and statement of claim**).

plenary summons and statement of claim: a plenary summons is a document which initiates ordinary proceedings in the High Court. It contains only a brief statement of the relief sought by the plaintiff and is followed by a more elaborate description of the plaintiffs case contained in a statement of claim.

precedent: a report or judgment from a previous case which is cited or quoted to a judge in support of a legal argument. preferential creditor: a creditor of a company, of a bankrupt or of a deceased person who is entitled by statute to rank higher than ordinary creditors in the queue for payment out of the assets available.

preferential creditor: a creditor of a company, of a bankrupt or of a deceased person, who is entitled by statute to rank higher than ordinary creditors in the queue for payment out of the assets available.

private international law: the body of law dealing with relations and disputes between private citizens or companies of different countries.

private law: the law dealing with civil disputes between private citizens or companies and not usually involving the state, e.g. tort, contract, etc.

privilege: (1) the right not to produce documents for discovery on the basis that they contain information which should not be disclosed to the other party for reasons of fairness or public policy; (2) a defence to a claim for defamation which admits the statement made and that it was defamatory but asserts the rights of the defendant to make the statement under various categories of exceptional circumstances recognised by law. Such a privilege can be absolute or qualified and if qualified the protection of the privilege will be lost if the plaintiff can show malice on the part of the defendant.

probate: a general term to describe the legal distribution of the assets of a deceased person.

product liability: the civil liability falling on the retailer, manufacturer, producer, importer, distributor, etc. for damage or injury caused by a defect in a product (generally including a service) supplied by that person. Now covered by the Liability for Defective Products Act 1991.

promoter: a person who takes it upon himself to set up a company. Promoters have a fiduciary duty to the company.

public law: constitutional law, criminal law and administrative law. That body of law which deals with the relations between the State and citizens.

quasi-judicial: a process or power or function the exercise of which requires the person presiding to exercise his/her/its power in a judicial manner. This means that fair procedures must be applied before a decision is taken.

quia timet: a form of legal order granted to prevent an anticipated wrongful act by another, e.g. a *mareva* injunction, an *Anton Piller* order.

rape: unlawful sexual intercourse, penetration of the anus or mouth by the penis, penetration of the vagina by an object. Criminal Law (Rape) (Amendment) Act 1990.

ratio decidendi: the precise legal basis for a court's decision in a previous case. Binding as a precedent on a lower court unless it can be distinguished from, the facts of the subsequent case or can be shown to be erroneous (*see* **precedent, obiter dicta**).

receiver: a person appointed to take charge of a company's assets or part thereof with a view to the paying of a debt owed to a particular creditor. A receiver has no power to wind up a company.

reckless trading: a statutory civil liability in company law whereby any officer of the company was responsible for carrying on business, or for involving the company in a transaction, which was likely to cause loss to the company's creditors.

recklessness: an act of gross carelessness filling just short of an intentional act.

recognisance: a promise made to a court to do a certain thing, e.g. to appear in court on a particular date.

recreational user: a category of entrant onto a person's land (*see* **occupier's liability**).

Regulation: a piece of EC legislation which is binding on all Member States without the need for national legislation to implement it into a Member State's law.

remand: the sending back of an accused person (either in custody or on bail) to appear in court on a later date.

res ipsa loquitur: a rule of evidence which presumes that certain accidents could not happen in the absence of negligence. Once the rule is found to apply to a defendant's conduct the onus of proof shifts to him to prove that he was not negligent.

res judicata: a legal argument seeking to end proceedings on the basis that the same issue between the same parties has been decided already by another court.

rescission: the setting aside of a contract on equitable grounds and the restoration of the parties to the position they occupied prior to entering into the contract (restitution)

reserved judgment: a judgment which is delivered in open court some time (but not immediately) after the conclusion of the hearing of a case.

restriction order: an order made by the High Court in company law matters against an officer or servant of a company which is insolvent and in liquidation where the officer or servant has been irresponsible in his handling of a company's affairs. The order restricts the activities of that person for a specified time in relation to the management of the affairs of any other company.

Rights Commissioner: a statutory officer appointed by the Labour Relations Commission responsible for the investigation of and adjudication on individual grievances relating to employment. A right of appeal exists to the Employment Appeals Tribunal.

robbery: an act of larceny involving violence to the victim or the perception by the victim of a threat of violence.

Rylands v Fletcher, **the Rule in**: the common law tort whereby a landowner is made responsible for loss or damage sustained as a result of the escape from his premises of a dangerous thing or substance which he has brought onto or collected on his premises.

safety statement: a statement dealing with hazards and precautions in the workplace which must be drafted with the co-operation of employees and displayed at the place of work or otherwise communicated to employees

scheduled offence: an offence declared by the Government to be one which is triable in the Special Criminal Court and to which the powers of arrest and detention conferred by section 30 of the Offences Against the State Act 1939 apply.

sequestration: a special type of order resulting from contempt of court whereby a person's assets are seized until he has complied with the court order.

seriatim: one by one in order, e.g. a defence can traverse (deny) a series of allegations in a statement of claim *seriatim.*

shadow director: a person who though not a director is capable of exerting a controlling influence on a company.

sheriff: a court officer whose principal function is to oversee the execution of judgments by taking possession of a debtor's assets.

specific performance: an equitable remedy which forces a party in breach of contract to carry out his obligations under the contract.

Statute of Frauds 1695: an Act which requires certain contracts to be reduced to writing before they will be legally enforceable.

Statute of Limitations: a period prescribed by statute within which a civil claim must be initiated.

statutory declaration: a sworn written statement usually declaring that a certain state of affairs exists, e.g. that a house is not a family home.

strict liability: liability in tort which is established without proof of fault on the part of the person found liable, e.g. nuisance, *Rylands v. Fletcher.*

subordinated liabilities order: an order made under the Credit Institutions (Stabilisation) Act 2010 which may direct the postponement termination suspension or other modification of specific rights, liabilities or obligations of what are termed subordinated liabilities of a financial institution. Subordinated liabilities are obligations of those institutions, which rank as subordinate to the claims of depositors and unsubordinated creditors of those institutions.

subpoena: (called a witness summons if issued by the Circuit or District Courts), a document summoning a person to court at a particular date and time to give evidence and sometimes to bring documents as well. A witness failing to appear can be jailed for contempt.

subrogation: the right of one person to "stand in the shoes" of a second person and so enforce rights against a third party normally only exercisable by the second person.

substantive: pertaining to the actual substance of a particular dispute rather than to the procedure by which the dispute is to be heard.

summary: used in various contexts but usually meaning a legal process which is shortened by cutting out an element of the procedure, e.g. summary trial cuts out a jury; summary dismissal is dismissal without notice; summary judgment is judgment without contest by the defendant. Summary proceedings are heard without oral evidence and affidavits are used instead.

summons: the method of initiation of certain (usually minor) criminal proceedings in the District Court.

surety: a person into whose charge an accused person is released on bail. The surety will also usually post a bail bond which is forfeited if the accused fails to appear.

taxation of costs/Taxing Master: where an award of costs is made against an unsuccessful party and that party disputes the amount of the costs he is being asked to pay the dispute will be referred to the Taxing Master for adjudication if the case was in the High Court or to the County Registrar or District Court Registrar if the case was heard in those courts. Prior to submitting the costs the solicitor will refer his file to a costs drawer or legal costs accountant who will provide specialist advice on the appropriate fee. The cost drawer will also usually represent the solicitor before the Taxing Master.

testimony: oral evidence given by a witness in court.

trade union: the most common and most important is a registered trade union which is the only type of trade union which benefits from statutory immunity in tort (*see* **conspiracy**). A registered trade union holds a licence to negotiate on behalf of its members and must post a bond with the Registrar of Friendly Societies. The rules relating to companies are analogous to those regulating trade unions.

transfer of undertaking: where a business is taken over as a going concern by another business EC law protects the employees of the business from compulsory redundancy.

transfer order: an order made under the Credit Institutions (Stabilisation) Act 2010 which directs the transfer of assets or liabilities of a financial institution to a transferee as permitted by the Act.

trespasser: a person who enters the land of another without permission or who enters initially with permission but then engages in an unlawful activity. The duty of care owed to a trespasser by an occupier of land is merely not to intentionally or recklessly injure him (*see* **occupier's liability**).

trust: an equitable concept where a person known as a trustee holds property for the benefit of another person or persons called a *cestui que trust*.

uberrimae fidei: utmost good faith; a principle applying to some contracts especially insurance contracts where both parties have an obligation to disclose to each other all matters relevant to the contract. The opposite of caveat emptor where it is up to the buyer to make full enquiry and the seller is not obliged to disclose matters relevant to the contract which the buyer could discover for himself.

ultra vires: in company law where a company engages in activities which is beyond the scope of the objects of that company as stated in its memorandum of association it is acting *ultra vires* and any contract entered into by the company in pursuance of such an *ultra vires* activity is void. In administrative law an administrative body or person with delegated authority acts *ultra vires* when it goes beyond the terms of reference of the delegated power conferred.

victim impact statement: a court is obliged to receive (if proffered) from the victim of a crime, a statement of the impact of the crime for specific offences such as sexual offences involving violence or the threat of violence. Members of a victim's family following a murder conviction may also make such a statement.

volenti non fit injuria: a defence to a claim in negligence to the effect that the plaintiff voluntarily brought the risk of injury upon himself.

voluntary liquidation: a liquidation initiated by a company's members or creditors where the liquidator is appointed by the creditors or members but not by the court. Unlike a compulsory liquidation there is no direct court supervision of the procedure.

visitor: a category of entrant onto the land of another under the Occupiers Liability Act 1995.

without prejudice: a form of privilege over a written or oral communication where it is understood that the details of the communication will not be disclosed to a court.

writ: civil legal proceedings.

INDEX